How to Cook

by

Olive Green

The Echo Library 2007

Published by

The Echo Library

Echo Library
131 High St.
Teddington
Middlesex TW11 8HH

www.echo-library.com

Please report serious faults in the text to complaints@echo-library.com

ISBN 978-1-40683-772-8

CONTENTS

THE CATCHING OF UNSHELLED FISH

"First catch your hare," the old cookery books used to say, and hence it is proper, in a treatise devoted entirely to the cooking of Unshelled Fish, to pay passing attention to the Catching, or what the Head of the House terms the Masculine Division of the Subject. As it is evident that the catching must, in every case precede the cooking—but not too far—the preface is the place to begin.

Shell-fish are, comparatively, slow of movement, without guile, pitifully trusting, and very easily caught. Observe the difference between the chunk of mutton and four feet of string with which one goes crabbing, and the complicated hooks, rods, flies, and reels devoted to the capture of unshelled fish.

An unshelled fish is lively and elusive past the power of words to portray, and in this, undoubtedly, lies its desirability. People will travel for two nights and a day to some spot where all unshelled fish has once been seen, taking $59.99 worth of fishing tackle, "marked down from $60.00 for to-day only," rent a canoe, hire a guide at more than human life is worth in courts of law, and work with dogged patience from gray dawn till sunset. And for what? For one small bass which could have been bought at any trustworthy market for sixty-five cents, or, possibly, some poor little kitten-fish-offspring of a catfish—whose mother's milk is not yet dry upon its lips.

Other fish who have just been weaned and are beginning to notice solid food will repeatedly take a hook too large to swallow, and be dragged into the boat, literally, by the skin of the teeth. Note the cheerful little sunfish, four inches long, which is caught first on one side of the boat and then on the other, by the patient fisherman angling off a rocky, weedy point for bass.

But, as Grover Cleveland said: "He is no true fisherman who is willing to fish only when fish are biting." The real angler will sit all day in a boat in a pouring rain, eagerly watching the point of the rod, which never for an instant swerves a half inch from the horizontal. The real angler will troll for miles with a hand line and a spinner, winding in the thirty-five dripping feet of the lure every ten minutes, to remove a weed, or "to see if she's still a-spinnin'." Vainly he hopes for the muskellunge who has just gone somewhere else, but, by the same token, the sure-enough angler is ready to go out next morning, rain or shine, at sunrise.

It is a habit of Unshelled Fish to be in other places, or, possibly, at your place, but at another time. The guide can never understand what is wrong. Five days ago, he himself caught more bass than he could carry home, at that identical rocky point. A man from La Porte, Indiana, whom he took out the week before, landed a thirty-eight pound "muskie" in trolling through that same narrow channel. In the forty years that the guide has lived in the place, man and boy, he has never known the fishing to be as poor as it is now. Why, even "ol' Pop Somers" has ceased to fish!

But the real angler continues, regardless of the local sage. He who has heard the line sing suddenly out of his reel, and, after a hard-fought hour, scooped a six-pound black bass into the landing net, weary, but still "game," is not dismayed by bad luck. He who can cast a fly a hundred feet or more finds pleasure in that, if not in fishing. Whoever has taken in a muskellunge of any size will ever after troll patiently, even through masses of weed. Whoever has leaned over the side of a sailboat, peering down into the green, crystalline waters of the Gulf, and seen, twenty feet down, the shimmering sides of a fifteen-pound red grouper, firmly hooked and coming, will never turn over sleepily, for a last nap, when his door is almost broken in at 5 A.M.

And, fish or no fish, there are compensations. Into a day of heart-breaking and soul-sickening toil, when all the world goes wrong, must sometimes come the vision of a wooded shore, with tiny dark wavelets singing softly on the rocks and a robin piping cheerily on the topmost bough of a maple. Tired eyes look past the musty ledger and the letter files to a tiny sapphire lake, set in hills, with the late afternoon light streaming in glory from the far mountains beyond.

It may be cold up North, but down in the Gulf they are fishing—scudding among the Florida Keys in a little white sailboat, landing for lunch on a strand as snowy as the northern streets, where the shimmering distances of white sand are paved with shell and pearl, and the tide thrums out its old song under the palms. And fish? Two-hundred and fifty pounds is the average day's catch for a small sailboat cruising among the Florida Keys.

Yet, when all is said and done, the catching of fish is a matter of luck—a gambler's chance, if you will have it so. The cooking, in unskilled hands, is also a lottery, but, by following the appended recipes, becomes an art to which scientific principles have been faithfully applied.

Having caught your fish, you may cook him in a thousand ways, but it is doubtful whether, even with the finest sauce, a pompano will taste half as good as the infantile muskellunge, several pounds under the legal weight, fried unskilfully in pork fat by a horny-handed woodsman, kneeling before an open fire, eighteen minutes after you had given up all hope of having fish for dinner, and had resigned yourself to the dubious prospect of salt pork, eggs, and coffee which any self-respecting coffee-mill would fail to recognize.

All of which is respectfully submitted by

O.G.

FISH IN SEASON

Bass—All the year.
Blackfish—April 1 to November 1.
Bluefish—May 1 to November 1.
Butterfish—October 1 to May 1.
Carp—July 15 to November 1.
Codfish—All the year.
Eels—All the year.
Flounder—All the year.
Haddock—All the year.
Halibut—All the year.
Herring—October 1 to May 1.
Kingfish—May 1 to November 1.
Mackerel—April 1 to October 1.
Mullet—June 1 to November 1.
Perch—September 1 to June 1.
Pickerel—June 1 to January 1.
Pike—June 1 to January 1.
Pompano—May 1 to August 1 and November 15 to January 1.
Red Snapper—October 1 to April 1.
Salmon—All the year.
Salmon Trout—October 1 to April 1.
Shad—January 1 to June 1.
Sheepshead—June 15 to November 15.
Skate—September 1 to July 1.
Smelts—August 15 to April 15.
Sole—November 1 to May 1.
Sturgeon—June 1 to October 15.
Trout—April 1 to September 1.
Turbot—January 1 to July 15.
Weakfish—May 15 to October 15.
Whitebait—May 1 to April 1.
Whitefish—November 1 to March 1.
Salt, smoked, and canned fish are never out of season.

ELEVEN COURT BOUILLONS

I

Put into the bottom of the fish-kettle a thick layer of sliced carrots and onion, and a sliced lemon. Season with parsley, thyme, a bay-leaf, half a dozen whole peppers, and three or four whole cloves. Lay the fish on top of this and cover with equal parts of cold water and white wine, or with water and a little lemon-juice or vinegar. Put the kettle over the fire and let it heat slowly. The fish must always be put into it while cold and after boiling allowed to cool in the water.

II

Cut fine a stalk of celery, a carrot, an onion, and a small sweet pepper. Fry in butter, and add eight cupfuls of water, one cupful of vinegar, and the trimmings of fish. Season with salt and pepper, add half a bay-leaf, four cloves, and two sprigs of parsley. Boil for ten minutes and let cool thoroughly before cooking the fish in it.

III

One pint of water, one quart of white wine, one tablespoonful of butter, a bunch of parsley, four young onions, a clove of garlic, a bunch of thyme, a bay-leaf, a carrot, and a blade of mace. Bring to the boil and let cool thoroughly before cooking the fish in it.

IV

Fry a large onion in two tablespoonfuls of butter. Add half a can of tomatoes, salt, pepper, allspice, and minced parsley to season, and half a cupful of tomato catsup. Add also one cupful of sliced carrot and sufficient water to cover the fish.

V

One onion, two bay-leaves, four whole cloves, a stalk of celery, two sprigs of parsley and three quarts of cold water. Add any trimmings of fish at hand, simmer for two hours, season with salt and pepper, and strain. Cool before using.

VI

Chop fine one onion, one stalk of celery, and two or three sprigs of parsley. Fry in butter, add two tablespoonfuls of salt, six pepper-corns, a bay-leaf, three cloves, two quarts of boiling water, and two cupfuls of vinegar or sour wine. Boil for fifteen minutes, strain, and cool. Rub the fish with salt and lemon-juice before cooking.

VII

Chop fine a large onion and a carrot. Add three bay-leaves, a few sprigs of parsley, a pinch of powdered thyme, and three tablespoonfuls of tarragon vinegar. Add enough water to cover the fish. The vinegar may be omitted and equal parts of water and white wine used for liquid.

VIII

Chop fine a quarter of a pound of bacon and an onion. Fry, add a can of tomatoes, a chopped clove of garlic, and cayenne, salt, and pepper to season. Add sufficient boiling water and cook for fifteen minutes. Cool before putting in the fish.

IX

Half a carrot, half an onion, two cloves, three sprigs of parsley, three pepper-corns, two tablespoonfuls of lemon-juice or vinegar, a teaspoonful of salt, a blade of mace, half a bay-leaf, half a teaspoonful of paprika, a dash of celery salt, and two quarts of cold water. Bring to the boil and cool before using.

X

Fry an onion in butter. Add half a teaspoonful of beef extract, a pinch of celery seed, a few drops of Worcestershire, a tablespoonful of tomato catsup, half a cupful of vinegar, and salt and pepper to season. Add two quarts of cold water, bring to the boil, and cool before using.

XI

Four quarts of water, one onion, one slice of carrot, two tablespoonfuls of salt, one tablespoonful of pepper, two cloves, one tablespoonful of vinegar, the juice of half a lemon, and a bouquet of sweet herbs. Boil for an hour before putting in the fish.

ONE HUNDRED SIMPLE FISH SAUCES

ADMIRAL SAUCE

Add two pounded anchovies, four chopped shallots, a teaspoonful of chopped capers, and a little grated lemon-peel to one cupful of Drawn-Butter Sauce. Reheat, season with salt and pepper and lemon-juice. Serve hot.

ALBERT SAUCE

Boil three chopped shallots with a tablespoonful of butter and one-fourth cupful of vinegar. Add one cupful of freshly grated horseradish, half a cupful of white stock and one cupful of Veloute Sauce. Boil until thick, rub through a sieve, reheat, add the yolks of three eggs beaten with a cupful of cream, two tablespoonfuls of butter in small bits, and a little minced parsley.

ALLEMANDE SAUCE—I

Put two cupfuls of white stock into a saucepan with half a dozen mushrooms, chopped fine, a two-inch strip of lemon-peel, salt and pepper to season, and a teaspoonful of minced parsley. Simmer for an hour and strain. Thicken with a teaspoonful of flour, rubbed smooth in a little cold stock or water, take from the fire, and add the yolks of three eggs beaten with the juice of half a lemon. Reheat, but do not boil. Take from the fire and add a tablespoonful of butter.

ALLEMANDE SAUCE—II

Cook together two tablespoonfuls of butter and three of flour. Add two cupfuls of white stock and cook until thick, stirring constantly. Beat the yolks of three eggs and add the sauce gradually to the eggs, beating constantly. Strain, add the juice of half a lemon and a tablespoonful of butter. Serve hot.

ANCHOVY BUTTER

Soak, bone, dry, and pound eight salted anchovies. Add twice their bulk of fresh butter, mix thoroughly, press forcibly through a fine sieve, add a little more butter and the juice of a lemon. Make into small pats and keep in a cold place.

ANCHOVY BUTTER SAUCE

Prepare a pint of Brown Sauce according to directions elsewhere given and season with melted butter, lemon-juice, and anchovy essence.

ANCHOVY SAUCE—I

Stir two tablespoonfuls of anchovy essence into one cupful of melted butter. Season with cayenne and powdered mace.

ANCHOVY SAUCE—II

Pound three anchovies smooth with three tablespoonfuls of butter, add two teaspoonfuls of vinegar and a quarter of a cupful of water. Bring to the boil and thicken with a tablespoonful of flour rubbed smooth in a little cold water. Strain through a sieve and serve hot.

ANCHOVY SAUCE—III

Add a tablespoonful of anchovy paste to a cupful of Drawn-Butter Sauce and season with lemon-juice and paprika.

AURORA SAUCE

Add one half cupful of mushroom liquor to one cupful of Béchamel Sauce. Add also three tablespoonfuls of stewed and strained tomatoes, and one tablespoonful of butter. Reheat, add a few cooked mushrooms cut into dice, and serve.

AVIGNONNAISE SAUCE

Chop together four shallots and two beans of garlic. Fry in olive-oil, add two cupfuls of Béchamel Sauce, bring to the boil, add the yolks of three eggs, two tablespoonfuls of grated Parmesan cheese, and a little minced parsley. Heat, but do not boil, and use as soon as it thickens.

BEARNAISE SAUCE—I

Bring to the boil two tablespoonfuls each of vinegar and water. Simmer in it for ten minutes a slice of onion. Take out the onion and add the yolks of three eggs beaten very light. Take from the fire, add salt and pepper to season, and four tablespoonfuls of butter beaten to a cream. The butter should be added in small bits.

BEARNAISE SAUCE—II

Beat the yolks of five eggs, add a pinch of salt and one tablespoonful of butter. Heat in a double-boiler until it begins to thicken, then take from the fire and add two more tablespoonfuls of butter. Season with minced fine herbs and parsley and add a teaspoonful of tarragon vinegar.

BEARNAISE SAUCE—III

Beat the yolks of two eggs very light and put into a double-boiler. Add gradually three tablespoonfuls of olive-oil, then the same quantity of boiling water, then one tablespoonful of lemon-juice. Season with salt and cayenne and serve immediately.

QUICK BEARNAISE SAUCE

Beat the yolks of four eggs with four tablespoonfuls of oil and four of water. Add a cupful of boiling water and cook slowly until thick and smooth. Take from the fire, and add minced onion, capers, olives, pickles, and parsley and a little tarragon vinegar.

BÉCHAMEL SAUCE

Cook together two tablespoonfuls each of butter and flour, add two cupfuls of white stock and cook until thick, stirring constantly. Season with salt, pepper, and grated nutmeg.

BOMBAY SAUCE

Season Drawn-Butter Sauce highly with chopped pickle, curry powder, and tarragon vinegar.

BORDELAISE SAUCE

Fry in butter a tablespoonful of chopped shallots and two minced beans of garlic. Add half a cupful of Claret, a pinch of red pepper, and a pint of Espagnole Sauce. Boil until thick, take from the fire and add lemon-juice and minced parsley to season. Add also a quarter of a pound of beef marrow cut in small pieces and parboiled in salted water. Serve at once.

WHITE BORDELAISE SAUCE

Fry a tablespoonful of chopped onions in butter, add a wineglassful of white wine and a cupful of Veloute Sauce. Season to taste, boil for five minutes, take from the fire, add one tablespoonful each of minced parsley, lemon-juice, and butter.

BROWN SAUCE—I

Brown two tablespoonfuls of flour in butter. Add two cupfuls of milk or cream and cook until thick, stirring constantly.

BROWN SAUCE—II

Fry in pork fat two slices of onion, a slice of carrot, a bay-leaf, and a sprig of parsley. Add a heaping teaspoonful of flour and, when brown, a cupful of stock. Cook until thick, stirring constantly. Take from the fire, strain, add the juice of half a lemon, and salt and pepper to season.

BROWN BUTTER SAUCE

Melt butter in a frying-pan and cook until brown, taking care not to burn. Take from the fire and add lemon-juice or vinegar and salt and pepper to taste. Serve hot.

BUTTER SAUCE

Mix chopped hard-boiled eggs with a liberal amount of melted butter. Season with salt, pepper, and minced parsley.

CAPER SAUCE—I

Add half a cupful of capers to two cupfuls of Drawn-Butter Sauce.

CAPER SAUCE—II

Prepare a pint of Drawn-Butter Sauce and add to it two tablespoonfuls of capers, a tablespoonful of anchovy essence, and salt and pepper to season.

CLARET SAUCE

Reheat one cupful of Brown Sauce, season with grated onion, add half a cupful of Claret, bring to the boil, and serve.

COLBERT SAUCE

Put into a saucepan one cupful of Espagnole Sauce, two tablespoonfuls of beef extract, the juice of a lemon, red and white pepper and minced parsley to season, and half a cupful of butter in small bits. Heat, but do not boil, and serve at once.

CREAM SAUCE

Cook together one tablespoonful of butter and two of flour. Add two cupfuls of cream or milk and cook until thick, stirring constantly Season with salt and pepper.

CUCUMBER SAUCE—I

Chop two cucumbers, drain, and add one tablespoonful of grated onion and half of a minced bean of garlic. Season with salt, pepper, and vinegar, and add enough olive-oil to make a smooth paste. Serve immediately.

CUCUMBER SAUCE—II

Grate four large cucumbers and drain. Season the pulp with salt, pepper, grated onion, and tarragon vinegar. Add enough whipped cream to make a smooth mixture and serve at once.

CUCUMBER SAUCE—III

Chop a cucumber finely, season with salt, pepper, and vinegar and add it to Hollandaise Sauce.

CURRY SAUCE

Fry a tablespoonful of chopped onion in butter and add a tablespoonful of flour mixed with a teaspoonful of curry powder. Mix thoroughly, add one cupful of cold water, and cook until thick, stirring constantly. Take from the fire, season with salt and onion juice, and serve hot.

DRAWN-BUTTER SAUCE

Cook to a smooth paste two tablespoonfuls of butter and two of flour. Add two cupfuls of cold water and cook until thick, stirring constantly. Season with salt and pepper.

DUTCH SAUCE

Cook together two tablespoonfuls each of butter and flour, add one cupful of white stock, and cook until thick, stirring constantly. Season with salt and pepper, take from the fire and add the yolks of three eggs beaten with half a cupful of cream. Cook in a double-boiler for three minutes, take from the fire, add a tablespoonful of lemon-juice and strain.

DUXELLES SAUCE—I

Cook in butter one cupful of chopped mushrooms; and one tablespoonful each of minced onion and parsley. Add to one pint of Spanish Sauce and serve.

DUXELLES SAUCE—II

Prepare a pint of Veloute Sauce, add a wineglassful of white wine and two tablespoonfuls of beef extract. Boil for five minutes, add two tablespoonfuls each of chopped mushrooms and cooked beef tongue or ham. Add a little minced parsley, reheat, and serve.

EGG SAUCE—I

Add one half cupful of sliced or chopped hard-boiled eggs to two cupfuls of Drawn-Butter Sauce.

EGG SAUCE—II

Prepare a Cream Sauce according to directions previously given, and add the yolks of two raw eggs, a tablespoonful of grated onion, a hard-boiled egg, chopped fine, and a teaspoonful of minced parsley.

ESPAGNOLE SAUCE

Add a small bay-leaf, a blade of mace, and two cloves, to two cupfuls of white stock. Simmer for fifteen minutes. Cook together two tablespoonfuls of butter and three of flour; add the heated stock and cook until thick, stirring constantly. Add one tablespoonful each of chopped ham, onion, celery, carrot, and parsley, with salt and paprika to season. Simmer for an hour, strain, and serve very hot.

FINE HERB SAUCE—I

Fry in butter one tablespoonful each of minced parsley and onion. Add to one pint of White Sauce and reheat. Season with salt and pepper, and serve.

FINE HERB SAUCE—II

Prepare according to directions given for Brown Italian Sauce, using butter instead of oil and half a cupful of minced parsley instead of the thyme and bay-leaf. Season with grated nutmeg and add to either Spanish or Veloute Sauce.

FLEMISH SAUCE

Prepare a cupful of Drawn-Butter Sauce, take from the fire, add the yolks of two eggs well-beaten, and pepper, grated nutmeg, made mustard, vinegar, and minced parsley to season. Add gradually half a cupful of melted butter and serve.

GARLIC SAUCE

Peel the garlic and boil for an hour, changing the water four times. Drain, chop, and mix to a smooth paste with melted butter. The flavour is mild and resembles almond.

SAUCE À LA GASCONNE

Chop together a tablespoonful of capers and a bean of garlic. Fry in olive-oil, seasoning with pepper and grated nutmeg. Add a wineglassful of white wine, a cupful of Veloute Sauce, a bay-leaf, and a sprig of thyme. Boil for fifteen minutes, skim, add another wineglassful of white wine, strain, and add the yolks of three eggs well beaten. Season with lemon-juice, butter, anchovy essence, and minced parsley.

GENEVA SAUCE

Brown one tablespoonful of flour in butter, add two cupfuls of thick stock and one cupful of red wine, and cook until thick, stirring constantly. Add two small onions chopped, a bunch of sweet herbs, two tablespoonfuls of chopped mushrooms, and salt and pepper to season. Simmer for half an hour, add a wineglassful of Madeira, strain, and serve.

GOOSEBERRY SAUCE

Boil a pint of green gooseberries for ten minutes in water to cover. Drain, press through a sieve, and mix with an equal quantity of White Sauce.

HESSIAN SAUCE

Mix four tablespoonfuls of freshly grated horseradish with an equal quantity of fresh bread-crumbs, a tablespoonful of sugar, and a little salt and pepper. Mix to a smooth paste with sour cream and serve with baked fish.

HOLLANDAISE SAUCE—I

Beat half a cupful of butter to a cream and add gradually the yolks of two eggs well beaten. Then add the juice of half a lemon and pepper and salt to season. Place the bowl over boiling water and beat with an egg-beater until thick and smooth. Take from the fire and beat for a few moments. Be careful not to cook it too long.

HOLLANDAISE SAUCE—II

Put a bay-leaf and a chopped onion in two tablespoonfuls of tarragon vinegar, bring to the boiling point, strain and cool. Cook together two tablespoonfuls of butter and one of flour, add a half cupful of cold water, and cook until thick, stirring constantly. Take from the fire and add the yolks of two eggs beaten with the vinegar. Reheat for a moment, seasoning with salt and pepper, strain, and serve immediately. Lemon-juice may be used in place of the vinegar.

HORSERADISH SAUCE—I

Add half a cupful of freshly grated horseradish to a cupful of Drawn-Butter Sauce. Season with lemon-juice and beat until smooth.

HORSERADISH SAUCE—II

Prepare a Cream Sauce according to directions previously given, and add three tablespoonfuls of freshly grated horseradish and half a cupful of melted butter. Serve with boiled fish.

HORSERADISH SAUCE—III

To one cupful of Spanish Sauce add two tablespoonfuls of prepared horseradish, two tablespoonfuls of bread-crumbs, a teaspoonful of powdered sugar, and salt, pepper, and made mustard to season. Heat in a double-boiler, and just before serving add one-half cupful of whipped or cold cream. (Cow cream, not cosmetic.)

ITALIAN SAUCE

Fry in butter two tablespoonfuls of minced parsley and one tablespoonful of chopped mushrooms and shallots. Add two cupfuls of white wine and boil until reduced half. Add one cupful of Veloute Sauce and one half cupful of stock. Boil until thick, skim, and serve.

BROWN ITALIAN SAUCE

Fry in olive-oil half a cupful of chopped mushrooms, four chopped shallots, a sprig of thyme, and a bay-leaf. Add half a cupful of white wine and simmer until the liquid is reduced half. Take out the thyme and bay-leaf, add a cupful of Spanish Sauce, skim, boil, and serve.

JAPANESE SAUCE

Chop fine a shallot and two cloves of garlic. Add two tablespoonfuls each of walnut catsup, soy, and Worcestershire sauce. Season highly with paprika, add two cupfuls of tarragon vinegar, and let stand for two weeks. Strain, and serve with fish.

JERSEY SAUCE

Brown four tablespoonfuls of flour in butter, add two cupfuls of brown stock and cook until thick, stirring constantly. Season with salt, pepper, and Worcestershire.

LEMON SAUCE—I

Melt half a cupful of butter and add to it the juice of a large lemon. When very hot take from the fire and pour over the well-beaten yolks of two eggs.

LEMON SAUCE—II

Prepare a pint of Drawn-Butter Sauce according to directions previously given, season with salt, pepper, grated nutmeg, and lemon-juice, and add half a cupful of melted butter.

LIVOURNAISE SAUCE

Soak, bone, and pound to a pulp eight salted anchovies. Add the yolks of two eggs, well beaten. Add slowly half a cupful of olive-oil and two tablespoonfuls of vinegar. Season with pepper, grated nutmeg, and minced parsley. Serve very cold.

LOBSTER SAUCE—I

Add half a cupful of chopped cooked lobster meat and the pounded coral to each cupful of Drawn-Butter Sauce. Season with paprika, butter, and lemon-juice.

LOBSTER SAUCE—II

Prepare a Hollandaise Sauce and mix with finely-cut cooked lobster meat. Season with melted butter, lemon-juice, tabasco, and Worcestershire.

MAÎTRE D'HÔTEL SAUCE

Work into half a cupful of butter all the lemon-juice it will take and add a teaspoonful or more of minced parsley. Or, melt the butter without burning, take from the fire, add the juice of half a lemon and a teaspoonful of minced parsley.

MAYONNAISE

Put into an earthen bowl the yolk of a fresh egg and a pinch of salt, a dash of red pepper, and half a teaspoonful of dry mustard. Place the bowl on ice or in ice-water. Pour one cupful of olive-oil into a small pitcher from which it will drop easily. When the egg and seasoning are thoroughly mixed, begin to add the oil, using a silver teaspoon, and rubbing rather than stirring. Add the oil until a clear spot is formed upon the egg, and then mix until smooth. Only a few drops can be added at first, but the quantity may be gradually increased. The clear spot on the egg is an infallible test of the right quantity of oil. If too much oil is added the dressing will curdle. A few drops of lemon-juice and long beating will usually make it right again. If this fails, set the bowl directly on the ice in the refrigerator, and let stand for half an hour. If it is still curdled, begin again with the yolk of another egg and add the curdled mayonnaise by degrees to the new dressing.

When the mayonnaise is so thick that it is difficult to stir it, add the juice of half a lemon, if desired.

MILANAISE SAUCE

Melt two tablespoonfuls of butter, add two chopped mushrooms and two boned and pounded anchovies. Add two tablespoonfuls of flour and cook until the flour is brown. Add one cupful of brown stock and one tablespoonful each of sherry and vinegar drained from capers. Cook until thick, stirring constantly, seasoning with salt, cayenne, and made mustard. Simmer for twenty minutes, strain, add one tablespoonful of capers, boil for five minutes, and serve.

MUSHROOM SAUCE

Prepare a Drawn-Butter Sauce according to directions previously given and add to it one cupful of chopped cooked mushrooms.

NIÇOISE SAUCE

Rub through a fine sieve the yolks of three hard-boiled eggs. Put into a deep bowl, with two raw yolks, a tablespoonful of made mustard, and salt and pepper to season. Add gradually half a cupful of olive-oil and a little vinegar, finishing with two tablespoonfuls of minced fine herbs.

NONPAREIL SAUCE

Add chopped hard-boiled eggs and chopped cooked mushrooms to Hollandaise Sauce.

NORMANDY SAUCE

Add one tablespoonful of mushroom catsup to one pint of Veloute Sauce and cook for ten minutes. Add one fourth cupful of strong fish stock, bring to the boil, take from the fire and add the yolks of two eggs beaten with the juice of half a lemon. Strain, add a tablespoonful of butter, and serve.

OLIVE SAUCE

Prepare according to directions given for Jersey Sauce, adding half a dozen chopped olives instead of the Worcestershire.

OYSTER SAUCE—I

Prepare a Cream Sauce according to directions previously given, using the oyster liquor for part of the liquid. Add parboiled oysters cut fine, and season with paprika and lemon-juice.

OYSTER SAUCE—II

Cook two dozen oysters in their liquor with a little water, butter, white and red pepper, and grated nutmeg. Thicken with a tablespoonful each of butter and flour cooked together, take from the fire, add the yolks of two eggs well beaten, the juice of a lemon, and two tablespoonfuls of butter. Serve with boiled fish.

PARSLEY SAUCE—I

Prepare a Drawn-Butter Sauce according to directions previously given, add half a cupful of fine minced parsley, and season with lemon-juice.

PARSLEY SAUCE—II

Boil two large bunches of parsley in water to cover for five minutes. Strain the water, and thicken with a tablespoonful each of butter and flour cooked together. Season with salt, pepper, and grated nutmeg, take from the fire, add the yolks of two eggs beaten with a little vinegar, three tablespoonfuls of butter in small bits, and a little minced parsley.

PARSLEY AND LEMON SAUCE

Squeeze the juice out of a lemon, remove the seeds, and chop the pulp fine with a bunch of parsley. Add a little of the grated peel. Cook together one tablespoonful each of butter and flour, add the parsley and lemon and one and one half cupfuls of stock. Season with salt, pepper, and powdered mace, and boil for ten minutes. Take from the fire, add the yolks of two eggs beaten with a little cold stock, and serve.

PERSILLADE SAUCE

Put into a bowl one fourth cupful of olive-oil with a tablespoonful of made mustard, the juice of two lemons, two tablespoonfuls of minced parsley, and salt and pepper to season. Add a few drops of tarragon vinegar, mix thoroughly, and serve.

PIQUANT SAUCE—I

Cook together a teaspoonful of chopped onion, a pinch of sugar, a few drops of Worcestershire sauce, and one tablespoonful each of chopped capers and pickles, with two tablespoonfuls of tarragon vinegar, and salt and cayenne to season. Prepare a Spanish Sauce and add the mixture to it.

PIQUANT SAUCE—II

Mix together half a cupful of beef stock, two tablespoonfuls of tarragon vinegar, two tablespoonfuls of chopped pickle, one tablespoonful each of chopped onion, capers, and parsley, a teaspoonful each of sugar and salt, and paprika to season.

POOR MAN'S SAUCE

Brown a tablespoonful of flour in butter, add two cupfuls of stock, and cook until thick, stirring constantly. Add two tablespoonfuls of tomato catsup and one of anchovy essence. Strain and serve.

PORTUGUESE SAUCE

Put six tablespoonfuls of butter into a saucepan with the yolks of two eggs beaten with the juice of half a lemon. Season with salt and pepper and heat thoroughly but do not boil. Take from the fire, stir until thick, and serve immediately.

POULETTE SAUCE

Simmer for ten minutes a pint of White Sauce, seasoning with salt, pepper, and lemon-juice. Beat the yolks of three eggs light and pour the hot sauce over them slowly. Cook for two minutes in a double boiler, and serve immediately.

RAVIGOTE SAUCE

Put one cupful of stock into a saucepan with two tablespoonfuls of white wine and three tablespoonfuls of chopped chives and parsley. Season with salt and pepper and simmer for twenty minutes. Thicken with one tablespoonful each of butter and flour cooked together. Take from the fire, add the juice of half a lemon, and serve.

COLD RAVIGOTE SAUCE

Chop together a tablespoonful each of parsley, chives, chervil, tarragon, and shallot. Add to a stiff mayonnaise and tint green, if desired, with color paste.

REMOULADE SAUCE

Mix two tablespoonfuls each of capers and minced anchovies, add a tablespoonful of minced parsley, a teaspoonful of dry mustard, and salt and pepper to taste. Add one half bean of garlic, chopped very fine, and enough olive-oil to make a smooth paste. Add a few drops of vinegar and serve.

ROYALE SAUCE

Cook together half a cupful of butter and the beaten yolks of three eggs until the yolks begin to thicken. Take from the fire and add by degrees two tablespoonfuls of tarragon vinegar, two tablespoonfuls of Indian soy, one finely chopped small pickle, and cayenne and salt to season. Mix thoroughly and cool. Serve cold.

SARDINE SAUCE

Add skinned, boned, and mashed sardines to Mayonnaise. Beat until smooth and serve with cold fish.

SHAD ROE SAUCE

Boil, drain, skin, and mash a shad roe. Season with salt, pepper, grated onion, and powdered mace. Add half a cupful of Madeira and half a cupful or more of melted butter. Serve with shad or any other fish.

SHRIMP SAUCE

Add one cupful of chopped cooked shrimps to each pint of White Sauce. Season with lemon-juice, paprika, and tabasco sauce.

SICILIAN SAUCE

Slice four onions, fry brown and drain carefully. Put into a saucepan with two cupfuls of Espagnole Sauce, a wineglassful of sherry, and a pinch of cayenne pepper. Reheat, strain, and serve.

SPANISH SAUCE

Prepare according to directions given for Brown Sauce, using one cupful of highly seasoned stock for liquid.

SUPREME SAUCE

Prepare according to directions given for Drawn-Butter Sauce, using chicken stock and a little cream for liquid. Take from the fire, and add two tablespoonfuls of butter and the juice of half a lemon.

TARTAR SAUCE—I

Chop together capers, olives, parsley, and pickles. Add one half cupful of the mixture to a cupful of Mayonnaise.

TARTAR SAUCE—II

Mix together one tablespoonful each of vinegar and Worcestershire sauce, add a teaspoonful of lemon-juice and a pinch of salt. Brown half a cupful of butter and strain into the hot vinegar. Serve hot.

TARTAR SAUCE—III

Prepare a cupful of Drawn-Butter Sauce and add to it a teaspoonful each of made mustard, grated onion, and chopped pickle. Take from the fire, season with salt and cayenne, add the beaten yolk of an egg, and serve.

TOMATO SAUCE—I

Prepare according to directions given for Drawn-Butter Sauce, using tomato-juice or stewed and strained canned tomatoes for liquid.

TOMATO SAUCE—II

Chop together capers, pickles, onion, and olives. There should be half a cupful in all. Add one half cupful of stewed and strained tomatoes, a teaspoonful each of made mustard and sugar, and salt and cayenne to season highly. Serve very hot.

TOMATO SAUCE—III

Chop fine an onion and a clove of garlic. Fry in butter and add half a can of stewed and strained tomatoes. Thicken with butter and flour cooked together, season with salt and pepper and serve.

BROWN TOMATO SAUCE

Fry a tablespoonful of chopped onion in butter, add one tablespoonful of flour and one half cupful each of stock and stewed and strained tomato. Cook until thick, stirring constantly. Season with salt, pepper, and kitchen bouquet. Strain and serve.

VELOUTE SAUCE

Cook together three tablespoonfuls each of butter and flour, add one cupful of white stock and one quarter cupful of cream. Cook until thick, stirring constantly. Season with salt, cayenne, grated nutmeg, and minced parsley. Simmer for an hour, strain, and serve.

VENETIENNE SAUCE—I

Cook together for five minutes two tablespoonfuls of tarragon vinegar, six pepper-corns, a tablespoonful of chopped ham, six parsley roots, a sprig of thyme and a bay-leaf. Strain, and add to one cupful of Veloute Sauce. Reheat, add a teaspoonful of minced parsley and serve.

VENETIENNE SAUCE—II

Add minced parsley, tarragon vinegar, grated nutmeg, and a tablespoonful of butter to Allemande Sauce.

VINAIGRETTE SAUCE

Mix four tablespoonfuls of olive-oil with one tablespoonful of vinegar. Season with salt and paprika and add to it minced parsley, pickle, and capers.

WHIPPED CREAM SAUCE

Mix a teaspoonful of dry mustard with a tablespoonful of vinegar and two tablespoonfuls of freshly grated horseradish. Mix with one fourth cupful of Mayonnaise, and when smooth fold in carefully one cupful of whipped cream. Season with salt and red pepper and serve very cold with cold fish.

WHITE SAUCE

Cook together two tablespoonfuls each of butter and flour, add one cupful of white stock and one half cupful of cream. Cook until thick, stirring constantly. Season with salt and pepper. One and one half cupfuls of milk may be used instead of the stock and cream.

TEN WAYS TO SERVE ANCHOVIES

I

Clean, bone, and trim the fish. Arrange on a dish, alternating with quarters of hard-boiled eggs. Moisten with olive-oil, sprinkle with parsley, and serve with toasted crackers.

II

Split the anchovies, wash in white wine, and bone them. Make a paste with the yolks of eggs, equal parts of minced cooked fish, and bread-crumbs. Stuff the anchovies, dip into batter, and fry in deep fat.

III

Pound the fish in a mortar, seasoning with minced parsley, grated onion, and cayenne. Serve on small circles of fried bread, as a first course at dinner.

IV

Drain a bottle of anchovies and mash fine with enough butter to make a smooth paste. Season with lemon-juice and cayenne. Spread on fingers of toast and lay a whole anchovy on each piece.

V

Wash eight salted anchovies, remove the skin and bones, and soak in clear water for an hour. Drain and wipe dry. Arrange on lettuce leaves with sliced hard-boiled eggs and pour over a French dressing.

VI

Toast circles of bread, spread with butter, cover with chopped hard-boiled eggs, make a hollow in the egg, lay an anchovy upon it, and set into a hot oven for five minutes.

VII

Toast thin circles of graham bread, butter, and cover each piece with anchovies. Sprinkle with lemon-juice and paprika and put into hot oven for five minutes.

VIII

Clean and rinse the fish and dry on a cloth. Butter a small baking-dish, put in a layer of cracker crumbs, then a layer of anchovies, then sugar and crumbs. Repeat until the dish is full, having crumbs and butter on top. Beat the yolks of two eggs with half a cupful of cream and a little sugar. Pour over the fish and bake in the oven.

IX

Use salted Norwegian anchovies soaked for two hours in cold water. Split down the back, bone and skin, cut into strips, and arrange on a platter. Mince separately parsley, capers, boiled carrots, beets, and the whites and yolks of hard-boiled eggs. Arrange small piles of contrasting colors among the fish and pour over a French dressing.

X

Fry thin circles of bread, put a pimola in the centre, and curl an anchovy around it. Fill the remaining space with chopped hard-boiled eggs and serve as a first course at dinner or luncheon.

FORTY-FIVE WAYS TO COOK BASS

BAKED BASS—I

Scale, wash, and clean, leaving the head intact. Make a stuffing of two cupfuls of bread-crumbs, one cupful of butter, two eggs well beaten, and enough cold water to make a smooth paste. Season with pepper, salt, grated lemon, minced parsley, thyme, and marjoram. Split the fish, stuff, and sew up. Lay thin slices of salt pork over the fish and put into a baking-pan with a little boiling water seasoned with wine and tomato juice. Bake carefully, basting frequently. The gravy may be thickened and served with the fish.

BAKED BASS—II

Split the fish and stuff with seasoned mashed potatoes. Put a little boiling water and a tablespoonful of butter into the baking-pan, and baste frequently while cooking.

BAKED BASS—III

Rub the inside of the fish with salt, sprinkle the outside with pepper and salt, cover with sliced onion and salt pork. Dredge with flour and put into the baking-pan with sufficient boiling water to keep from burning. Baste frequently while cooking, remove the pork and onion, thicken the sauce with a tablespoonful each of butter and flour blended and mixed with a little tomato catsup. Pour the hot sauce over the fish and serve.

BAKED BASS—IV

Make a stuffing of one cupful of bread-crumbs, one teaspoonful each of melted butter, Worcestershire sauce, tomato catsup, minced parsley, minced onion, minced olives or pickles, lemon-juice, salt, black pepper, and paprika to taste, and sufficient cold water to moisten. Sew up the fish and bake as usual. Serve with Tartar Sauce.

BAKED BASS WITH WHITE WINE

Put a bass into a baking-dish with salt, pepper and mushroom liquor to season, and enough white wine to moisten. Cover with buttered paper and bake for fifteen minutes. Melt two tablespoonfuls of butter, add three tablespoonfuls of flour, and cook thoroughly. Add two cupfuls of white stock and cook until thick, stirring constantly. Take from the fire and add the yolks of three eggs beaten with a little cold water, and the juice of half a lemon. Add a tablespoonful of butter and the juice in the baking-pan. Pour over the bass and serve.

BAKED BASS WITH SHRIMP SAUCE

Marinate the cleaned fish for an hour in oil and vinegar. Put into a baking-pan with slices of salt pork underneath and on top and sufficient boiling water to keep from burning. Add a teaspoonful of butter to the water and baste two or three times during the hour of baking. Strain the gravy and set aside. Melt one tablespoonful of butter, add one tablespoonful of flour and cook until brown. Add one cupful of the liquid left in the baking-pan, making up the required quantity with boiling water if necessary. Cook until thick, stirring constantly; season with cayenne and lemon-juice, and add half a can of shrimps chopped fine. Bring to the boil, pour over the fish, and serve.

BAKED AND STUFFED BLACK BASS

Mix together one cupful of bread-crumbs, two small onions chopped, two eggs well beaten, and cold water to moisten. Season with Worcestershire, tabasco and minced parsley. Stuff a bass with this mixture, rub with melted butter, and bake with a little boiling water, basting as required.

BAKED BASS À LA NEWPORT

Clean the fish, gash the top, season with salt and pepper, and cover with thin slices of salt pork. Pour a little boiling water into the pan and bake slowly, basting as required. Serve with the pork. Bacon may be used instead.

BAKED BASS À LA MANHATTAN

Butter a baking-dish, put in the cleansed fish, rub with melted butter, season with salt and pepper, and cover with thin slices of bacon and bread crumbs. Add a little boiling water and bake in a very hot oven, basting as required.

BAKED BASS AND TOMATOES

Select one large black bass or two small ones; clean the head and let it remain on the fish. Slice four tomatoes and cut in halves. Make a plain bread dressing; open the fish, rub the inside lightly with salt and soft butter; lay a thick layer of tomatoes in, then a layer of the bread dressing, alternating them until the fish is well stuffed; then bind with a tape. Lard the fish with strips of salt pork. Lay in a baking-pan, add one cupful of hot water and one tablespoonful of butter, and bake, basting often. In fifteen minutes take the pan out of the oven and spread the fish with a layer of thinly sliced tomatoes, seasoned with a sprinkling of salt, some melted butter, and a light sprinkling of grated cheese. Bake until the tomatoes are done, then carefully remove to a platter, taking off the tape first. Garnish with parsley and serve.

BAKED BLACK BASS À LA BABETTE

Clean the fish, salt it well, and put into a baking-pan with a cupful of water. Put lumps of butter on top, and season with salt, pepper, and minced parsley. Bake for an hour, basting often. Add a wineglassful of Sherry and a little catsup to the sauce remaining in the pan. Thicken with a teaspoonful of flour, rubbed smooth with a little cold water.

BAKED FILLETS OF BASS

Cut bass into small fillets, sprinkle with salt and pepper, put into a shallow pan, cover with buttered paper and bake for twelve minutes in a hot oven. Serve with a border of boiled rice and Hollandaise Sauce.

BLACK BASS À LA MONTMORENCY

Clean, skin, and bone a bass, and cut into pieces. Butter a baking-dish, put in the fish, season with salt, pepper, and white wine; cover with buttered paper and set in the oven until the fish is partly cooked. Take out the fish and arrange in a baking-pan. Add to the remaining liquor a chopped onion, half a dozen mushrooms, and two sprigs of parsley finely chopped. Add a little stock and thicken with a teaspoonful of flour rubbed smooth in a little cold water. Pour this sauce over the fish, lay a large mushroom on each piece, cover with crumbs, dot with butter, and bake in the oven. Sprinkle with lemon-juice before serving.

STUFFED SEA-BASS

Clean the fish and cover it with a marinade of olive-oil and vinegar. Soak for an hour. Fill the fish with chopped salt pork and mushrooms, put into a baking-pan with slices of salt pork underneath and on top, and sufficient boiling water. Bake for forty minutes, cover with slices of tomatoes and half of a sweet green pepper chopped fine. Dot with butter and bake for twenty minutes more. Take up the fish and rub the sauce through a colander. Stir in a tablespoonful of butter rolled in flour, add one teaspoonful of sugar and two teaspoonfuls of grated onion. Dilute with boiling water if too thick, bring to the boil, pour over the fish, and serve.

BASS À LA BORDELAISE

Split a large sea-bass. Put into a baking-dish with a wineglassful of Claret and salt and pepper to season. Sprinkle with chopped shallot, cover with buttered paper, and cook in a moderate oven for fifteen minutes. Lay the bass on a platter, put the juice in a saucepan with half a teaspoonful of beef extract, four chopped mushrooms, and a bruised bean of garlic. Thicken with flour browned in butter, bring to the boil, pour over the fish, and serve very hot.

BOILED BASS

Clean the fish, put it into warm salted water and simmer for twenty minutes.

BOILED SEA-BASS WITH EGG SAUCE

Boil the fish according to directions previously given. Melt one tablespoonful of butter, add two tablespoonfuls of flour, and cook thoroughly. Add two cupfuls of the water in which the fish was boiled, and cook until thick, stirring constantly. Season with salt, pepper, minced parsley, and lemon-juice; add three hard-boiled eggs coarsely chopped, pour over the fish, and serve.

BOILED BASS WITH MUSHROOMS

Boil a bass in water to cover, adding to the water four tablespoonfuls of vinegar, six pepper-corns, and a little salt. Melt one tablespoonful of butter, add one tablespoonful of flour and cook thoroughly. Add one cupful or more of boiling water and cook until thick, stirring constantly. Add the juice of half a lemon, half a can of mushrooms chopped fine, and pepper and salt and minced parsley to season. Bring to the boil, pour over the fish, and serve.

BOILED BLACK BASS WITH CREAM SAUCE

Clean the bass and sew it up in coarse cheese-cloth. Boil in enough water to cover, adding half a cupful of vinegar, a sliced onion, six or eight whole peppers, a blade of mace, and salt to season. Take up the fish and reduce the liquid by rapid boiling. Strain and set aside. Melt one tablespoonful of butter, add one tablespoonful of flour and cook thoroughly. Add a cupful of the strained liquid and cook until thick, stirring constantly. Season to taste, add half a cupful of cream, bring to the boil, pour over the fish, and garnish with sliced lemons.

BLACK SEA-BASS À LA POULETTE

Prepare a Poulette Sauce and pour over a black sea bass boiled according to directions previously given.

COLD BASS WITH TARTAR SAUCE

Boil the fish in court bouillon and drain. Chop fine parsley, pickles, olives, and capers. Mix with a stiff Mayonnaise and spread over the fish. Serve with a border of sliced cucumbers.

BROILED BASS

Clean the fish, split it, and cut each half into two or three pieces. Dip in oil or melted butter, sprinkle with flour, and broil carefully.

BROILED BLACK BASS

Clean and split the fish, remove the bone, rub with melted butter or oil, and broil carefully. Pour over a little melted butter, and garnish with lemon and parsley.

BASS STEWED WITH TOMATOES

Clean the fish, remove the bones and cut into square pieces. Fry two sliced onions in olive-oil. Lay the fish upon it, season with salt and pepper and pour over a can of tomatoes which have been rubbed through a sieve. Season with salt and pepper, cover closely, and cook for an hour. Serve in the same dish.

FRIED BASS WITH BACON

Clean and cut up the fish, season with pepper and salt, roll in flour, and fry in hot lard. Serve with rashers of bacon fried separately. Garnish with parsley and lemon.

FRIED BLACK BASS

Scale, clean, and cut up the fish, season with salt and pepper, dredge with flour, and fry in deep fat.

BREADED FILLET OF BASS

Clean the fish and cut into convenient pieces. Season with salt and pepper, dip in beaten egg, then in crumbs, and fry in deep fat. Serve very hot with Tartar Sauce.

BREADED BASS WITH BACON

Clean the fish and cut into pieces. Season with pepper and salt, roll in flour, then in beaten egg, then in bread-crumbs. Fry in deep fat and serve with a border of rashers of bacon fried separately. Garnish with parsley.

BOILED SEA-BASS WITH PARSLEY SAUCE

Put two medium-sized cleaned sea-bass into a fish-kettle with a bunch of parsley. Cover with salted and acidulated water, bring to the boil, simmer for half an hour, drain, garnish with lemon and parsley, and serve with a parsley sauce.

FRIED SEA-BASS WITH TARTAR SAUCE

Clean and wipe small sea-bass, score the sides deeply, dip in milk, roll in flour, fry in deep fat, drain, sprinkle with salt, and garnish with quartered lemons and fried parsley. Serve with Tartar Sauce.

MATELOTE OF SEA-BASS

Clean three pounds of sea-bass and cut in convenient pieces for serving. Put into a saucepan with a bunch of parsley, salt and pepper to season, and a teaspoonful of sweet herbs. Add two onions, sliced, and two small cloves of garlic. Cover with equal parts of stock and Claret and simmer slowly until the fish is done. Move the fish carefully to a serving-dish and strain the liquid into another saucepan. Brown two tablespoonfuls of flour in as much butter as is required to make a smooth paste, add the liquid, and cook until thick, stirring constantly. Add to the sauce three tablespoonfuls of essence of anchovy and some mushrooms and small button onions fried brown in butter. Pour over the fish and serve.

BROILED SEA-BASS

Select a large fish, clean, and split. Season with salt and pepper, rub with olive-oil, and broil carefully. Serve with Maître D'Hôtel Sauce and garnish with lemon and parsley.

SEA-BASS À LA BUENA VISTA

Prepare and clean a large sea-bass. Cut a long, deep incision lengthwise on each side. Place in a buttered baking-dish with a chopped onion, a bunch of parsley, a pinch of sweet herbs, half a can of tomatoes and a small green pepper, shredded. Sprinkle with salt and pepper, add two cupfuls of stock and one cupful of Port wine. Dot with butter and bake in a moderate oven for forty minutes, basting freely. Take up the fish, and strain the sauce. Melt a tablespoonful of butter, brown in it a tablespoonful of flour, add two cupfuls of well-seasoned beef stock and cook until thick, stirring constantly. Combine these two sauces, cover the fish with broiled tomatoes, pour the sauce over, sprinkle with parsley and lemon-juice, and serve.

BOILED SEA-BASS WITH MELTED BUTTER SAUCE

Boil the fish in acidulated water according to directions previously given. Drain, garnish with parsley, and serve with a sauce made by melting half a cupful of butter with the juice of a lemon, and seasoning with white pepper and a little grated nutmeg.

SEA-BASS À LA FRANCAISE

Clean and trim two large sea-bass. Put into a saucepan, with salt and pepper to season, three tablespoonfuls of butter, two large onions, sliced, a bunch of parsley, and enough Claret to cover the fish. Simmer for forty minutes, drain, and place on a serving-dish. Take out the parsley and keep the liquid warm. Brown two tablespoonfuls of flour in two tablespoonfuls of butter, add the onions and liquid and cook until thick, stirring constantly. Add stock or water if there is not enough liquid. Add a tablespoonful each of melted butter and minced parsley, pour over the fish, and serve.

SEA-BASS WITH BLACK BUTTER

Boil medium-sized sea-bass in salted and acidulated water, drain, and marinate with salt, pepper, and vinegar. Brown a cupful of butter in a saucepan, skim, pour the top part over the fish, leaving the sediment in the pan, garnish with fried parsley, and serve.

STRIPED BASS WITH SHAD ROE

Clean a four-pound striped bass and soak the soft roes of four shad in cold water. Put the bass into a fish-kettle with an onion, salt and pepper to season, a small bunch of parsley, a tablespoonful of butter, two wineglassfuls of white wine, and enough white stock to cover. Cover, cook for half an hour or more, basting as required, and drain. Strain the liquid and add it to a tablespoonful each of butter and flour cooked together. Cook until it thickens, stirring constantly. Add the juice of a lemon and two tablespoonfuls of butter. Cook the roes for five minutes in salted and acidulated water, drain, cut in two, and arrange around the fish. Pour the sauce over, sprinkle with minced parsley, and serve.

FILLETS OF STRIPED BASS À LA BORDELAISE

Clean two striped bass and cut into fillets. Cover the trimmings with water, add one cupful of white wine, two cupfuls of white stock, a sliced onion, a bay-leaf, a sprig of thyme, a tablespoonful of butter, and salt and pepper to season. Skin the fillets, season with salt, and marinate for half an hour in oil and lemon-juice. Drain, sprinkle with flour, dip in egg yolks beaten smooth with a little melted butter, then in crumbs. Broil carefully, basting with melted butter as required. Fry a tablespoonful of chopped onion in two tablespoonfuls of flour and cook to a smooth paste. Add the liquid strained from the fish trimmings and cook until thick, stirring constantly. Add half a cupful of stewed and strained tomato, a tablespoonful of minced parsley, and two tablespoonfuls of butter. Season with red pepper and lemon-juice, pour over the fish, and serve.

FILLETS OF STRIPED BASS À LA MANHATTAN

Clean and trim a four-pound bass, skin, remove the bones, and chop very fine. Add four tablespoonfuls of butter, season with salt, pepper, and grated nutmeg, and add enough cream to make a stiff paste. Shape into cutlets, dip in egg and crumbs and fry in deep fat, or sauté in clarified butter. Drain. and serve with Tomato Sauce.

STRIPED BASS WITH CAPER SAUCE

Clean and trim a large striped bass, cut two incisions across the back, tie in a circle, and boil slowly in salted and acidulated water for forty minutes. Drain, pour over a Caper Sauce, garnish with parsley, and serve.

STRIPED BASS À LA DAUPHINE

Clean and trim a striped bass. Put into a fish-kettle with salt, pepper, a bunch of parsley, a pinch of sweet herbs, a sliced onion, two cupfuls of white wine, two cupfuls of water, and four tablespoonfuls of butter. Cook for forty minutes in a moderate oven, basting frequently. Drain the fish, strain the liquor, and add enough white stock or oyster liquor to make the required quantity of sauce. Cook two tablespoonfuls of flour in one tablespoonful of butter, add the liquid, and cook until thick, stirring constantly. Add three egg yolks well beaten with four tablespoonfuls of butter, a tablespoonful of anchovy essence, the juice of half a lemon, and a pinch of paprika. Bring to the boiling point, pour over the fish, and serve. Garnish with fried mushrooms.

STRIPED BASS À LA CARDINAL

Clean and trim a striped bass. Cook in a fish-kettle with two cupfuls of water, one cupful of white wine, four tablespoonfuls of butter, a bunch of parsley, an onion, and a carrot, sliced, and salt and pepper to season. Simmer for forty minutes and drain. Add two cupfuls of white stock to the liquid, strain, and skim off the fat. Cook two tablespoonfuls of flour in a tablespoonful of butter, add the strained liquid and cook until thick, stirring constantly. Take from the fire and add the yolks of four eggs, beaten with the juice of a lemon, four tablespoonfuls of melted butter, and a pinch of paprika. Bring to the boil, then take from the fire, add sufficient dried and pounded lobster coral to color, pour over the fish, and serve.

STRIPED BASS À LA HOLLANDAISE

Clean and trim a striped bass and simmer half an hour in salted and acidulated water to cover. Drain, garnish with parsley, and serve with Hollandaise Sauce.

STRIPED BASS À LA COMMODORE

Clean and stuff a striped bass. Put into a fish-kettle with a bunch of parsley, a cupful of mixed vegetables cut fine, a cupful of white wine, a cupful of oyster liquor, and enough water or stock to cover. Simmer for forty minutes and drain. Strain the gravy, skim off the fat, and set aside. Brown two tablespoonfuls of flour in one tablespoonful of butter, add one cupful of stock and cook until very thick, stirring constantly. Add the strained sauce and reheat, stirring until smooth. Add a tablespoonful of anchovy essence, four tablespoonfuls of butter, and lemon-juice to taste. Pour over the fish and serve.

STRIPED BASS À L'AMERICAINE

Cook together one tablespoonful each of butter and flour, add a pint of oysters, with their liquor, and the yolks of two eggs, well beaten. Cook until thick, stirring constantly. Prepare and trim a striped bass, fill with the oyster mixture, season, and sew up. Put into a fish-kettle with enough white wine and water, in equal parts, to cover. Add a sliced onion, a bunch of parsley, a little salt and pepper and a tablespoonful of butter. Simmer for an hour and drain. Strain the gravy and skim off the fat. Cook together two tablespoonfuls of flour and one of butter, add the strained liquid and cook until thick, stirring constantly. Take from the fire, add the yolks of four eggs beaten with four tablespoonfuls of melted butter, the juice of a lemon, and a tablespoonful of minced parsley. Bring to the boil, pour over the fish, and serve. Garnish with fried oysters.

STRIPED BASS À LA MARSEILLES

Clean a large striped bass and divide into fillets. Put into a fish-boiler with three tablespoonfuls of butter, two large onions, sliced, a bunch of parsley, a bay-leaf, salt and pepper to season, and red wine and water, in equal parts, to cover. Simmer for an hour, drain the fish, take out the parsley, strain the liquid, and spread the cooked onions over the fish. Cook three tablespoonfuls of flour in two tablespoonfuls of butter, add the strained liquid and cook until thick, stirring constantly. Take from the fire, add the juice of a small lemon, a tablespoonful of anchovy essence, and two tablespoonfuls of butter. When the butter is melted, pour over the fish and serve.

STRIPED BASS À LA CONTI

Clean and trim a large striped bass. Put into a baking-pan with four tablespoonfuls of olive-oil, a small onion, chopped fine, salt and pepper to season, a bunch of parsley, and two cupfuls each of white wine and white stock. Cover and cook for an hour in a moderate oven, basting often. Drain the fish and remove the parsley. Strain the sauce. Brown two tablespoonfuls of flour in one of butter, add the strained liquid, and cook until thick, stirring constantly. Add the juice of half a lemon and a tablespoonful of minced parsley. Pour over the fish and serve.

EIGHT WAYS TO COOK BLACKFISH

BLACKFISH À L'AMERICAINE

Draw two large blackfish, trim, and clean thoroughly. Put into a baking-dish with two chopped onions fried in butter. Add two cupfuls of cold water and half a cupful of Port wine. Season with salt and pepper, a pinch of powdered cloves, mace, allspice, and thyme, two bay-leaves, a small bunch of parsley, and two leeks. Cover tightly and cook for an hour. Lift out the fish and strain the liquid. Thicken it with a tablespoonful of butter, blended with an equal quantity of flour. Bring to the boil, add two tablespoonfuls of butter, and minced parsley and lemon-juice to season. Pour over the fish and serve.

BLACKFISH WITH FINE HERBS

Put the cleaned fish into a baking-dish with chopped onions, parsley and mushrooms. Gash the fish and fill the incisions with butter and chopped onion. Moisten with equal parts of white wine and stock, cover with buttered paper, and cook in a moderate oven for half an hour, basting frequently. Take out the fish, strain the sauce, and add stock to make the necessary quantity. Thicken with a tablespoonful of butter rolled in flour, and pour over the fish. Cover with crumbs, dot with butter, and brown in the oven. Sprinkle with lemon-juice before serving.

BROILED BLACKFISH WITH CHILLI SAUCE

Clean the fish, season with salt and pepper, rub with oil, and broil slowly. Fry in butter a chopped shallot and two chilli peppers. Add two chopped tomatoes, a wineglassful of Catawba wine, and a cupful of stock. Boil to the consistency of a thick sauce, add two tablespoonfuls of butter and a little chopped parsley. Spread over the fish.

MATELOTE OF BLACKFISH

Cover four pounds of cleaned blackfish with equal parts of Claret and water. Add salt and pepper to season, two small cloves of garlic, two onions sliced, and a bunch of parsley. Boil for half an hour and strain the liquid. Thicken it with two tablespoonfuls of butter blended with a little flour. Add two tablespoonfuls of butter, a tablespoonful of anchovy paste, and lemon-juice to season. Strain over the fish and garnish with fresh fried mushrooms and small white onions sprinkled with sugar and fried brown in clarified butter.

STEWED BLACKFISH À LA NEWPORT

Cook four pounds of blackfish in Catawba wine and water to cover, seasoning with parsley and onion, three cloves, salt, and half a dozen pepper-corns. Boil for half an hour, strain the sauce, and thicken with two tablespoonfuls of flour browned in butter. Cook until thick, add two tablespoonfuls of butter and the juice of half a lemon. Strain over the fish and surround with a border of baked tomatoes.

BAKED BLACKFISH—I

Put two cleaned blackfish into a buttered baking-pan with one cupful of Port wine and two cupfuls of water. Add salt, white and red pepper, grated nutmeg, minced parsley, and sweet herbs to season. Dot the fish with butter, cover with buttered paper, and bake for forty-five minutes, basting as required. Take out the fish, strain the sauce, and put it into a saucepan with two cupfuls of stock. Thicken with two tablespoonfuls of butter blended with an equal quantity of flour, and boil for ten minutes. Skim, add two tablespoonfuls each of butter and anchovy paste, and lemon-juice to taste. Reheat, pour over the fish, and serve.

BAKED BLACKFISH—II

Remove the skin and fins from a six-pound fish and place in a baking-pan. Cover with two cupfuls of bread-crumbs moistened with hot water, and seasoned with butter, salt, pepper, sage, summer savory, and sweet marjoram. Bake for an hour and a half and serve with any preferred sauce.

BLACKFISH WITH PORT WINE SAUCE

Put two cleaned blackfish into a pan with one cupful of Port wine, one cupful of water, one cupful of white stock, and salt, pepper, minced parsley, and sweet herbs to season. Cover and simmer for forty minutes. Take out the fish, add two cupfuls of stock to the sauce, thicken with one tablespoonful of butter blended with two of flour, and cook until of the proper consistency. Strain through a cloth, add two tablespoonfuls of butter, and lemon-juice and red pepper to season. Pour over the fish and serve.

TWENTY-SIX WAYS TO COOK BLUEFISH

BAKED BLUEFISH À L'ITALIENNE

Score and scale the bluefish and put it into a buttered pan with three tablespoonfuls each of white wine and mushroom liquor, a tablespoonful of chopped onion, half a dozen chopped mushrooms and salt and pepper to season. Cover with buttered paper and bake for fifteen minutes. Take out the fish and add to the sauce half a teaspoonful of beef extract, dissolved in half a cupful of boiling water. Add a wineglassful of white wine and thicken with one tablespoonful each of butter and browned flour. Pour the sauce over the fish, sprinkle with chopped parsley, and serve.

BAKED BLUEFISH—I

Clean, scrape, and split the fish and take out the backbone. Gash the flesh and insert a thin slice of salt pork under the skin. Make a stuffing of one cupful of bread-crumbs, two tablespoonfuls of chopped salt pork, and salt, minced parsley, chopped onion, red pepper, kitchen bouquet, and tomato catsup to season. Add one egg well beaten. Fill the fish and sew up. Lay on thin slices of salt pork and bake, basting frequently with the fat. Garnish with cress and lemon.

BAKED BLUEFISH—II

Clean a large bluefish, put into a baking-pan, pour over it a cupful of boiling salted water, cover and bake for an hour, basting frequently. Put on a serving platter, and thicken the sauce with browned flour, seasoning with salt, pepper, Worcestershire and tomato catsup. Serve with a garnish of sliced lemon.

BAKED BLUEFISH—III

Make a stuffing of bread-crumbs, two tablespoonfuls of minced onion, a teaspoonful of minced parsley, three tablespoonfuls of butter, one egg well-beaten, and salt and pepper to season. Stuff the fish and tie securely. Bake in a pan with a cupful of hot water and a tablespoonful of butter, basting frequently. Take out the fish, boil up the sauce, add a tablespoonful of catsup, a tablespoonful of browned flour wet with four tablespoonfuls of cold water, and the juice of a lemon. Cook until thick, and strain.

BAKED BLUEFISH—IV

Prepare a stuffing of crumbs, grated onion, beaten egg and capers. Stuff a large bluefish and sew up. Season with salt and pepper, rub with butter, and add sufficient boiling water. Bake, baste frequently, and serve with any preferred sauce.

BAKED BLUEFISH—V

Make a stuffing of one cupful of bread-crumbs, a tablespoonful of melted butter, and salt and pepper to season. Fill the fish and sew firmly. Gash the fish and lay strips of pork in the gashes. Cover with crumbs, dot with butter and add sufficient boiling water to keep from burning. Bake for an hour, basting frequently. Garnish with parsley and lemon and serve with tomato sauce.

BAKED BLUEFISH—VI

Slit a large bluefish, take out the bone, put in a buttered baking-dish and season with salt and pepper. Fry a chopped onion in butter, add half a dozen chopped mushrooms, three tablespoonfuls of chopped cooked egg-plant, and a teaspoonful of minced parsley. Add two cupfuls of stock, and cook for fifteen minutes. Thicken with a tablespoonful or more of flour rubbed smooth in cold water, and pour over the fish. Sprinkle with crumbs, dot with butter, and bake for an hour in a moderate oven.

BAKED BLUEFISH WITH WHITE WINE SAUCE

Put a cleaned bluefish into a buttered pan with salt, pepper, minced parsley, sweet herbs, a sliced onion, two cupfuls of white wine, and one cupful of white stock. Cover with a buttered paper and cook for forty minutes, basting as required. Take out the fish, strain the sauce, and thicken with a tablespoonful of flour cooked in butter. Boil for ten minutes, add three tablespoonfuls of butter, the juice of half a lemon and three egg yolks well beaten. Bring to the boil, pour over the fish, and serve.

BAKED BLUEFISH À LA NAPLES

Prepare the fish according to directions given for Baked Bluefish—II. Fry in butter for five minutes two tablespoonfuls each of chopped onion, carrot, and lean raw ham. Add twelve pepper-corns, two cloves, and a sprig of marjoram. Add two and one half tablespoonfuls of flour and cook until brown. Add gradually one cupful of brown stock and one and one fourth cupfuls of white wine. Cook until thick, stirring constantly, strain, reheat, pour over the fish, sprinkle with minced parsley, and serve.

BOILED BLUEFISH

Prepare according to directions given for Boiled Bass.

BROILED BLUEFISH—I

Split the fish down the back and soak for half an hour in brine. Rinse in fresh water, dry on a towel and broil on a buttered broiler. Serve on a hot platter with melted butter poured over, and garnish with watercress and sliced lemon.

BROILED BLUEFISH—II

Clean and split down the back, season with salt and pepper, and broil according to directions previously given. Sprinkle with minced parsley and lemon-juice and pour over a little melted butter. Serve with a border of mashed potatoes.

PAN-BROILED BLUEFISH

Lay the fish flesh side down in a well greased, very hot pan. Turn with a pancake-turner.

BROILED BLUEFISH AU BEURRE-NOIR

Broil a bluefish according to directions previously given. Mix together one tablespoonful each of vinegar and minced parsley, one teaspoonful of lemon-juice, and salt and pepper to season. Put two tablespoonfuls of butter into a frying-pan and when it browns add the other ingredients. Bring to the boil and pour it over the broiled fish.

BROILED BLUEFISH WITH MUSTARD SAUCE

Broil a bluefish according to directions previously given, and sprinkle with lemon-juice. Pour over a Cream Sauce to which prepared mustard has been added.

MATELOTE OF BLUEFISH

Prepare according to directions given for Matelote of Blackfish, using white wine instead of Claret.

STUFFED BLUEFISH—I

Prepare according to directions given for Stuffed Sea-Bass.

STUFFED BLUEFISH—II

Scrape, clean, and dry a large bluefish. Chop three onions fine and fry in butter. Add enough mashed potatoes to make the required quantity of stuffing, and season with salt, pepper, minced parsley, and melted butter. Fill the fish and sew up. Rub with melted butter, put a little hot water into the pan, and bake for thirty minutes, basting as required. Garnish with lemon and parsley.

ESCALLOPED BLUEFISH

Flake cold cooked bluefish and mix it with an equal quantity of mashed potatoes. Fill buttered shells, sprinkle with grated cheese, cover with crumbs, dot with butter, and brown in the oven.

FILLETS OF BLUEFISH À LA DUXELLES

Skin, bone, and fillet a bluefish. Season with salt and pepper, and cook with melted butter and lemon-juice until firm. Take from the fire and cool. Prepare a Duxelles Sauce, boil down until thick, and cook the fish with it. Dip in crumbs, then in beaten egg, then in crumbs, and fry in deep fat. Serve with the diluted sauce poured around the fish.

FILLETS OF BLUEFISH WITH ANCHOVY SAUCE

Prepare the fish according to directions given in the preceding recipe, cooking with white wine as well as lemon-juice. Prepare a Cream Sauce, and add to it two tablespoonfuls each of butter and anchovy paste. Pour over the fish and serve.

BLUEFISH À L'ICARIENNE

Scale and score a two-pound bluefish, and put in a buttered baking-dish with three tablespoonfuls each of mushroom liquor and white wine, and salt and pepper to season. Cover with a buttered paper and bake for fifteen minutes. Take out the fish and add to the sauce three tablespoonfuls of stewed and strained tomatoes and one tablespoonful of chopped, cooked, smoked beef tongue. Bring to the boil, pour over the fish, and serve.

BLUEFISH À LA VENETIENNE

Prepare according to directions for Baked Bluefish à la Italienne, adding to it a chopped tomato and six whole mushrooms. Sprinkle with crumbs, dot with butter, brown in the oven, and sprinkle with minced parsley.

FRIED FILLETS OF BLUEFISH

Cut the fish into fillets and soak for half an hour in olive-oil and lemon-juice. Dip in crumbs, then in beaten egg, then in seasoned cracker crumbs, and set into a cold place for an hour. Fry in deep fat and serve with Tartar Sauce.

FRIED BLUEFISH

Clean the fish, season with salt and pepper, dredge with flour and fry in plenty of hot lard. Drain on brown paper and garnish with parsley.

STEAMED BLUEFISH

Season the fish with salt and pepper and pour over it a cupful of vinegar. Let stand for an hour, pour off the vinegar, and steam for twenty minutes. Serve with any preferred sauce.

FIVE WAYS TO COOK BUTTERFISH

FRIED BUTTERFISH—I

Trim, draw, and clean the fish. Wipe dry, dip in milk, roll in flour and fry in a frying-pan in plenty of clear hot fat. Drain on a cloth, sprinkle with salt, and garnish with lemon and parsley.

FRIED BUTTERFISH—II

Clean, wash and dry the fish, rub with flour, season with salt and pepper, dip in beaten egg, then in cracker dust or sifted bread-crumbs. Fry in deep fat.

FRIED BUTTERFISH—III

Clean and gash the fish, roll in corn-meal and sauté in hot salt pork fat. Serve with Tartar Sauce.

BUTTERFISH WITH FINE HERBS

Prepare according to directions given for Sole with Fine Herbs.

BOILED BUTTERFISH

Cover well-cleaned and lightly-gashed butterfish with boiling water, season with one chopped onion, parsley and thyme, salt and pepper. Boil gently for about ten minutes if small. Take from the water, and serve with scalded milk seasoned with butter, pepper, salt, and minced parsley.

TWENTY-TWO WAYS TO COOK CARP

BAKED CARP—I

Clean a carp and cover it with salted cold water and vinegar. Soak for an hour, then drain and dry. Stuff with seasoned crumbs, sew up, and put into a deep baking-pan. Brush with beaten egg, sprinkle with bread-crumbs and dot with butter. Add two sliced onions and a pinch of sweet herbs, a cupful each of sweet wine and stock, and a teaspoonful of anchovy paste. Bake for an hour, basting as needed. Take out the fish, strain the liquor, thicken with a tablespoonful of butter rolled in flour, and season with salt, pepper, lemon-juice, and a pinch of sugar.

BAKED CARP—II

Let the fish stand in vinegar for fifteen minutes. Stuff with seasoned crumbs and sew up. Brush with beaten egg, cover with crumbs, and dot with butter. Put into a baking-pan with two chopped onions, a bunch of parsley, a cupful of water, and a teaspoonful of Worcestershire sauce. Bake in a moderate oven, basting as required. Add enough water to make a cupful of the liquid remaining after taking up the fish. Thicken with a tablespoonful of flour blended with an equal quantity of butter, strain, add the juice of a lemon, and pepper and salt to season.

STEWED CARP—I

Clean and scale a carp, pouring boiling vinegar over the fish to facilitate the process. Wrap in a cloth and cook it gently in court bouillon. Serve with a sauce made of court bouillon, strained and thickened, with a few capers and a little anchovy sauce added.

STEWED CARP—II

Mix together one tablespoonful of salt, half a teaspoonful of pepper, and a pinch of powdered mace. Rub a cleaned fish with it, both inside and out. Leave it in a cold place for two hours. Then put into a kettle, cover with boiling water, add a small onion sliced, a sprig of parsley, a bay-leaf, and a teaspoonful of marjoram. Simmer until done, drain, and serve with Cream Sauce.

BOILED CARP

Put a cleaned carp into a saucepan with sufficient beef stock to cover. Add an onion, four cloves, a bunch of sweet herbs, and salt to season. Simmer until the fish is done. Take out the fish and strain the sauce. Add two cupfuls of beef stock and thicken with browned flour. Boil until thick, add a wineglassful of white wine and the juice of half a lemon. Pour the sauce over the fish and serve.

PICKLED CARP

Put a cleaned carp into a fish-kettle and pour over it boiling vinegar and a cupful of Claret. Add two carrots and three onions chopped fine, and sage, thyme, bay-leaves, parsley, cloves, and bruised garlic to season. Simmer for an hour and let cool in the liquid.

CARP À L'ITALIENNE

Clean, scale, and slice the fish. Fry with onion, parsley, thyme, salt, and pepper, using plenty of butter. Add white wine to cover and simmer for ten minutes; then put in the oven and bake until tender. Add two lemons sliced and one cupful each of chopped almonds and currants. Cook long enough to soften the currants, adding stock if necessary.

CARP À L'ALLEMANDE

Clean and cut into strips two pounds of carp. Add one wineglassful of Claret, one cupful of beef stock, one cupful of chopped mushrooms, a carrot and an onion chopped fine, and salt, pepper, thyme, clove and parsley to season. Simmer for an hour, add a tablespoonful of capers, and serve on buttered toast.

CARP À LA BORDELAISE

Chop fine an onion, a carrot, and a bunch of parsley. Add two cupfuls of white wine, a clove of garlic, three cloves, and salt and pepper to season. Cook for fifteen minutes, then add two quarts of cold water. Boil the carp in this sauce and drain. Prepare a sauce as follows: Chop fine a small onion and a shallot. Season with salt and pepper, and cook until soft with a wineglassful of Claret. Add two cupfuls of beef stock and bring to the boil. Thicken with two tablespoonfuls of browned flour rubbed smooth in a little cold water, season with salt, red pepper, minced parsley, and chives, and add a small piece of cooked chopped marrow. Pour over the fish and serve very hot.

BROILED CARP

Broil as usual and serve with melted butter, lemon-juice, and minced parsley poured over it.

CARP À LA FRANÇAISE

Cut the cleaned fish into square pieces and put it into a saucepan with four tablespoonfuls of olive-oil, one cupful of Claret, and a tablespoonful of butter blended with an equal quantity of flour. Add a chopped clove of garlic, a shallot, a quarter of a pound of mushrooms, and salt, pepper, and minced parsley to season. Cook for twenty minutes and serve.

FRIED CARP—I

Soak the fish over night in salt water. Drain, rinse in cold water, season with pepper and salt, dredge in flour, and fry in butter.

FRIED CARP—II

Cook the carp in court bouillon, drain, and cut in slices. Cover with a very thick Cream Sauce and let cool. Dip in crumbs, then in egg and crumbs, and fry in deep fat.

FRIED CARP—III

Clean the fish and cut it into convenient pieces. Dip in milk then in seasoned flour, and fry in hot fat.

CARP À LA COBLENTZ

Boil the fish with one cupful of Rhine wine, two cupfuls of white stock, two carrots and two onions sliced, half a cupful of sliced mushrooms and minced parsley, salt, pepper, and sweet herbs to season. Add water if the stock is not sufficient to cover. Boil for half an hour, take the fish up, then thicken the sauce with butter and flour, and add the juice of half a lemon with another tablespoonful of butter. Pour over the fish and serve.

BAKED CARP À LA MARINIÈRE

Clean the fish and line it with bacon. Boil carefully in court bouillon to which one quarter of the quantity of white wine has been added. Boil for five minutes, then put the pan into the oven and bake for an hour and a half, basting frequently. Take out the fish, strain the liquid, thicken with browned flour, add a wineglassful of white wine, and boil until thick. Rub through a sieve and add three tablespoonfuls of butter. Pour over the fish and serve.

STEAMED CARP

Scale and clean the fish and steam until done. Serve with sour cream or with a Drawn-Butter Sauce seasoned with lemon-juice.

CARP IN MATELOTE

Cook the cleaned carp in a fish-kettle with two sliced onions, a bunch of parsley, a little salt, a few pepper-corns, two cloves of garlic, a quart of red wine and a pint of water. Cook slowly for forty minutes and take out the fish. Strain the sauce and reduce by rapid boiling to one quart. Thicken with butter and browned flour and boil for half an hour. Skim, add three tablespoonfuls of butter, one tablespoonful of anchovy paste, and the juice of a lemon. Pour over the fish and serve.

CARP À LA BOURGUINOTTE

Stew the carp in red wine, drain, and place on a platter. Cook four shallots, two cloves, a blade of mace, a pinch of thyme, a bay-leaf, and a mushroom for five minutes in enough red wine to cover. Add enough beef stock to make the required quantity of sauce, and thicken with butter and browned flour. Cook until thick, strain, and pour over the fish.

CARP À LA PÉRIGUEUX

Cook the carp in wine and drain. Chop six truffles fine, add a tablespoonful of chopped raw ham, a pinch of thyme, and a bay-leaf. Cook for ten minutes in sufficient white wine to cover. Add a cupful of beef stock and thicken with butter and browned flour. Cook until thick, rub through a sieve, add a tablespoonful of butter and a little anchovy paste and the juice of half a lemon.

CARP À LA LYONS

Clean the fish and cut into thick slices. Soak for an hour in a marinade of oil and vinegar, season with salt, pepper, thyme, bay-leaves, and chopped onion. Drain, dip in flour, then in beaten egg, then in bread-crumbs, mixed with Parmesan cheese. Fry in deep fat and garnish with lemon and parsley.

CARP À LA PROVENÇALE

Stew the carp in court bouillon and white wine. Drain and place on a platter. Cook together two tablespoonfuls each of chopped ham and olive-oil, four bruised cloves of garlic, a pinch of thyme, a bay-leaf, a tablespoonful of capers, a peeled lemon sliced, a small bunch of parsley, and paprika to season. Cook for five minutes, add enough beef stock to make the required quantity of sauce, and cook for ten minutes. Thicken with browned flour, rub through a sieve, skim, add a tablespoonful of butter and a little anchovy paste, and pour over the fish.

SIX WAYS TO COOK CATFISH

CATFISH STEWED WITH TOMATOES

Slice the fish and fry in butter. When half cooked, add a cupful of water, a chopped onion, a red pepper, and a can of tomatoes. Cook slowly for half an hour and serve with buttered toast.

FRIED CATFISH—I

Clean and cut the fish in squares. Season with salt, pepper, and Worcestershire sauce. Dip in egg, then in crumbs or corn-meal, and fry in deep fat.

FRIED CATFISH—II

Prepare the fish according to directions given above, dredge with seasoned flour, and fry in butter in a frying-pan.

FRIED CATFISH—III

Skin and clean the fish, cut into pieces. Soak for an hour in olive-oil and vinegar, dip in egg and crumbs, and fry in deep fat.

STEWED CATFISH

Soak the skinned fish in brine for an hour. Put into a saucepan with a chopped onion, cover with cold water, and simmer until they are tender. Take out the fish, season with salt, pepper, and butter, and thicken the liquid in which they were cooked with a tablespoonful each of butter and flour cooked together and mixed with half a cupful of boiling cream. Bring to the boil, add a teaspoonful of minced parsley and one egg well beaten. Pour the sauce over the fish and serve.

BOILED CATFISH

Boil the fish according to directions previously given. Thicken the remaining liquid with butter rolled in flour, season with salt, pepper, and lemon-juice, add two chopped hard-boiled eggs, pour over the fish, and serve.

SIXTY-SEVEN WAYS TO COOK CODFISH

BAKED CODFISH—I

Rub the inside of a small fresh cod with butter and lemon-juice and put on a buttered drainer in a fish-kettle. Rub with butter, sprinkle with chopped mushrooms, shallots, and parsley, lemon-juice, and minced garlic. Pour over the fish three cupfuls of white wine, bring to the boil, and simmer for an hour and a half. Baste as required. Thicken the liquor with butter and flour and serve with the sauce.

BAKED CODFISH—II

Stuff the fish with seasoned crumbs and season with pepper and salt. Pour over two cupfuls of Sherry and a tablespoonful of mushroom catsup. Add two cupfuls of stock, cover with buttered paper, and bake, basting often. When nearly done, sprinkle with bread-crumbs and dot with butter, and bake until brown. Take up the fish carefully, add a teaspoonful of beef extract and a little anchovy paste to the liquor in the baking-pan, strain, add two tablespoonfuls of butter and the juice of half a lemon, bring to the boil, pour over the fish, and serve.

BAKED CODFISH—III

Prepare according to directions given for Baked Codfish—I, adding a pint of parboiled oysters to the sauce.

BAKED SALT CODFISH

Prepare the fish according to directions given in the recipe for Boiled Salted Cod. Mix with an equal quantity of mashed potatoes, season, add two tablespoonfuls of melted butter and enough hot milk to make very soft. Put into a buttered baking-dish, rub with butter, and bake until brown. Serve with Cream or Drawn-Butter Sauce.

CREAMED AND BAKED CODFISH

Put into a stoneware platter creamed codfish prepared according to directions elsewhere given, and surround with a border of mashed potatoes beaten light with an egg. Cover with crumbs, dot with butter, and brown in the oven.

BAKED CODFISH À LA MONTREAL

Butter a baking-dish and put in the centre a large piece of prepared codfish. Surround with boiled potatoes, rub all thoroughly with butter, season with pepper and salt, and bake in the oven, basting frequently. Serve in the same dish, sprinkling with minced parsley.

BAKED CODFISH À LA NANTUCKET

Prepare a stuffing of one cupful of cracker crumbs, one cupful of oysters, one quarter of a cupful of melted butter, and salt, pepper, minced parsley, and lemon-juice to season. Clean a four-pound cod, sprinkle with salt and pepper, brush over with lemon-juice, stuff, and sew. Rub with butter, sprinkle with crumbs, and add sufficient boiling water to keep from burning. Bake until done, basting as required.

BAKED CODFISH WITH CHEESE SAUCE

Rub the fish with butter and lemon-juice, put it on the grating in the baking-pan, season with salt and pepper, and bake, pouring a cupful of white stock under the grating. Take up the fish, cover with crumbs, dot with butter, and brown in the oven. Strain the liquid, thicken with butter rolled in flour, and season with lemon-juice, grated onion, and four tablespoonfuls of grated Parmesan cheese. Bring to the boil and serve poured around the fish.

QUICK BAKED CODFISH

Put a thick slice of codfish into a baking-pan. Rub with butter, season with pepper and salt, and add sufficient boiling water to moisten. Bake for half an hour, basting frequently. Thicken the gravy with butter and flour, pour over the fish, and serve.

BAKED ROCK COD WITH DRESSING

Season bread-crumbs with grated onion, sage, salt, and pepper. Add a tablespoonful of butter broken into bits, and sufficient milk to moisten. Fill and sew up the fish. Lay in a baking-pan on thin slices of salt pork, rub with butter, and cover with thin slices of pork. Pour over two tablespoonfuls of tomato catsup and half a cupful of boiling water. Bake for an hour, basting frequently.

BAKED COD À LA BEDFORD

Soak the cleaned fish for two hours in olive-oil seasoned with salt, pepper, and Worcestershire. Drain and put into a baking-dish, rub with butter, and sprinkle with crumbs. Add two wineglassfuls of Catawba wine and two cupfuls of oyster liquor. Cover with buttered paper and bake for forty minutes. Take up the fish, thicken the sauce with butter and flour, season with lemon-juice and minced parsley, pour around the fish, and serve.

BAKED CODFISH WITH CREAM

Parboil part of a codfish in salted water. Remove the bones and put the pieces into a baking-dish in layers with Cream Sauce and seasoning between. Cover with crumbs, dot with butter, sprinkle with grated nutmeg, and bake.

BOILED SALT CODFISH—I

Soak two pounds of salted cod over night, put into fresh water, bring to the boil and serve with melted butter.

BOILED SALT CODFISH—II

Soak the fish over night, change the water, and simmer until done. Serve with a Drawn-Butter Sauce.

BOILED SALTED CODFISH WITH EGG SAUCE

Prepare the fish according to directions given in the preceding recipe. Cook one teaspoonful of corn-meal until thick in one cupful of milk, add one cupful of mashed potatoes, the codfish chopped, two tablespoonfuls of butter, two well-beaten eggs, and pepper to taste. Prepare an Egg Sauce, pour over the fish, and serve.

BOILED CODFISH WITH OYSTER SAUCE

Boil the fish in salted water, seasoned with pepper, cloves, and lemon peel. Prepare a Cream Sauce, and cook oysters in it until the edges curl, pour over the fish, and serve.

BOILED CODFISH WITH CREAM SAUCE

Boil the codfish slowly in salted water. Melt two tablespoonfuls of butter, add two tablespoonfuls of flour, and cook thoroughly. Add two cupfuls of cream and cook until thick, stirring constantly. Add salt, pepper, and anchovy paste to season, pour over the fish. sprinkle with minced parsley, and serve.

BOILED CODFISH À LA HOLLANDAISE

Boil the fish according to directions previously given and serve with Hollandaise Sauce.

BOILED CODFISH WITH CAPER SAUCE—I

Prepare according to directions given for Boiled Codfish with Cream Sauce, omitting the anchovy paste, and adding two tablespoonfuls each of capers and melted butter.

BOILED CODFISH WITH CAPER SAUCE—II

Boil a small fresh codfish in court bouillon, and allow it to cool partially in the liquor. Serve with Caper Sauce.

BOILED CODFISH CREAMED

Sew up the fish in a cloth dredged with flour, and boil in salted and acidulated water. Unwrap, and serve with sauce made of half a cupful each of milk and boiling water, thickened with two tablespoonfuls of butter rolled in flour. Take from the fire, add two eggs well-beaten, and salt, pepper, and minced parsley to season. Add a tablespoonful of capers or tarragon vinegar, pour over the fish, and garnish with slices of hard-boiled eggs.

BOILED CODFISH WITH EGG SAUCE

Prepare the fish according to directions given in the recipe for Boiled Codfish with Oyster Sauce. Serve with Egg Sauce.

CODFISH BALLS WITH EGG SAUCE

Free two pounds of fresh cod from all bones; chop it and season with salt, pepper, grated nutmeg, and a little finely chopped lemon peel, adding chopped parsley, marjoram, a little soaked bread-crumbs with the water drained well out; mix with two unbeaten eggs and form into balls the size of a tomato. Fry a large sliced onion in two ounces of butter, add a cupful of boiling water, let it boil up, then put in the balls. When cooked, beat three eggs, strain in the juice of two large lemons, adding a little chopped parsley; stir this well in without letting it boil, then dish up the balls and strain the sauce over. Garnish with parsley. If liked, add three or four cut-up tomatoes to the balls.

CODFISH À LA CREOLE—I

Flake one pound of cooked codfish, add to it one cupful of boiled rice, half a can of tomatoes strained, a chopped onion, two tablespoonfuls of butter, and salt and pepper to season. Cook slowly for half an hour.

CODFISH À LA CREOLE—II

Soak over night two pounds of salt codfish. Fry brown in lard a chopped onion and a bean of garlic. Mix with three tablespoonfuls of browned flour and cook thoroughly. Add a can of tomatoes which have been rubbed through a sieve and simmered until very thick. Drain and rinse the fish, pour boiling water upon it and let stand until cool. Pick out the bones, add to the sauce, and reheat.

CODFISH PUFFS

Prepare the fish according to directions given in the preceding recipe. Mix with an equal quantity of mashed potatoes, add a heaping tablespoonful of butter, and mix thoroughly, using a little hot cream to moisten it. Add four eggs well beaten and mix thoroughly. Drop by spoonfuls into boiling fat and fry brown.

CODFISH AU GRATIN

Cook in court bouillon and cool in the liquor. Scrape off the skin, take out the bones, and put in the baking-dish in which it is to be served. Sprinkle it thickly with grated cheese and pour over a Béchamel Sauce. Sprinkle with crumbs and bake golden brown.

ESCALLOPED CODFISH AND MACARONI

Mix together equal parts of cooked and broken macaroni and flaked boiled cod. Mix with Cream Sauce. Fill a buttered baking-dish, sprinkle thickly with grated cheese, cover with crumbs, dot with butter, and brown in the oven.

FRICASSÉED SALT CODFISH

Soak over night in cold water two pounds of salt codfish. Take out the bones, cover with fresh water, and bring to the boil. Fry in olive-oil two chopped onions and a green pepper, with a sliced tomato, a bruised clove of garlic, and a chilli pepper. Add six cupfuls of stock, three tablespoonfuls of tomato catsup, a tablespoonful of minced parsley, and two cupfuls of peeled raw potatoes cut into dice. Cook until the potatoes are nearly done, then add the codfish and boil for five or ten minutes.

CREAMED CODFISH

Flake cold cooked codfish, or salted codfish which has been soaked and boiled. Mix with a Cream Sauce, adding one or two well-beaten eggs to the sauce just before serving.

ESCALLOPED CODFISH WITH CHEESE

Prepare according to directions given for Creamed Codfish. Cover with grated cheese, crumbs, and butter, and bake in the oven.

BROILED SALT CODFISH

Soak two pounds of salt codfish over night. In the morning change the water, add a chopped onion, bring to the boil, and cool. Drain, wipe dry, rub with melted butter, and broil. Serve with Drawn-Butter Sauce.

CODFISH SOUFFLÉ

Boil half a pound of salt codfish according to directions previously given. Mash the fish and mix with two cupfuls of mashed potatoes, pepper to season, and the yolks of two eggs well beaten. Beat thoroughly, fold in the stiffly beaten whites of the eggs, and bake in a hot oven until well puffed and brown.

CODFISH AND MACARONI

Soak over night half a pound of salt codfish. Boil for twenty minutes two ounces of broken macaroni. Melt one tablespoonful of butter, add one of flour, and cook thoroughly. Add one cupful of stewed and strained tomatoes and cook until thick, stirring constantly. Season with salt, pepper, and grated onion, add the fish and macaroni, and cook for an hour in a double-boiler.

CODFISH À LA BONNE FEMME

Soak over night three pounds of salt codfish. Boil for twenty-five minutes a quart of peeled potatoes, with salt, parsley, a clove, and an onion in the water. Add the fish and cook for ten minutes longer. Arrange the fish on a platter with the drained potatoes for a border. Melt one teaspoonful of butter, add one of flour, and cook thoroughly. Add two cupfuls of water in which the fish was cooked and cook until thick, stirring constantly. Take from the fire and add the yolks of two eggs beaten with a teaspoonful of vinegar and a tablespoonful of melted butter. Season with pepper, pour over the fish and the potatoes, and serve.

CODFISH À LA BEAUREGARD

Prepare according to directions given for Creamed Codfish, using fresh codfish and omitting the egg. Serve on buttered toast and cover with hard-boiled eggs rubbed through a sieve.

STEWED CODFISH À LA LINCOLN

Clean and bone four pounds of fresh codfish. Slice and scald two small onions, drain and fry soft in salt pork fat. Cut the fish into cubes and season with salt and pepper. Boil the bones in water to cover, with onion and pork fat. Put the fish into a buttered sauce-pan and strain the boiling liquid over it, using enough to cover. Add the juice of half a lemon, and thicken with one heaping tablespoonful of butter cooked with two of flour. Season with salt, pepper, minced parsley, and tomato or mushroom catsup. Just before the fish is done add one quart of drained oysters and cook until the oysters are plump.

BOILED CODS' TONGUES WITH EGG SAUCE

Soak the tongues over night, change the water, and boil for ten minutes. Serve with Drawn-Butter Sauce.

FRIED CODFISH TONGUES

Wash the tongues, dip in cold milk and roll in seasoned flour. Fry in butter, and serve with tomato sauce.

CODS' TONGUES À LA POULETTE

Prepare according to directions given for boiled Cods' Tongues with Egg Sauce and serve with a Poulette Sauce, using for liquid the water in which the tongues were boiled.

CODFISH TONGUES À LA BEURRE NOIR

Prepare the tongues according to directions given in the recipe for Boiled Cods' Tongues with Egg Sauce. Drain and serve with brown butter, seasoned with salt, pepper, minced parsley, and lemon-juice.

CODFISH FRITTERS

Cut into strips fresh boiled cod, or freshened and boiled salt cod. Dip in fritter batter and fry in deep fat.

DEVILLED CODFISH

Flake cold cooked fish. Mix with an equal quantity of bread-crumbs the yolks of two hard-boiled eggs, and melted butter, grated onion, minced parsley, and pepper and salt to season. Add milk or oyster liquor to moisten and fill buttered shells. Cover with crumbs, dot with butter, and brown in the oven.

CODFISH À LA SEVILLE

Wash and dry one cupful of rice, brown it in olive-oil, and drain. Put into a stewpan and cover with fillets of fresh cod, fried in the oil. Add a sliced onion fried, half a dozen sliced tomatoes, and salt, cayenne, and lemon-juice to season. Add two cupfuls of stock, put a buttered paper on top, cover the pan, and bake half an hour in the oven. Take out the fish carefully, mix the rice and seasoning together, and serve as a border around the fish.

CODFISH À LA BÉCHAMEL

Prepare according to directions given for Creamed Codfish, omitting the egg and using white stock and milk in equal parts instead of cream.

ESCALLOPED CODFISH À LA BÉCHAMEL

Prepare according to directions given for Codfish à la Béchamel, adding the yolks of three eggs. Arrange in a baking-dish with layers of seasoned crumbs, and add sufficient milk to moisten. Cover with crumbs, dot with butter, and brown in the oven.

CODFISH À LA FLAMANDE

Prepare boiled codfish according to directions previously given. Melt one tablespoonful of butter and cook in it a teaspoonful of flour. Add one cupful of boiling water and cook until thick, stirring constantly. Take from the fire, add the yolks of two eggs well beaten, four tablespoonfuls of made mustard, and pepper, vinegar, grated nutmeg, and minced parsley to season. Add gradually half a cupful of melted butter, pour over the fish, and serve.

STEWED CODFISH À LA SHREWSBURY

Stuff the fish with drained oysters and seasoned crumbs, adding two tablespoonfuls of butter in small bits. Sew up, put on the grating in a fish-kettle, seasoning with salt, pepper, and minced parsley. Dot with butter and add the oyster liquor, and two cupfuls each of stock and water. Simmer for forty minutes, basting as required. Take up the fish, thicken the sauce with butter and flour cooked together, and boil for ten minutes. Take from the fire, add a tablespoonful of butter, the juice of a lemon, and the yolks of two eggs well beaten. Strain over the fish and serve.

SALT CODFISH À LA BRANDADE

Cut the fish in pieces and soak in cold water for twenty-four hours. Put into fresh cold water, bring to the boil, and simmer for twenty minutes. Drain, bone, and cool. Mix to a cream with lemon-juice and olive-oil, adding a little milk if it becomes too thick. Season with salt, pepper, minced parsley, and garlic. Serve with toasted crackers and cheese.

STEWED COD WITH OYSTERS

Cut fresh cod into fillets, and put in a baking-pan, with salt, pepper, and chopped onion to season. Add one cupful of white wine and the liquor of two dozen parboiled oysters. Cook slowly for fifteen minutes, take out the fish, thicken the sauce with butter and flour cooked together, add two tablespoonfuls of melted butter, season with lemon-juice, and pour the sauce over the fish. Garnish with the parboiled oysters and serve.

SALTED COD WITH BROWN BUTTER

Soak the fish for twenty-four hours and prepare according to directions given for Boiled Salted Cod. Drain, wipe dry, and fry brown in butter, adding a little minced parsley.

CODFISH STEAK

Cut the fish into steaks, about two inches thick, season with salt and pepper, and let stand for two hours. Dredge with corn-meal and fry in salt pork fat. Sprinkle with lemon-juice and serve.

BROILED CODFISH STEAKS WITH BACON

Prepare the steaks according to directions previously given and serve with a border of thin slices of bacon fried crisp.

BROILED CODFISH STEAKS

Soak in salted water for fifteen minutes, wipe dry, and let stand for an hour in olive-oil and vinegar. Drain, season, and broil on a well-buttered gridiron. Serve with melted butter and minced parsley.

BREADED CODFISH STEAKS

Season the steaks with salt, pepper, and lemon-juice, dip in egg and crumbs, and fry in deep fat. Serve with any preferred sauce.

FRIED CODFISH STEAKS

Clean the steaks, sprinkle with salt and pepper, and dip into flour. Sauté in salt pork fat.

CODFISH STEAKS À LA NARRAGANSETT

Fry the steaks with a chopped onion in butter, seasoning with salt and pepper. Take out and put a tablespoonful of flour into the frying-pan. Cook thoroughly, add two cupfuls of water and half a cupful of wine, and cook until thick, stirring constantly. Add two tablespoonfuls of butter, season with minced parsley and lemon-juice, pour over the fish, and serve.

CODFISH HASH

Flake cold cooked cod, mix with an equal quantity of mashed potatoes, and season to taste. Cook until light brown in butter.

MATELOTE OF CODFISH

Mix together one cupful of oysters, two cupfuls of bread-crumbs, two tablespoonfuls of butter, one egg, and a small onion, chopped. Stuff a small boned codfish and sew up. Lay the fish on slices of bacon in a baking-pan and cover the top with bacon. Add sufficient boiling water and bake for an hour, basting as required.

STEWED CODFISH

Flake cold cooked cod and reheat with butter, pepper, salt, minced parsley, cayenne, and lemon-juice. Serve very hot on toast.

FILLETS OF CODFISH

Clean and bone the fish and cut into thick strips. Put into a buttered saucepan with a little stock, season, sprinkle with minced parsley, and set into the oven, covered with a buttered paper. Serve in a deep platter with a border of mashed potatoes.

FRIED COD

Prepare the fish according to directions given for Fillet of Codfish. Season, dredge with flour, dip in egg and bread-crumbs, and fry in deep fat.

FRIED CODFISH À LA MAÎTRE D'HÔTEL

Prepare according to directions given for Fried Codfish. Serve with a sauce of melted butter, lemon-juice, and minced parsley.

FRIED FILLETS OF CODFISH

Mix together one tablespoonful of olive-oil, two tablespoonfuls of lemon-juice, and salt, grated onion, and paprika to season. Soak fillets of codfish in this for an hour, then drain, dip into beaten egg, then into crumbs, and fry in deep fat. Drain on brown paper and serve with Tartar Sauce.

BROILED CODFISH

Split the tail end of the fish and broil. Serve with melted butter, lemon-juice, and minced parsley.

CODFISH PIE

Prepare Creamed Codfish according to directions previously given, seasoning with grated onion. Fill a buttered baking-dish and cover with mashed potato, beaten very light with an egg and a little cream. Rub with melted butter, sprinkle with grated cheese, and bake in a quick oven.

ESCALLOPED CODFISH

Prepare the fish according to directions previously given. Flake and prepare according to directions given for Creamed Codfish. Put into a buttered baking-pan with layers of seasoned crumbs between, add milk to moisten, cover with crumbs, dot with butter, and brown in the oven.

FORTY-FIVE WAYS TO COOK EELS

BRAISED EEL

Skin and clean an eel, cut it into two-inch pieces, sprinkle with salt, and let stand for an hour. Soak in cold water for ten minutes, drain, and dry. Put into a buttered saucepan, seasoning with grated nutmeg, salt, and pepper. Cover with sliced lemon, chopped shallot, minced parsley, and a few pepper-corns. Cover the pan and bake in the oven until the fish is brown. Take out the eel and put into a deep dish. Add to the sauce one cupful of stock, bring to the boil, and thicken with a tablespoonful each of butter and flour cooked together. Boil until thick, take from the fire, add the yolks of three eggs beaten smooth with a little stock, bring to the boil, add a little lemon-juice, strain over the fish, and serve.

BROILED EELS—I

Skin, clean and cut up a large eel. Dip into beaten egg, then into crumbs seasoned with grated lemon rind, nutmeg, minced parsley, sweet herbs, pepper, and salt. Broil skin side down on a buttered gridiron, turning when done. Serve with Anchovy or Tartar Sauce.

BROILED EELS—II

Clean and cut the eels into three-inch lengths. Let stand for half an hour in a marinade of oil and lemon-juice, seasoned with pepper and salt. Drain, broil, and garnish with fried parsley.

BROILED EELS WITH SOUR SAUCE

Clean the eels and cut into five-inch lengths. Boil for ten minutes in one cupful of vinegar and enough cold water to cover, seasoning with salt, pepper-corns, carrot, onion, and parsley. Cool in the water, dip in crumbs, then in eggs beaten with a tablespoonful of olive-oil for each egg, then in bread-crumbs. Broil as usual. Serve with a sauce made of two tablespoonfuls of chopped shallots, fried in two tablespoonfuls of butter, added to a wineglassful each of white wine and vinegar. Add two cupfuls of stock and thicken with browned flour cooked in butter. Boil for five minutes, add one tablespoonful each of chopped mushrooms, parsley, pickles, and capers, and two tablespoonfuls of butter. Garnish with lemons and parsley.

FRIED EELS—I

Prepare and cut up the fish according to directions previously given and soak for several hours in vinegar with salt, pepper, and grated lemon-peel. Drain, dip into batter, and fry in deep fat. Serve with any preferred sauce.

FRIED EELS—II

Prepare according to directions previously given and cut into two-inch pieces. Dredge with flour and sauté in hot lard, or dip into egg and bread-crumbs and fry in deep fat. They may also be dipped into corn-meal before frying.

FRIED EELS—III

Prepare the eels according to directions given for Stewed Eels à la Americaine, sprinkling with shallot and parsley also. Let stand for several hours, dip into egg and crumbs, and fry in deep fat. Serve with any preferred sauce.

FRIED EELS—IV

Clean the eels, cut into two-inch pieces, and parboil for eight minutes. Sprinkle with salt and pepper, dip into corn-meal, and sauté in salt pork fat.

EELS FRIED IN BATTER

Cut a large cleaned eel into joints, and soak for several hours in cold water, to which salt, pepper, and vinegar have been added. Drain dip in batter, and fry in hot fat. Drain on brown paper and serve with Tomato Sauce.

EELS À LA LYONNAISE

Clean two large eels, cut into four-inch lengths and remove the bones. Cook in equal parts of white wine and water to cover, adding salt, pepper, a sliced onion, a clove of garlic, and a bunch of parsley. Drain the fish and strain the liquid. Thicken with two tablespoonfuls of flour rubbed smooth with two tablespoonfuls of butter. Boil for fifteen minutes and skim. Add two tablespoonfuls of butter and the juice of a lemon. Bring to the boil, pour over the fish, and serve with a garnish of small onions fried in butter and sugar.

EELS À LA VILLEROY

Clean two large eels and cut into lengths. Cover with salted and acidulated water, add a bunch of parsley, a sliced onion, and a pinch of powdered sweet herbs. Boil slowly for ten minutes, cool, and drain. Melt one tablespoonful of butter and cook in it two tablespoonfuls of flour. Add two cupfuls of white stock and cook until thick, stirring constantly. Take from the fire and season to taste. Add the yolks of four eggs well beaten and cool. Dip the pieces of eel in this sauce, and set on ice. Roll in cracker crumbs, dip in beaten egg, then in bread-crumbs, and fry brown in deep fat.

EELS À LA TARTAR

Cut up the eel and cook in court bouillon with wine. Drain, dip in egg and crumbs, and fry in deep fat. Serve with a stiff Mayonnaise mixed with chopped parsley, olives, pickles, and capers.

EELS À L'INDIENNE

Chop fine an onion, half a carrot, and a stalk of celery. Fry in butter, dredge with flour, and cook thoroughly. Add enough stock to make the required quantity of sauce, and cook until thick, stirring constantly, Season with mace, thyme, a bay-leaf, minced parsley, and curry powder. Strain through a sieve and pour over eels stewed in wine and seasoned with vegetables according to directions previously given. Serve with a border of boiled rice sprinkled with grated Parmesan cheese.

EELS À LA NORMANDY

Fry in butter a pound and a half of prepared eels. Add a wineglassful of white wine or cider, a tablespoonful of mushroom catsup, and salt, pepper, and grated nutmeg to season. Simmer for ten minutes, add one cupful of white stock, half a dozen mushrooms, a dozen oysters, and half a dozen shrimps. When cooked take from the fire, add the yolks of two eggs well beaten, and serve at once.

STUFFED EELS À L'ITALIENNE

Skin the eel but keep the head on. Remove the back-bone and stuff with seasoned crumbs, mixed with minced parsley and mushrooms. Skewer in the form of a circle; put into a saucepan with two ounces of butter, a small bunch of parsley, a chopped onion, two cupfuls of white wine, and salt, pepper, and grated nutmeg to season. Bake for an hour, basting as required. Drain, take out the parsley, and add to the sauce two cupfuls of brown stock, and one cupful of chopped mushrooms. Boil for five minutes and thicken with browned flour cooked in butter. Season with minced parsley and lemon-juice, pour the sauce around the eel, and serve.

EELS À LA LONDON

Fry four chopped onions in butter, dredge with flour, and cook thoroughly. Add two cupfuls of stock, half a cupful of Port wine, two bay-leaves, and salt and pepper to season. Cook until thick, stirring constantly. Add one large cleaned eel, cut into two-inch lengths, cover, and cook for fifteen minutes. Serve on toast.

EELS À LA REINE

Prepare and cut up the eels. Fry in butter with half a can of mushrooms, and dredge with flour. Add one cupful of stock and half a cupful of white wine. Bring to the boil, season with salt, pepper, and a chopped onion, and cook until the eel is tender. Skim, take from the fire, and add the juice of half a lemon, beaten smooth with the yolks of two eggs.

EELS À LA POULETTE

Stew the eels in white wine with carrot, onion, parsley, bay-leaf, thyme, pepper-corns, and salt to season. Drain and serve with Poulette Sauce.

FRICASSÉE OF EEL

Prepare the eel according to directions previously given, cook in equal parts of white wine and water, seasoning with mace, pepper, nutmeg, cloves, sweet herbs, allspice, and salt. Boil until the eels are tender, then skim out. Add a little anchovy paste to the sauce, with a tablespoonful of butter, bring to the boil, take from the fire, add the yolks of two eggs well beaten, pour over the fish, and serve.

FRICASSÉED EELS

Skin, clean, and cut up. Cover with cold water, add salt, and minced parsley to season, cover, and cook slowly for an hour. Thicken with a tablespoonful each of butter and flour blended together and made smooth with cold water. Season highly with pepper, and serve.

STEWED EELS WITH CUCUMBERS

Clean and skin two eels, cut into pieces and soak in cold water for an hour. Drain, cover with wine and water, seasoning with salt, pepper, onion, and parsley, and simmer for fifteen minutes. Take out the fish and add three sliced and parboiled cucumbers. Strain the sauce, thicken with flour cooked in butter, and boil for ten minutes. Skim, add the yolks of four eggs well beaten and take from the fire. Season with red pepper and lemon-juice, strain over the fish, and serve.

STEWED EELS—I

Put into a saucepan three fourths of a cupful of butter and fry in it four small chopped onions. Add a tablespoonful of flour, cook through, and add two cupfuls of boiling water or stock. Cook until thick, stirring constantly, then put in one large cleaned eel cut into inch pieces; cover and cook for fifteen minutes.

STEWED EELS—II

Wash and skin a pint of eels, cut them in pieces three inches long, pepper and salt them, and put them into a stewpan. Pour in one pint of good soup stock, adding one large onion, shredded, three cloves, a teaspoonful of grated lemon-peel, and a wineglassful of Port wine. Stew slowly for half an hour, and pour into a hot dish. Strain the liquor and add a wineglassful of cream thickened with flour, and boil up once. Pour over the eels and serve.

STEWED EELS—III

Clean, skin, and joint the eels. Cover with boiling water, add a tablespoonful of vinegar, and cook for ten minutes. Drain, cook together one tablespoonful of butter and two of flour. Add two cupfuls of the water in which the eels were cooked. Cook until thick, stirring constantly. Season with salt, pepper, and grated onion, then add the eels and reheat. Simmer for twenty minutes, add a tablespoonful of minced parsley, and serve.

STEWED EELS—IV

Prepare according to directions given above, using veal or fish stock, instead of water, and adding a bay-leaf to the seasoning.

STEWED EELS À L'ANGLAISE

Cook prepared eels in half a bottle of Port wine, seasoned with carrot, onion, parsley, bay-leaf, thyme, salt, pepper-corns, cloves, mace, and chopped mushrooms. Cover with buttered paper, simmer for half an hour and drain. Melt two tablespoonfuls of butter and cook in it two tablespoonfuls of flour. Add a chopped shallot and enough of the eel liquor to make the required quantity of sauce. Cook until thick, stirring constantly. Add half a cupful of stock, and two wineglassfuls of Port wine. Bring to the boil, strain, add a few chopped mushrooms, a tablespoonful of butter, and minced parsley, lemon-juice, and anchovy paste to season. Pour the sauce over the eels, and serve.

STEWED EELS À L'AMERICAINE

Use three pounds of cleaned and skinned eel with all the fat removed. Cut in two-inch pieces, season with pepper and salt and chopped onion, and put in a double-boiler with half a cupful of butter. Sprinkle with parsley, cover tightly, and cook for about an hour and a half. Serve in a deep dish.

STEWED EELS À LA POULETTE

Cut cleaned eels into two-inch pieces and cook until tender in stock. Thicken with butter and flour cooked together, add half a dozen chopped mushrooms, and salt, pepper, grated onion, and minced parsley to season. Boil for twenty minutes, add the juice of a lemon, and serve.

STEWED EELS À LA CANOTIERE

Fry a chopped onion in butter, add a pound of rice and cook brown. Add four cupfuls of fish stock, seasoning with red and white pepper, caver, and cook for twenty minutes. Take from the fire, add half a cupful each of butter and Tomato Sauce. Prepare the eels according to directions given for Eels à la Lyonnaise, adding a tablespoonful of anchovy essence to the sauce. Serve with a border of the rice.

STEWED EELS À LA GENEVOISE

Prepare two eels, cut into four-inch lengths. Put into a saucepan with a sliced carrot, an onion, a bunch of parsley, two cloves of garlic, and salt and pepper-corns to season. Put in enough cider to cover the fish, and simmer for fifteen minutes. Take up the fish, strain the sauce, and thicken it with two tablespoonfuls of butter. Add two tablespoonfuls of butter to the sauce, reheat, pour over the eels, and garnish with small onions fried brown in butter and sugar.

MATELOTE OF EELS—I

Prepare and cut up the fish according to directions previously given. Put into a saucepan with one cupful each of stock and Claret, a bruised clove of garlic, a whole pepper, a sliced onion, a bay-leaf, and a pinch each of thyme, cloves, parsley, and salt. Take out the fish, strain the sauce, add to it a tablespoonful each of butter and flour cooked together, and pour over the fish.

MATELOTE OF EELS—II

Cut a pound and a half of prepared eels into two-inch pieces and fry for two minutes in butter. Add a wineglassful of Claret, and three tablespoonfuls each of stock and mushroom liquor. Season with salt, pepper, and grated nutmeg, and a pinch of powdered sweet herbs. Add six small onions and six button mushrooms. Cook for half an hour and thicken with a tablespoonful each of butter and flour cooked together.

MATELOTE OF EELS—III

Prepare two eels and cut them into two-inch lengths. Cover with cold salted water and bring to the boil. Add an onion, a dozen cloves, and two tablespoonfuls of vinegar. Boil for fifteen minutes, drain, dry, roll in flour and fry brown in butter. Add two cupfuls of boiling water, and salt, pepper, and fine herbs to season. Add a cupful of button onions peeled and fried brown in butter and sugar. Cover and simmer for one hour. If the sauce should evaporate, add more boiling water. When done, add half a cupful of wine and serve.

MATELOTE OF EELS À LA PARISIENNE

Clean and cut the eels into four-inch pieces. Cover with white wine and season with sliced carrot and chopped mushrooms. Add also the liquor from three dozen parboiled oysters. Simmer until the eels are done and drain. Add to the liquor half a cupful of white stock, and thicken with flour cooked in butter. Add two wineglassfuls of white wine and boil until thick, stirring constantly. Take from the fire, and add the yolks of four eggs beaten smooth with the juice of half a lemon, a tablespoonful of butter, and a grating of nutmeg. Add the parboiled oysters, and a handful of button mushrooms. Reheat, pour over the fish, and serve.

MATELOTE OF EELS À LA GENOISE

Prepare the eels and cut into four-inch lengths. Cover with Claret or Burgundy and add sliced carrot, onion, minced parsley, chopped mushrooms, thyme, a bay-leaf, mace, cloves, and pepper-corns to season. Simmer until done and drain. Add to the liquor half a cupful of beef stock and thicken it with browned flour. Strain through a fine sieve, add a tablespoonful of butter, a little anchovy paste, a teaspoonful of minced parsley, a grating of nutmeg; and a little lemon-juice. Bring to the boil, pour over the fish, and serve.

MATELOTE OF EELS À LA BORDELAISE

Cut the eels into three-inch lengths, and cover with a bottle of Claret. Season with carrot, onion, parsley, chopped mushrooms, thyme, bay-leaf, mace, cloves, and peppercorns. Simmer for half an hour and drain. Thicken the liquor with browned flour rubbed smooth with butter, add two wineglassfuls of Claret, and bring to the boil. Skim, add a teaspoonful of capers, a pounded clove of garlic, a little butter, grated nutmeg, and anchovy paste to season. Reheat, pour over the fish, and serve.

BOILED EELS

Cut into short pieces a pound and a half of eels which have been skinned and cleaned. Put into a saucepan, cover with cold water, add a tablespoonful of salt, six whole peppers, one red onion, and a cupful of vinegar. Simmer for half an hour; drain and serve on a platter with melted butter, lemon-juice, and minced parsley.

PICKLED EELS

Clean and cut three pounds of eels into six-inch lengths. Cover with salt, let stand for three hours, then rinse thoroughly. Boil together for fifteen minutes one cupful of vinegar, one cupful of water, a sliced onion, two bay-leaves, three allspice, and a slice of lemon. Put in half of the eels and simmer until tender, take out, and cook the remaining half. Let the vinegar cool before pouring over the eels.

GREEN EELS

Boil together an onion, a bunch of parsley, a pinch of celery seed, and a teaspoonful of mixed spices in a little water. Add two cleaned and cut eels with water to cover and simmer until done. Strain the sauce, thicken with butter and flour cooked together, and pour over the eels. Serve with boiled potatoes and cucumber salad.

BAKED EELS

Skin and parboil, cut into two-inch pieces, and put into a baking-pan. Dredge with flour, season with salt and pepper and add half a cupful of water.

Bake for twenty minutes and take out. Thicken the gravy with a tablespoonful of flour rubbed smooth with a little of the liquid. Add a tablespoonful of butter, a teaspoonful of Worcestershire sauce, and enough boiling water to make the sauce of the proper consistency. Bring to the boil and pour around the eels.

BAKED EELS WITH TARTAR SAUCE

Clean and skin two large eels. Wrap in a wet cloth and simmer for fifteen minutes in court bouillon. Cook in the liquor. Take out, wipe dry, and cover with seasoned crumbs. Spread with two eggs beaten with one tablespoonful of olive-oil and sprinkle with crumbs. Put into a baking-pan with two tablespoonfuls of butter, and bake for half an hour, basting twice. Serve with Tartar Sauce.

ENGLISH EEL PIE

Skin, clean, and cut up two large eels. Cook with one tablespoonful of butter, half a cupful of chopped mushrooms, a tablespoonful of chopped parsley, a minced onion, a bay-leaf, salt, pepper, the rind of a lemon, a wineglassful of Sherry and a cupful of beef stock. Cook until the eels are tender, strain the sauce, and thicken with butter and flour. Line a baking-dish with pastry, put the eels in it, and pour the sauce over, with sliced hard-boiled eggs on top. Cover with pastry, brush with yolk of egg, and bake for an hour in a moderate oven. Serve either hot or cold.

COLLARED EELS

Clean, split, and bone one large eel, and season with salt and pepper. Chop together three hard-boiled eggs, a beet, a tablespoonful of capers, two pickles, one onion, and three anchovies. Add salt and pepper, cover the eel with the mixture, tie in a cloth, and cook with a bay-leaf for half an hour in equal parts of vinegar and water. Drain, untie, and put into a mould with aspic jelly, or with beef stock to which sufficient dissolved gelatine has been added. Serve cold with Mayonnaise.

EELS EN BROCHETTE

Boil the eel in a court bouillon and cut into two-inch pieces. Dip into egg and crumbs and string on steel skewers, alternating with squares of bacon. Bake in the oven and serve on toast.

CREAMED EELS

Clean and cut up the eels, and stew according to directions previously given. Pour over a Cream Sauce, seasoned with salt, paprika, onion juice, and minced parsley.

FIFTEEN WAYS TO COOK FINNAN-HADDIE

BOILED FINNAN-HADDIE—I

Divide into convenient pieces, cover with boiling water, add a teaspoonful of sugar, and boil for fifteen minutes. Take up on a hot platter, remove the skin, and dot with butter.

BOILED FINNAN-HADDIE—II

Cover the fish with boiling water, boil for five minutes, drain, cover with melted butter, and serve with plain boiled potatoes.

BROILED FINNAN-HADDIE—I

Brown a haddie on a greased broiler. Cover with hot water, let stand for ten minutes and drain. Spread with butter and sprinkle with pepper.

BROILED FINNAN-HADDIE—II

Cut the haddie into small squares, skin and parboil it. Wipe dry, broil on a buttered gridiron and serve with melted butter.

BROILED FINNAN-HADDIE—III

Wash the fish thoroughly, and let stand in cold water for three quarters of an hour, then cover with boiling water for five minutes, wipe dry, rub with butter and lemon-juice, and broil for fifteen minutes. Serve with melted butter or Tartar Sauce.

BROILED FINNAN-HADDIE—IV

Wash the fish and soak for half an hour in cold water, skin side up. Cover with water just below the boiling point, and let stand for fifteen minutes. Wipe dry, brush with olive-oil, and broil slowly. Serve with melted butter and lemon-juice.

BAKED FINNAN-HADDIE—I

Pour boiling water over the fish, and let it stand for ten minutes. Take it out of the water, lay it in a baking-pan, brush with butter and pepper, and bake for fifteen minutes.

BAKED FINNAN-HADDIE—II

Put a haddie into a frying-pan, pour over it half a cupful of milk, and half a cupful of water. Heat slowly and let stand just below the boiling point for half an hour. Pour off the liquid, spread with butter, and bake for twenty-five minutes in a hot oven.

ESCALLOPED FINNAN-HADDIE

Prepare the fish according to directions given in the preceding recipe. After drying, remove the skin and bones and flake with a fork. Butter a baking-dish and put the fish into it. Pour over it a sauce made of two tablespoonfuls each of butter and flour cooked together and added to two cupfuls of milk. Bring to the boil, pour over the fish, cover with crumbs, dot with butter, and brown in the oven.

TOASTED FINNAN-HADDIE

Brush the fish with butter and sprinkle it with pepper. Broil until cooked through, and serve with toast.

FINNAN-HADDIE À LA DELMONICO

Flake half a pound of freshened finnan-haddie, and fry in a little butter. Add one cupful of cream beaten with the yolk of a raw egg. Thicken with a tablespoonful of flour rubbed smooth with a little of the cream. Add a hard-boiled egg chopped fine, and a teaspoonful of grated cheese. Serve on toast.

SAVORY FINNAN-HADDIE

Dip the fish in boiling water, take out all the bones and skin. Mash the meat with a tablespoonful each of butter and cream, seasoning with salt, pepper, and lemon-juice. Cook until thick and pour over slices of buttered toast.

FINNAN-HADDIE HASH

Prepare the fish according to directions given for Boiled Finnan-Haddie. Mix with an equal quantity of hot mashed potatoes, moisten with cream, and season with chopped green peppers fried in oil.

FINNAN-HADDIE WITH TOMATOES

Lay a haddie in a deep dish, cover with boiling water, and let stand for ten minutes. Drain and remove skin and break in good-sized flakes. Cook two level tablespoonfuls of butter and a tablespoonful of finely minced onion in a saucepan until golden brown. Add one cupful of the solid part of canned tomatoes. When it begins to simmer, add salt and pepper to taste. Then add the prepared fish and simmer for five minutes. Add one tablespoonful of finely minced parsley and serve.

CREAMED FINNAN-HADDIE

Parboil, drain, and flake the fish. Reheat with shredded fried green peppers in a Cream Sauce. Canned pimentos may be used instead of the green peppers.

THIRTY-TWO WAYS TO COOK FLOUNDER

BAKED FLOUNDER

Clean and split two flounders and take out all the small bones. Lay the fish in a buttered dish, sprinkle with chopped mushrooms, minced parsley, onion, and grated bread-crumbs, season with salt, pepper, and grated nutmeg. Dot with butter and bake. Cook together two tablespoonfuls each of butter and flour, and thicken two cupfuls of milk with it. Season with salt, pepper, lemon-juice, anchovy paste, and minced parsley. Add a tablespoonful of capers, drain the butter from the fish, pour over the sauce, and serve.

BAKED FLOUNDER À L'ITALIENNE

Cook together a tablespoonful of butter, two tablespoonfuls of chopped parsley, one tablespoonful each of chopped mushrooms and shallots, and two cupfuls of white wine. Reduce half by rapid boiling. Add one cupful of chicken stock and half a cupful of milk or beef stock, and thicken with flour blended with butter. Season with salt and pepper and boil down until very thick. Prepare a flounder according to directions given in the preceding recipe. Season with salt and pepper, rub with butter, pour over one cupful of white wine, cover with the sauce, and sprinkle thickly with crumbs. Bake in a moderate oven until done. Serve in the same dish.

BAKED FLOUNDER À LA BONVALLET

Put a cleaned flounder into a baking-pan with salt, pepper, grated nutmeg, chopped onion, a tablespoonful of butter, a wineglassful of white wine, and a cupful of white stock. Bake carefully, basting as required. Take up the fish, add another cupful of stock, and thicken the sauce with two tablespoonfuls of flour, blended with an equal quantity of butter. Take from the fire, add the yolks of three eggs well beaten and a tablespoonful of minced parsley. Spread this sauce over the fish, cover with crumbs, dot with butter, and brown in the oven. Sprinkle with lemon-juice and serve.

BAKED FLOUNDER À LA PARISIENNE

Stuff a cleaned flounder with seasoned crumbs and put into a buttered baking-dish. Dot with butter, sprinkle with salt and pepper, and pour over half a cupful each of oyster liquor and white wine. Cover with buttered paper and bake for forty minutes, basting as required. Take up the fish, strain the sauce, and prepare a sauce according to directions given in the first part of the recipe for Flounder Pie à la Normandy. Add the strained liquid to the sauce, pour over the fish, cover with crumbs, and brown in the oven.

BAKED FLOUNDER À LA ST. MALO

Put the cleaned fish into a buttered baking-dish with chopped onions, parsley, salt, pepper, a tablespoonful of butter and two cupfuls of cider. Add also a little mussel or oyster liquor if at hand. Bake for half an hour in a moderate oven, basting as needed. Drain the sauce, thicken with a tablespoonful of butter cooked with an equal quantity of flour, add more butter and a squeeze of lemon-juice. Pour the sauce over the fish and serve.

BAKED FILLETS OF FLOUNDER IN WINE

Fillet the fish. Mix together four tablespoonfuls of Sherry, half a cupful of butter, one tablespoonful each of onion-juice, lemon-juice, and salt, and add pepper to season. Bring to the boil, dip the fillets into it, arrange in a baking-dish, cover with the remaining sauce and bake in a hot oven for ten minutes. Fry in butter a slice each of onion and carrot, a bay-leaf, and a sprig of parsley. Add a tablespoonful of flour and cook thoroughly. Add one cupful of chicken stock and half a cupful of cream. Cook until thick, stirring constantly, and seasoning with salt, pepper, and grated nutmeg. Add the gravy from the baking-pan, strain, reheat, pour over the fish, and serve.

BAKED FILLETS OF FLOUNDER

Remove the back-bone and cut the fish into four pieces. Roll up each piece and pin with a toothpick. Soak for an hour in oil and lemon-juice. Roll in seasoned crumbs, then in beaten egg, then in crumbs. Put into a baking-pan, upon thin slices of salt pork, sprinkle with chopped onion and olives, cover, and bake. Garnish with sliced lemons.

FLOUNDER WITH FINE HERBS

Put the prepared fish into a pan with two tablespoonfuls of butter, the juice of a lemon, and salt and pepper to season. Add one cupful each of water and white wine, cover and cook for half an hour. Drain the fish, thicken the sauce with a tablespoonful of flour cooked in butter, boil, strain, add two tablespoonfuls of butter, and two tablespoonfuls of chopped parsley, pour over the fish, and serve.

FLOUNDER À LA FRANÇAISE

Cover a flounder with white wine, sprinkle with salt and pepper, add a bunch of parsley, a few chives, a bay-leaf, and a little chopped onion. Boil for ten minutes. Take up the fish carefully, rub the sauce through a sieve, thicken with a tablespoonful of flour rubbed smooth with half a cupful of butter, bring to the boil, pour over the fish, and serve.

FLOUNDER À LA JANIN

Fill a flounder with seasoned crumbs mixed with chopped mushrooms, shallots, and parsley. Put on a buttered baking-dish, season with salt and pepper, dot with butter, and pour over half a cupful each of Sherry and oyster liquor. Bake until done, basting as required. Take up the fish, add a cupful of stock to the sauce, and thicken with browned flour. Add two tablespoonfuls of butter and a little lemon-juice. Strain over the fish and garnish with parboiled oysters.

FLOUNDER À LA PROVENÇALE

Clean two flounders and let stand for four hours in a marinade of olive-oil and lemon-juice, seasoned with salt, pepper, onion, parsley, thyme, bay-leaves, and bruised garlic. Put into a baking-dish with the seasoning, a teaspoonful of butter and one cupful each of stock and white wine. Bake for half an hour, basting as needed. Drain, strain, and skim the sauce, thicken with butter and flour, take from the fire, add the yolks of four eggs well beaten and lemon-juice to taste. Season with red pepper and minced parsley, pour over the fish, and serve.

BREADED TURBANS OF FLOUNDER

Fillet three flounders, season with salt and pepper, dip into melted butter, roll up and fasten with a toothpick. Dip into egg and crumbs and fry in deep fat. Serve with Tartar Sauce.

TURBANS OF FLOUNDER WITH ANCHOVIES

Drain a bottle of anchovies from the oil. Mix with two tablespoonfuls of butter, half a cupful of stock, a tablespoonful of lemon-juice, and salt and pepper to season. Pound to a paste, and add the yolks of two raw eggs. Prepare the fillets of flounder according to directions given in the preceding recipe. Spread with the forcemeat, roll up, and pin with toothpicks. Roll in melted butter, then in flour, and bake in a hot oven for twenty minutes.

TURBANS OF FLOUNDER WITH OYSTERS

Prepare according to directions given above, stuffing with chopped oysters and seasoned crumbs.

FRICASSÉE OF FLOUNDER

Clean the flounders, cut into convenient pieces, season with salt, dredge with flour, and fry in boiling fat. Chop a dozen oysters, and put into a saucepan with their liquor, one cupful of white wine, a tablespoonful of anchovy paste, and salt, pepper, and grated nutmeg to season. Bring to the boil, pour over the fish, and serve.

FRIED FLOUNDER

Prepare the fish according to directions given in the preceding recipe. Sprinkle with salt and pepper, dip into milk, then into flour, and sauté in pork fat. Or, dip in beaten egg and bread-crumbs and fry in deep fat. Garnish with lemon and parsley.

FRIED FILLETS OF FLOUNDER

Prepare the fillets according to directions given in the preceding recipe. Keep in a cold place for half an hour, fry in deep fat, and serve with Tartar Sauce.

FILLETS OF FLOUNDER AU GRATIN

Cook together three tablespoonfuls of butter, one tablespoonful of flour, a slice of onion, and a bay-leaf. Add two cupfuls of chicken stock and cook until thick, stirring constantly. Strain, and add a tablespoonful of lemon-juice. Dip the fillets of fish into melted butter, season with salt and pepper, cover with sauce and bread-crumbs. Bake for twenty minutes in a very hot oven.

FILLETS OF FLOUNDER À LA LYONS

Bone the fish and cut into fillets. Wash in cold salted water and wipe dry. Dip in egg and seasoned bread-crumbs, and fry in hot drippings. Serve with melted butter, lemon-juice, and minced parsley, or Tomato Sauce, or a sauce made as follows: Cook together one tablespoonful each of butter and flour and thicken with it a cupful of cream or milk. Add a tablespoonful each of lemon-juice chopped pickles, and capers, a teaspoonful each of minced parsley and mustard, and the mashed yolk of a hard-boiled egg. Beat thoroughly together and serve either hot or cold.

FILLETS OF FLOUNDER À LA NORMANDY

Prepare the fillets according to directions previously given, and season with pepper and salt. Fry a small chopped onion in butter and add two chopped hard-boiled eggs, and one tablespoonful of minced parsley. Season with pepper and salt, add a tablespoonful of butter, and cook to a smooth paste. Spread the fillets with this paste, put a parboiled mussel on each one, roll and tie with a string. Add to the mussel liquor one cupful of cream and simmer the fillets in it for six minutes. Take out and cut the strings. Thicken the sauce with the yolks of two eggs beaten with four tablespoonfuls of cream, add a teaspoonful of butter and a few drops of lemon-juice. Add a few parboiled mussels to the sauce, reheat, pour over the fish, and serve.

STUFFED FILLETS OF FLOUNDER—I

Prepare the fillets according to directions previously given, season with salt and pepper, and dredge with flour. Put half of the fillets into a buttered baking-dish. Chop together a button onion, a small bunch of parsley, half a stalk of celery and half a can of mushrooms. Mix two tablespoonfuls of butter with one teaspoonful of flour, and add to the chopped mixture with the yolks of two raw eggs. Season with salt, red and black pepper, and mix thoroughly. Spread the fillets in the pan with this stuffing and lay the other fillets on top. Cover with buttered paper and cook for twelve minutes. Serve with the remaining mushrooms heated and sprinkle with lemon-juice.

STUFFED FILLETS OF FLOUNDER—II

Prepare the fillets according to directions previously given. Put each two together, with mashed potato beaten light with egg between. Cover with crumbs, dip in egg and crumbs, and fry in deep fat. Serve with Tartar Sauce.

FILLETS OF FLOUNDER WITH GREEN PEAS

Prepare the fillets according to directions previously given, dip into melted butter, and season with salt, pepper, and lemon-juice. Skewer into shape with toothpicks and arrange in a baking-dish. Half cover with stock made from the fish trimmings and bake for ten minutes. Arrange in a circle on a platter, and fill the centre with green peas seasoned with salt, pepper, and butter. Strain the stock, thicken with butter and flour cooked together, and serve separately as a sauce.

STEAMED FILLETS OF FLOUNDER

Prepare the fillets according to directions previously given, and spread with chopped pickles, olives, capers, parsley, and onions. Roll up, fasten with toothpicks, and steam or bake, basting with stock, or dip in egg and crumbs and fry in deep fat. Serve with any preferred sauce.

STUFFED FILLETS OF FLOUNDER À LA DELMONICO

Prepare the fillets according to directions previously given. Cover with half a cupful of white wine, one cupful of fish stock made from the bones, and salt and paprika to season. Simmer for twenty minutes. Cook together one tablespoonful each of butter and flour, add half a cupful of stock and cook until very thick, stirring constantly. Add half a cupful each of shrimps and oysters chopped fine, a teaspoonful of Worcestershire sauce, the yolk of an egg, and two drops of tabasco sauce. Dip the fillets in this mixture and cool. When cold dip in crumbs, then in egg, then in crumbs, and fry in deep fat.

ROLLED FILLETS OF FLOUNDER

Prepare the fillets as directed and spread with anchovies, lobster, shrimps, or sardines, mashed to a paste with butter. Roll up, fasten with toothpicks, and bake, fry, sauté, or stew, as preferred.

BROILED FILLETS OF FLOUNDER À LA BRIGHTON

Season the fillets with salt, pepper, and oil. Broil carefully and put on slices of buttered toast. Surround with parboiled oysters and pour over a sauce made of water and the oyster liquor, thickened with butter and flour cooked together, and seasoned with anchovy paste.

FILLETS OF FLOUNDER À LA DIEP-POISE

Prepare the fillets as directed, seasoning with salt and pepper, brown in melted butter, and cool. Sprinkle with crumbs, dip in eggs beaten with an equal quantity of melted butter, roll in fresh crumbs and broil, basting with oil. Serve with melted butter, minced parsley, and lemon-juice.

FLOUNDER PIE À LA NORMANDY

Chop fine two carrots and two onions, two sprigs of parsley, a stalk of celery and a bit of bay-leaf. Fry in butter, seasoning with salt and pepper, and powdered mace. Add two cupfuls of boiled milk and cook slowly for twenty-five minutes. Press through a sieve, add two cupfuls of cream, and reheat. Add the fillets of a two-pound flounder, the mussels taken from a quart of mussel shells, a quart of oysters, parboiled in their liquor, and drained, and half a pound of cleaned fresh mushrooms. Cook for two minutes. Thicken with the yolks of two eggs beaten with one tablespoonful of butter and two of cream. Fill a baking-dish lined with pastry, cover with crust, and bake.

BROILED FLOUNDER À LA CHIVRY

Cut the flounder into fillets as previously directed. Soak for an hour in a marinade of oil and lemon-juice, seasoned with salt, pepper, onion, and parsley. Dip in crumbs and broil, basting with oil. Serve with quartered lemon.

FLOUNDER WITH WHITE WINE SAUCE

Put the prepared fish into a baking-dish with two tablespoonfuls of butter, two cupfuls of white wine, and salt and pepper to season. Cover and cook for twenty minutes, adding more water if necessary. Drain the fish, thicken the gravy with a tablespoonful of flour cooked in butter, bring to the boil, add the juice of a lemon and two tablespoonfuls of butter, pour over the fish, and serve.

FLOUNDER AU GRATIN

Fry in butter chopped parsley, shallot, and button mushrooms. Season with salt and pepper and spread on the bottom of a baking-dish. Lay on them a trimmed flounder, cover with crumbs, dot with butter, moisten with white wine, and cook carefully. Serve in the same dish.

TWENTY-SEVEN WAYS TO COOK FROG LEGS

FRIED FROG LEGS—I

Beat the yolk of an egg with a cupful of milk and add flour enough to make a smooth batter. Dip into the batter frog legs which have been marinated in oil and vinegar, and fry in deep fat.

FRIED FROG LEGS—II

Clean, season with salt and pepper, dip in egg and crumbs, and fry in deep fat. Serve with Tartar Sauce.

FRIED FROG LEGS—III

Parboil for three minutes, drain, wipe dry, dip in crumbs, then in beaten egg, then in seasoned crumbs, and fry in deep fat. Serve with a border of green peas, or with Cream Sauce.

FRIED FROG LEGS—IV

Parboil for five minutes, blanch in cold water, drain, and wipe dry. Season with salt and pepper, dredge with flour, and sauté in butter. Serve with a garnish of fried parsley.

FRIED FROG LEGS—V

Soak the prepared legs in milk for fifteen minutes. Dip in seasoned flour without wiping and fry in deep fat.

FRIED FROG LEGS—VI

Parboil for five minutes in salted and acidulated water. Drain, dip into beaten egg, then in corn-meal, and fry golden-brown in salt pork fat.

FROG LEGS SAUTÉ

Put a tablespoonful of butter into a saucepan, and when it bubbles put in the frog legs with a sprig of parsley, and salt and pepper to season. Fry brown, and garnish with slices of lemon.

SOUTHERN FRIED FROG LEGS

Parboil the legs for three minutes in salted water. Beat together one egg and half a cupful of milk. Season the legs with salt and pepper, dip into the milk, then into cracker crumbs rolled fine, and fry in deep fat.

FRIED FROG LEGS À L'ANGLAISE

Season the frog legs with salt and pepper and soak for an hour in lemon-juice. Roll in flour, dip in beaten egg, then in crumbs, and fry in deep fat. Serve with Tomato Sauce.

FRIED FROG LEGS À LA FRANÇAISE

Marinate for an hour in vinegar with salt, pepper, parsley, chopped onion, bay-leaves, and thyme. Drain, roll in flour, and sauté in hot fat. Garnish with lemon and parsley.

BROILED FROG LEGS

Soak the legs for half an hour in a marinade of oil and lemon-juice, seasoned with salt and pepper. Broil on a double-broiler, and serve with Maître d'Hôtel Sauce.

BAKED FROG LEGS

Prepare and clean one dozen frog legs. Butter a baking-dish, sprinkle with chopped mushrooms and crumbs, and lay the frog legs on them. Season with salt and pepper and sweet herbs. Sprinkle with crumbs, squeeze over the juice of a lemon, and pour in a cupful of Brown Sauce. Cover and bake for half an hour in a moderate oven.

FRICASSÉE OF FROG LEGS—I

Simmer the prepared legs in milk until tender. Drain and put in a platter. Spread with butter and keep warm. Cook together one tablespoonful of flour and two of butter, add the milk in which the legs were cooked and enough more to make a pint. Cook until thick, stirring constantly. Season with salt, paprika, and minced parsley, take from the fire, and add two eggs well beaten with the juice of half a lemon. Bring to the boil, pour over the frog legs, and serve.

FRICASSÉE OF FROG LEGS—II

Prepare and skin the legs and boil until tender in veal stock to cover, with pepper and salt to season, a bunch of sweet herbs, and a bit of lemon-peel. Add a small slice of onion and cook until the legs are tender. Strain the liquid, thicken it with butter and flour and a little cream cooked together. Add the frog legs and a few canned mushrooms cut fine. Bring to the boil and serve.

FRICASSÉE OF FROG LEGS—III

Brown a dozen frog legs in butter with half a teaspoonful of chopped onions. Add one half cupful of water and one half cupful of Sherry. Cover and cook for twenty minutes. Beat the yolks of four eggs with two tablespoonfuls of cream, add a little of the hot liquid, pour into the pan, and bring to the boil. Skim out the frog legs, put on a platter, and strain the sauce over them.

BROWN FRICASSÉE OF FROG LEGS

Melt one tablespoonful of butter and brown in it two tablespoonfuls of flour. Add sufficient brown stock to make the required quantity of sauce and cook until thick, stirring constantly. Season with salt, pepper, grated lemon-peel, grated onion, sweet herbs, anchovy paste, and a pinch of allspice. Dip the frog legs in flour and fry brown. Arrange on a platter, cover with broiled mushrooms, pour the sauce over, and serve.

STEWED FROG LEGS—I

Soak the frog legs for an hour in a marinade of oil and lemon-juice, adding a teaspoonful of chopped onion. Fry brown in butter a small onion, a tomato, and a green pepper, all chopped fine. Add two tablespoonfuls of flour and cook to a smooth paste. Add the frog legs and enough water or stock to keep from burning. Cover and cook for ten or fifteen minutes.

STEWED FROG LEGS—II

Melt one tablespoonful of butter and brown in it one tablespoonful of flour, add one cupful of stock, and cook until thick, stirring constantly. Add a dozen prepared frog legs simmer for ten minutes, season with salt and pepper, take from the fire, add the yolk of an egg beaten smooth with a little cold water; bring to the boil and serve at once.

STEWED FROG LEGS—III

Soak the prepared legs in milk for fifteen minutes, dip in seasoned flour, and fry in hot butter for three minutes. Cover with hot water and simmer for twenty minutes. Bring half a cupful of cream to the boil, stir in a tablespoonful of butter rolled in flour, and cook until thick, stirring constantly. Add to the frog legs, cook three minutes longer, season with salt, pepper, and minced parsley, and serve.

STEWED FROG LEGS—IV

Brown a dozen frog legs in butter, sprinkle with flour, and add enough cream to make the required quantity of sauce. Cook until thick, stirring constantly. Add a teaspoonful each of onion-juice and minced parsley, and salt and pepper to season. Take from the fire, and add the yolks of two eggs beaten smooth with a little cold milk, bring to the boil, and serve very hot.

FROG LEGS À LA HOLLANDAISE

Fry the prepared frog legs in butter, seasoning with salt and pepper. Add half a wineglassful of white wine, cover, and simmer for five minutes; then add two cupfuls of Hollandaise Sauce, two teaspoonfuls of finely chopped parsley, and a little lemon-juice. Bring to the boil and serve very hot.

FROG LEGS À LA PROVENÇALE

Cover the bottom of a saucepan with olive-oil, and sprinkle with finely minced garlic. Lay the frog legs on this, cover and cook until brown. Squeeze over the juice of half a lemon, sprinkle with parsley, and serve.

FROG LEGS AU BEURRE NOIR

Boil the legs in court bouillon for five minutes. Drain, arrange on a serving-dish, sprinkle with minced parsley, and keep warm. Brown half a cupful of butter in a frying-pan, taking care not to burn. Add two tablespoonfuls of vinegar and salt and pepper to season. Pour over the frog legs and serve.

FROG LEGS À LA POULETTE—I

Parboil a dozen frog legs, drain and cool. Cook together one tablespoonful each of butter and flour, add one cupful of milk, or white stock, and cook until thick, stirring constantly. Add salt and pepper to season, and the frog legs. Cover and cook for twenty minutes. Take from the fire, add the yolk of an egg beaten smooth with a little cold water, and a tablespoonful of minced parsley. Bring to the boil, and serve at once.

FROG LEGS À LA POULETTE—II

Season prepared frog legs with salt, pepper, and nutmeg, and fry brown in butter. Add two tablespoonfuls of flour and two cupfuls of cream. Cook until thick, stirring constantly. Add a wineglassful of white wine, two tablespoonfuls of butter, a tablespoonful of minced parsley, and the yolks of four eggs beaten smooth with the juice of a lemon. Bring to the boil and serve.

FROG LEGS PATTIES

Boil the legs until the meat drops from the bone, remove the bone, reheat in Cream Sauce, and season to taste. Fill patty-shells and serve.

FROG LEGS À LA CREOLE

Melt a tablespoonful of butter in a saucepan and fry in it a chopped onion, a tablespoonful of chopped raw ham, and half a green pepper shredded. Season highly with salt and pepper, add four cupfuls of stock, a tablespoonful of rice, six sliced okras, and one sliced tomato. Cook thoroughly for twenty minutes. Add four cupfuls of prepared frog legs, and simmer until they are tender. Half of this recipe is sufficient for a small family.

TWENTY-TWO WAYS TO COOK HADDOCK

BROILED HADDOCK—I

Clean and dry a fresh haddock, rub with vinegar, sprinkle with flour, and broil on a well greased gridiron. Serve with Shrimp or Anchovy Sauce.

BROILED HADDOCK—II

Soak the fish for an hour in a marinade of oil and vinegar. Drain, wipe dry, broil, and serve with melted butter.

BROILED HADDOCK À LA MAÎTRE D'HÔTEL

Clean and split a haddock, season with salt and pepper, dredge with flour, and broil. Serve with Maître d'Hôtel Sauce.

BROILED SMOKED HADDOCK

Rub the fish with melted butter, season with pepper, and broil. Serve very hot.

FRIED FILLETS OF HADDOCK—I

Skin, clean and fillet a haddock. Season with pepper and salt, dip into egg and crumbs and fry brown in deep fat.

FRIED FILLETS OF HADDOCK—II

Cut the fish into fillets and marinate in oil and vinegar with a little onion. Drain, dip in batter, then in crumbs, and fry in deep fat. Serve with Tomato Sauce.

FRIED SMOKED HADDOCK

Soak a haddock for four hours in olive-oil to cover. Drain and fry in a frying-pan with a little of the oil. Season with pepper and serve very hot.

BAKED HADDOCK—I

Make a stuffing of equal parts of chopped bacon and bread-crumbs, season with salt and pepper, anchovy essence, and add a raw egg to bind. Stuff a cleaned haddock and sew up. Mix one tablespoonful of flour with one of cold water, add one cupful of boiling water, and cook until thick, stirring constantly. Add one tablespoonful of butter and two tablespoonfuls of essence of anchovy. Pour the sauce into a baking-pan, put the fish on it, and bake for an hour, basting as required.

BAKED HADDOCK—II

Make a stuffing of one cupful of cracker crumbs, one fourth of a cupful of butter, and salt, minced onion, pickles, pepper, and parsley to season. Stuff the fish, sew up, cover with strips of salt pork, dredge with flour, and bake until brown, basting as required. Serve with any preferred sauce.

BAKED HADDOCK—III

Stuff the fish with crumbs and chopped veal, seasoning to taste and using a raw egg to bind. Rub with beaten egg, sprinkle with crumbs, and bake in a moderate oven, basting with melted butter as required. Serve with Anchovy Sauce.

BAKED FILLETS OF HADDOCK

Clean and fillet a fish, put into a pan with melted butter, and season with pepper, salt, and lemon-juice. Sprinkle with minced parsley, cover with buttered paper, and bake in the oven. Serve with Italian Sauce.

BAKED HADDOCK WITH SAUCE

Clean and cut up the fish, and remove the bones. Cut into small pieces. Butter a baking-dish, sprinkle with crumbs, put in a layer of the fish, and spread with crumbs seasoned with salt, pepper, thyme and grated onion, and mixed to a paste with raw egg. Repeat until the dish is full, having crumbs and butter on top. Add enough milk to moisten, and bake. For the sauce, simmer the bones and trimmings of the fish, strain, season, and thicken with a tablespoonful each of butter and flour cooked together and blended with a little cold water.

BAKED HADDOCK WITH OYSTER STUFFING

Remove the skin, head, and tail, and take out as many bones as possible. Divide into two fillets. Sprinkle with salt and brush with lemon-juice. Lay one fillet on a greased fish sheet in a dripping-pan, and cover thickly with seasoned oysters dipped in buttered cracker crumbs. Cover with the other fillet, brush with egg slightly beaten, cover with buttered crumbs, and bake for fifty minutes in a moderate oven. Serve with Hollandaise Sauce.

HADDOCK RAREBIT

Cut the haddock into slices an inch thick. Free from bone and skin. Lay in a greased baking-dish, and season with salt and pepper. Grate sufficient cheese to cover, and season with salt, red pepper, and mustard. Make to a smooth paste with cream or beaten egg. Put into a hot oven and cook until the cheese melts and browns, and the fish is firm. Take up carefully on a platter, and pour one tablespoonful of Sherry over each slice.

BOILED HADDOCK WITH WHITE SAUCE

Boil the fish in salted and acidulated water, with a bunch of parsley to season. Cook together two tablespoonfuls of butter and one of flour, and add salt, pepper, and grated nutmeg to season. Add two cupfuls of boiling water, bring to the boil, strain, add two tablespoonfuls of butter and the juice of a lemon, pour over the fish and serve.

BOILED HADDOCK WITH EGG SAUCE

Mix finely grated bread-crumbs with half the quantity of chopped beef suet. Season with minced parsley, shallot, thyme, pepper, salt, and grated nutmeg. Bind with a raw egg. Stuff and sew up the fish and boil in salted water. For the sauce, melt one tablespoonful of butter, add two of flour, and cook thoroughly. Add two cupfuls of boiling water, and cook until thick, stirring constantly. Add two chopped hard-boiled eggs, season to taste, pour over the fish, and serve.

BOILED HADDOCK WITH LOBSTER SAUCE

Boil the fish gently in salted boiling water to cover. Melt three tablespoonfuls of butter, add two tablespoonfuls of flour, and cook thoroughly. Add gradually two cupfuls of boiling water and cook until thick. Season with lemon-juice and cayenne. Strain the sauce and reheat. Add the finely-cut meat of a small boiled lobster and the pounded coral. Pour over the fish and serve.

STEWED HADDOCK

Split the fish lengthwise and cut into pieces. Boil the bones and trimmings in water to cover, and strain. Butter a baking-dish, put the fish into it with the flesh downward, and sprinkle each piece with salt, cayenne, mace, and flour. Pour over it two cupfuls of the fish liquor, cover, and simmer for twenty minutes. Add two teaspoonfuls of anchovy essence and one cupful of Sherry. Blend together two tablespoonfuls each of flour and butter, make smooth with a little of the gravy, and thicken all of it. Simmer for ten minutes and serve with the gravy poured over the fish. Garnish with lemon and parsley.

HADDOCK AND OYSTERS

Clean and fillet a haddock. Cover the trimmings with water and add the liquor drained from a pint of oysters. Add a slice of onion, a pinch of powdered sweet herbs, and a slice of carrot. Simmer to form a stock. Put a layer of sliced onion into a saucepan, and arrange upon it the fillets of fish, and a pint of oysters; sprinkle with salt and pepper, add the juice of a lemon, cover with sliced onion, strain the stock over, cover and simmer until the fillets are tender. Arrange the fillets on a hot dish with the oysters, strain the liquid, thicken it with the yolks of four eggs, pour over, and serve.

FILLETS OF HADDOCK À LA ROYALE

Prepare the fillets and put into a basin with a marinade of oil and lemon-juice, seasoned with pepper, salt, minced parsley and chopped shallots. Drain, dip into batter and fry in deep fat. Serve with any preferred sauce.

HADDOCK À LA CRÈME

Boil the fish in salted and acidulated water. Melt two tablespoonfuls of butter and cook in it two heaping tablespoonfuls of flour. Add four cupfuls of milk and cook until thick, stirring constantly. Season with pepper, salt, grated onion, and minced parsley. Put the fish upon a serving-dish, skin it carefully, and pour the sauce over it. Put a border of mashed potatoes around the fish, rub with melted butter and put into the oven until the potato is brown.

HADDOCK CUTLETS

Prepare a sauce according to directions given in the preceding recipe, using one fourth the quantity of milk. Mix the sauce with cold cooked haddock, minced very fine, and cool. Shape into cutlets, dip into egg and crumbs, and fry in deep fat.

EIGHTY WAYS TO COOK HALIBUT

BROILED HALIBUT—I

Cut into steaks, dust with salt and pepper, cover with melted butter, and let stand for half an hour. Dredge with flour and broil. Serve with a garnish of sliced lemon and parsley.

BROILED HALIBUT—II

Freshen salt halibut for an hour or two in cold water, drain, season with pepper, and wrap each slice in tough paper well buttered, twisting the ends. Broil for eight minutes. Take from the papers and serve with any preferred sauce.

BROILED HALIBUT—III

Season with salt and pepper and broil on a buttered gridiron over a clear fire. Serve with plenty of melted butter.

BROILED HALIBUT—IV

Sprinkle halibut steaks with salt, rub thoroughly with melted butter and broil until brown. Garnish with lemon and parsley.

BROILED HALIBUT—V

Rub halibut steaks with olive-oil and lemon-juice, and broil over a clear fire. Season with pepper and salt and serve with melted butter.

BROILED HALIBUT À LA BOSTON

Broil one side of halibut steaks until heated through, then turn, and spread the other side with a paste of butter, flour, chopped onion, and tomato pulp. Cook until brown and serve with the crust side up.

HALIBUT À LA RAREBIT

Sprinkle two halibut steaks with salt and pepper, brush with melted butter, and bake until done. Arrange on a platter, pour over a Welsh rarebit, and serve.

HALIBUT À LA MAJESTIC

Skin and bone halibut steaks, and cut into fillets. Lay in a buttered baking-dish, spread with butter, and add a wineglassful of white wine, and a little boiling water. Cover with buttered paper, and set into a hot oven until cooked. Take the pan out, cover the fish with a layer of sweet Spanish peppers, spread with Cream Sauce, sprinkle with crumbs and grated cheese, dot with butter, and brown in a hot oven. Serve in the same dish.

HALIBUT À LA CONANT

In a buttered baking-pan put three thin slices of fat salt pork, three slices of onion and a bit of bay-leaf. On top of these lay a halibut steak and spread over it one tablespoonful each of butter and flour blended together. Cover with buttered cracker crumbs and small strips of salt pork, and bake for twenty minutes. Garnish with lemon and parsley.

HALIBUT À LA MAÎTRE D'HÔTEL

Soak two halibut steaks for an hour in lemon-juice, seasoned with salt, pepper, and minced parsley. Mix together two tablespoonfuls of butter, one tablespoonful of flour, and two cupfuls of boiling water. Cook until thick, stirring constantly. Put the slices of halibut into a buttered pan, cover with the sauce, and bake for twenty minutes, basting as required. Serve with any preferred sauce.

HALIBUT À LA CREOLE—I

Wash a thick piece of halibut, put on a buttered baking-dish, and season with salt and pepper. Cover with finely minced garlic, add one cupful of canned tomatoes and enough boiling water to keep from burning. Bake until done, basting as required.

HALIBUT À LA CREOLE—II

Lay halibut steak for an hour in oil and vinegar, adding chopped onion and minced parsley to the marinade. Drain and put the fish into a baking-pan. Turn over it a sauce made of one cupful of strained tomatoes, a tablespoonful of butter, a heaping teaspoonful of flour, and salt, paprika, and grated onion to season. Cover closely and bake until tender. Sprinkle with grated cheese and cook for five minutes longer. Transfer the fish carefully to a hot platter and pour the sauce around it.

HALIBUT À LA CREOLE—III

Boil together a pint of stewed tomatoes, a cupful of water, a slice of onion, and three cloves. Blend together two tablespoonfuls of butter and one of flour, and stir into the sauce when it boils. Season with salt and pepper, and cook for ten minutes. Strain and cool. Skin the fish according to directions given in the recipe for Baked Halibut—I. Put on a buttered tin sheet in a baking-pan, season with salt and pepper, and bake, basting frequently with the sauce.

BAKED HALIBUT—I

Take three or four pounds of the fish and remove the dark skin, by dipping it into boiling water and scraping. Rub the flesh with salt and pepper, put it into a baking-pan, and add enough milk to cover the bottom of the pan an inch deep.

Bake for an hour, basting frequently with the milk. Take out the fish, remove the bone and skin, and serve with Egg Sauce.

BAKED HALIBUT—II

Soak six pounds of halibut in salt water for two hours. Wipe dry and score the outer skin. Bake for an hour in a moderately hot oven, basting with melted butter and hot water. Add a little boiling water to the gravy, a tablespoonful of walnut catsup, a teaspoonful of Worcestershire Sauce, salt and pepper to season, and the juice of a lemon. Thicken with browned flour rubbed smooth with a little cold water.

BAKED HALIBUT—III

Take a thick cut of halibut and soak for half an hour in salted water. Put into a baking-pan with two slices of carrot, a slice of onion, and half a bay-leaf. Pour over it a cupful of boiling water and two tablespoonfuls of melted butter. Bake for an hour, basting frequently, and serve with any preferred sauce.

BAKED HALIBUT—IV

Lay a thick piece of halibut into a buttered pan, cover with thin slices of salt pork, and dredge with salt, pepper, and flour. Cover the bottom of the pan with boiling water, and bake for an hour. Baste with the gravy in the pan and melted butter, adding salt, pepper, and flour as needed. A bay-leaf, a sprig of parsley, two slices of carrot, and half an onion or a clove of garlic may be put into the dripping-pan.

BAKED HALIBUT—V

Prepare according to directions given for Baked Halibut—II, seasoning the gravy with lemon- and onion-juice, celery salt, and half a cupful of Claret.

BAKED HALIBUT WITH LOBSTER SAUCE

Put a piece of halibut on a buttered fish sheet, sprinkle with salt and pepper, and dredge with flour. Cover the bottom of the pan with water, add a sprig of parsley, a slice of onion, two slices of carrot, three tablespoonfuls of butter, and a bit of bay-leaf. Bake for an hour, basting as required, and serve with Lobster Sauce.

BAKED HALIBUT WITH TOMATO SAUCE

Cook together for twenty minutes two cupfuls of tomatoes, one cupful of water, a slice of onion, three cloves, and a teaspoonful of sugar. Cook together three tablespoonfuls each of butter and flour, stir into the hot mixture, and cook until thick. Strain, and pour half of the sauce around two pounds of halibut placed on a buttered tin sheet. Bake for thirty-five minutes, basting often. Transfer to a hot platter and pour the remaining sauce around.

BAKED HALIBUT WITH CREAM

Cover the fish with Cream Sauce, then with crumbs, dot with butter, and bake.

BAKED FILLETS OF HALIBUT AU GRATIN

Bake half a dozen fillets of halibut for half an hour, seasoning with salt and pepper and basting with milk. Cover with a Cream Sauce to which half a cupful of grated cheese has been added, then with fried crumbs. Reheat and serve in the same dish.

BAKED HALIBUT STEAKS WITH OYSTERS

Soak two halibut steaks for an hour in a marinade of oil and vinegar. Lay thin slices of salt pork upon a buttered tin sheet, and spread thin slices of salt pork upon it. Lay one of the steaks upon the pork. Dip oysters in melted butter, then in cracker crumbs, and cover the steak with them. Put the other steak on top, cover with thin slices of pork and bake for forty minutes, basting with the juice in the pan or with butter melted in hot water. A few minutes before taking up, remove the pork from the top and cover with cracker crumbs and melted butter. Serve with Hollandaise Sauce to which parboiled oysters have been added.

BAKED FILLETS OF HALIBUT

Skin, bone and fillet two halibut steaks. Dip in melted butter, season with salt, pepper, lemon- and onion-juice. Roll up each fillet, fasten with a wooden toothpick, and bake for twenty minutes, basting with butter melted in hot water. Serve with any preferred sauce.

BAKED HALIBUT STEAKS—I

Put a halibut steak into a buttered baking-dish, and spread with a dressing made of one cupful of crumbs, one tablespoonful of butter, and grated onion, minced parsley, grated nutmeg, salt, and red and black pepper to season. Lay another steak on top, season with salt and pepper, dot with butter, and bake for half an hour.

BAKED HALIBUT STEAKS—II

Wash the steaks and soak for an hour in olive-oil and lemon-juice. Put into a buttered baking-dish, sprinkle with minced onion and parsley, and pour over a Cream Sauce, using white stock instead of milk, if preferred. Put a layer of flaked cooked halibut into a buttered baking-dish, season with salt, pepper, and grated nutmeg, add a layer of chopped mushrooms and a few tablespoonfuls of the sauce. Repeat until the dish is full, having sauce on top. Sprinkle with crumbs, dot with butter, and brown in the oven.

BAKED HALIBUT STEAKS—III

Trim the steaks, lay them in a baking-pan, season with salt and pepper, dredge with flour, dot with butter, pour over one cupful of cream and bake for fifteen minutes in a quick oven, basting with cream.

BAKED CHICKEN HALIBUT

Prepare a dressing according to directions given in the preceding recipe. Stuff a chicken halibut, sew up and bake in a buttered pan, basting with melted butter and salted hot water. Serve with Hollandaise Sauce.

BAKED HALIBUT STEAKS WITH TOMATOES

Soak the steaks for an hour in olive-oil and lemon-juice. Cook together for fifteen minutes a can of tomatoes and a seeded chopped green pepper, half an onion, a teaspoonful of sugar, and pepper and salt to season. Rub through a colander and cool. Put the drained fish in a buttered baking-pan, pour the sauce over, and bake.

DEVILLED HALIBUT—I

Flake cold cooked halibut. Make a forcemeat of bread-crumbs, the yolks of two eggs, a tablespoonful of melted butter, and salt, paprika, grated onion, and minced parsley to season. Mix the fish, moisten with oyster liquor, and fill buttered individual shells. Cover with crumbs, season with salt and pepper, dot with butter, and brown in the oven.

DEVILLED HALIBUT—II

Flake a pound of cooked halibut. Mix together the pounded yolks of three hard-boiled eggs, one tablespoonful of olive-oil, two teaspoonfuls of sugar, a teaspoonful of made mustard, a pinch of cayenne, a teaspoonful of salt, a teaspoonful of Worcestershire sauce, half a teaspoonful of anchovy paste, and enough vinegar to make a smooth paste. Mix thoroughly with the fish, and garnish with hard-boiled eggs sliced or quartered.

MOULDED HALIBUT WITH GREEN PEAS

Chop a pound of raw halibut very fine. Add to it the yolk of an egg well beaten, and salt, red and white pepper to season. Add a teaspoonful of corn-starch rubbed smooth with two thirds of a cupful of milk and one third of a cupful of cream, whipped solid. Fill buttered individual moulds, put into a pan of hot water, and bake in a slow oven for twenty minutes. Turn out on a platter and surround with cooked peas, reheated in Cream Sauce.

SANDWICHES OF CHICKEN HALIBUT

Cut chicken halibut into thin fillets. Put together in pairs with chopped oysters between, rubbed to a paste with seasoned crumbs and cream. Rub with melted butter, sprinkle with lemon-juice, and season with salt and pepper. Put into a shallow pan with half a cupful of white wine, and bake for twenty minutes. Arrange on a platter, sprinkle with minced parsley, and serve with Hollandaise Sauce.

TURBANS OF HALIBUT

Have a slice of halibut cut two inches thick. Take off the skin and cut into cylinders with a small tin baking-powder box. Steam until firm and serve with a Cream Sauce flavored with parsley and lemon. Or, bake in milk and serve with Cream Sauce, using stewed and strained tomato for half of the liquid.

HALIBUT AND LOBSTER À LA HOLLANDAISE

Reheat equal quantities of boiled and flaked lobster and halibut in Hollandaise Sauce.

HALIBUT STEAK À LA JARDINIÈRE—I

Soak halibut steaks for an hour in salt and water. Wipe dry and rub with melted butter. Butter a china baking-dish, sprinkle chopped onion on the bottom and put in the steaks. On top put a boiled carrot cut into dice, half a dozen sliced tomatoes, a shredded green pepper, and half a cupful of green peas. Add enough salted boiling water to keep the fish from scorching, put a tablespoonful of butter on top, cover, and bake until done. Drain the liquor carefully from the pan, add three tablespoonfuls of white wine, and thicken with a teaspoonful of butter rolled in browned flour. Serve separately as a sauce.

HALIBUT À LA JARDINIÈRE—II

Cover two slices of halibut with a chopped onion, two tomatoes sliced, a shredded and seeded green pepper, a dozen chopped almonds, a tablespoonful of melted butter, and salt to season. Bake for half an hour, pour over the sauce from the pan, and serve.

HALIBUT IN CUCUMBERS

Cook the halibut until tender in court bouillon, drain, and flake with a fork. Make a Cream Sauce, seasoning with curry powder. Pare, cut in halves, and parboil in beef stock as many cucumbers as are required. Scoop out the inside of each half, fill with the creamed fish, cover with crumbs, dot with butter, and bake in the oven until the cucumbers are soft. Serve with a garnish of lemon and parsley.

HALIBUT WITH ANCHOVY SAUCE

Four tablespoonfuls of butter, four tablespoonfuls of flour, one eighth teaspoonful of pepper, one half teaspoonful of salt, two hard-boiled eggs chopped, two cupfuls of cream, two drops of tabasco, one teaspoonful of anchovy essence, one and one half cupfuls of cold cooked halibut, flaked. Mix the ingredients in the order given and cook for ten minutes. Serve with brown bread spread with cheese and chopped olives.

HALIBUT AU GRATIN

Flake cold cooked halibut and mix with an equal quantity of Cream Sauce. Put into buttered individual shells, sprinkle with crumbs, dot with butter, and brown in the oven.

ESCALLOPED HALIBUT

Prepare the fish according to directions given in the preceding recipe, and add the yolks of two eggs well beaten. Fill a baking-dish, using alternate layers of fish and grated cheese. Cover with crumbs, dot with butter, and brown in the oven.

HALIBUT STEAK À LA FLAMANDE

Butter a baking-pan, sprinkle with chopped onion, and lay a halibut steak upon it. Pour over the beaten yolk of an egg, season with salt and pepper, add the juice of half a lemon, and one tablespoonful of butter cut into small pieces. Bake for thirty minutes. Add to the liquid remaining in the pan enough boiling water to make the required quantity of sauce, and thicken it with browned flour.

CREAMED HALIBUT

Flake cold cooked halibut and mix with Cream Sauce. Add a tablespoonful of minced parsley, the juice of half a lemon, and three tablespoonfuls of grated Parmesan cheese. Spread on buttered toast, sprinkle with minced parsley and serve.

HALIBUT SALAD

Take cold cooked halibut cut small, salt and pepper lightly, and sprinkle with lemon-juice. For the dressing boil three large peeled potatoes until mealy. Drain, let dry, and beat to a dry powder with a fork. Add one saltspoonful of salt, the same of mustard and pepper, one rounding teaspoonful of powdered sugar, and two tablespoonfuls of vinegar beaten in gradually. Pour over the halibut and decorate with lettuce or green tops.

TURKISH HALIBUT

Place on the bottom of a baking-pan two or three slices of onion, then a cutlet of halibut, and put a tablespoonful of butter cut into small bits over the top of the fish. Cut three skinned tomatoes into quarters, slice a sweet green pepper into ribbons, and put the tomatoes and pepper on the fish. Put the pan on the shelf of the oven to cook first the vegetables, but do not let it remain there long enough to discolor or change their shape; then remove it to the bottom of the oven, baste it well, and finish the cooking. When done place it carefully on a hot dish, and pour over it the juice from the pan.

HALIBUT PIE

Butter a china baking-dish and sprinkle with chopped shallots and parsley. Add a layer of chopped halibut, and salt, pepper, grated nutmeg, chopped shallots, and parsley to season. Dot with butter and cover with sliced hard-boiled eggs. Add a cupful of Cream Sauce, and two wineglassfuls of white wine. Wet the edge, cover with pastry, gash, brush with egg and bake for an hour and a half in a moderate oven. Make a hole in the centre and moisten the pie with milk if it becomes too dry.

STEAMED HALIBUT

Put the prepared fish on a plate, cover with a cloth, and put in a steamer. Steam for two hours and pour over an Egg Sauce.

HALIBUT MOUSSELINES

Mince enough uncooked halibut to make two cupfuls, add one cupful of soft bread-crumbs and one half cupful of cream. Press through a colander, season with salt, pepper, lemon-juice, a suspicion of mace and Worcestershire Sauce. Fold in carefully the beaten whites of four eggs. Turn into buttered moulds (round-bottomed ones) and steam one half hour. Turn out on separate plates, surround with sauce, make a stock of the fish bones and water, and add it to two tablespoonfuls of butter and two of flour cooked together. There should be one and one half cupfuls of stock. Add one half cupful of cream, and when boiling add salt, pepper, and one tablespoonful of grated horseradish soaked in lemon-juice.

HALIBUT STEAKS À LA MAÎTRE D'HÔTEL

Season the steaks with salt and pepper, and rub thoroughly with oil. Broil in a double-broiler, and serve with melted butter, minced parsley, and lemon-juice.

TIMBALE OF HALIBUT

Chop half a pound of raw halibut and press it through a sieve. Mix a cupful of bread-crumbs to a smooth paste with half a cupful of milk, and cook until it thickens. Take from the fire, add the fish pulp and the stiffly beaten whites of five eggs. Fill buttered timbale moulds with the mixture and cook in a pan of hot water in a moderate oven for twenty minutes. Serve with Cream or Tomato Sauce.

FILLETS OF HALIBUT À LA POULETTE

Free the fish of skin and bones and cut it into fillets. Sprinkle with lemon-juice, salt, and pepper. Cover with sliced onion and let stand for half an hour.

Remove the onion, dip into melted butter, roll up each piece, and fasten with a wooden toothpick. Dip once more into the butter, dredge thickly with flour and bake for twenty minutes in a moderate oven. Cut the whites of three hard-boiled eggs into rings, and arrange around the fillets after taking up. Sprinkle the grated yolks over the fish and serve with Cream Sauce.

COLD HALIBUT FILLET

Prepare half a dozen fillets of halibut, remove the skin and bone, and boil in court bouillon. Drain and sprinkle with olive-oil, lemon-juice, minced parsley, and chopped onion. Serve with Tartar Sauce.

FILLETS OF HALIBUT WITH TOMATO SAUCE

Prepare the fillets according to directions previously given, and bake, basting with tomato-juice and melted butter. Serve with Tomato Sauce.

FILLETS OF HALIBUT STUFFED WITH OYSTERS

Prepare the fillets according to directions given for Fillets of Halibut à la Poulette. Roll each one around an oyster, fasten with a wooden toothpick, and bake as usual.

FILLETS OF HALIBUT WITH BROWN SAUCE

Put the seasoned fillets into a buttered pan with sufficient boiling water, and bake, basting as required. Drain off the water, add to it a teaspoonful of beef extract, and thicken with browned flour. Pour the sauce over the fish, cover with buttered crumbs, and bake until the crumbs are brown.

FILLETS OF HALIBUT WITH POTATO BALLS

Cut the solid meat into fillets, seasoning with salt, pepper, onion- and lemon-juice. Brown slightly in pork fat, then place in a baking-dish. Prepare a Cream Sauce, adding to it a slice each of carrot and onion, a bay-leaf, and minced parsley and grated nutmeg to season. Strain over the fish and bake for twelve minutes. Serve with a border of steamed potato balls.

FRIED FILLETS OF HALIBUT—I

Prepare the fillets according to directions previously given and soak for an hour in a marinade of oil, vinegar, and minced onion. Drain, dip in batter, then in crumbs, and fry in deep fat.

FRIED FILLETS OF HALIBUT—II

Clean and fillet the fish. Dip into beaten egg, then into crumbs, and fry in deep fat. Serve with melted butter, lemon-juice, and minced parsley.

MAYONNAISE OF HALIBUT WITH CUCUMBERS

Boil or steam halibut steaks according to directions previously given. Remove the skin, cover with thinly sliced cucumbers, and pour over a Mayonnaise dressing.

HALIBUT LOAF

Cook together two tablespoonfuls of butter and one tablespoonful of flour. Add half a can of chopped mushrooms, two cupfuls of chopped cooked halibut, pepper, salt, onion-juice, and anchovy paste to season, and two eggs beaten smooth with four tablespoonfuls of cream. Pour into a buttered mould, cover set into a pan of hot water and cook steadily for an hour. Turn out and garnish with potato balls.

HALIBUT AND EGGS

Flake a pound of cooked halibut and mix with six eggs well beaten. Season with salt and pepper and cook in butter, stirring constantly until the eggs set. Serve on buttered toast.

HALIBUT IN RAMEKINS

Prepare the fish according to directions given for Halibut in Cucumbers. Fill buttered individual dishes, cover with crumbs, dot with butter, and bake in the oven.

HALIBUT FISH BALLS

Flake cold cooked halibut and mix with an equal quantity of mashed potatoes beaten very light with egg. Season with salt, pepper, and melted butter. Shape into balls, dip into melted butter, dredge with flour, and fry in deep fat.

BREADED HALIBUT

Prepare according to directions given for Halibut à la Creole—I, sprinkling with minced parsley as well as garlic. Cover with crumbs, dot with butter, and bake in the oven.

COQUILLES OF HALIBUT

Flake cold cooked halibut, and mix with Cream Sauce. Season with mushroom catsup, fill buttered individual shells, cover with fried bread-crumbs and heat thoroughly in the oven.

HALIBUT WITH CAPER SAUCE

Boil the halibut in salted and acidulated water. Pour over a Caper Sauce.

HALIBUT PUDDING

Three pounds of halibut, six eggs, one quarter pound butter, one quart sweet milk, two tablespoonfuls of corn-starch, one tablespoonful of flour. Skin and bone the fish and run through a meat-chopper. Add flour and corn-starch, mixing well. Add butter, rubbing all to a cream; next the eggs, one at a time, thoroughly beating after each one. Add milk gradually, one quarter teaspoonful pepper and one and one half teaspoonfuls of salt. Beat until it thickens. Grease and line a deep baking-pan with browned bread-crumbs. Fill with the fish mixture and sprinkle crumbs on top. Bake for an hour and a half in a moderate oven; cover at first, then remove the cover and let it brown well.

BOILED HALIBUT—I

Put two pounds of halibut into a saucepan and cover it with fresh water. Add a sliced onion, half a carrot sliced, two tablespoonfuls of vinegar, a small bunch of parsley, a pinch of powdered sweet herbs, and two tablespoonfuls of salt. Simmer until done, drain, and serve with melted butter to which a little anchovy paste has been added.

BOILED HALIBUT—II

Rub the fish with salt, sprinkle with lemon-juice, and keep in a cool place for an hour. Cover with cold water, bring quickly to the boil, and simmer until done. Serve with Egg Sauce.

BOILED HALIBUT STEAKS AU GRATIN

Soak the steaks in salted water for an hour, drain, and sprinkle with oil and lemon-juice. Put into a covered baking-pan, sprinkle with chopped onion and a tablespoonful of melted butter, and add a cupful of boiling water. Cover and cook until nearly done, then uncover, sprinkle with crumbs, dot with butter, and bake brown. Serve with Tartar Sauce.

BOILED HALIBUT STEAKS

Cover the steaks with court bouillon or hot water, and add a slice each of carrot, onion, and celery, a bay-leaf, four cloves, six peppercorns, and the juice of half a lemon. Simmer until done, drain and serve with any preferred sauce.

BOILED HALIBUT À LA BECHAMEL

Prepare Boiled Halibut according to directions previously given, and serve with Bechamel Sauce, seasoning with salt, pepper, and grated nutmeg. Add four tablespoonfuls of butter and a pinch of sugar, and strain over the fish.

BOILED HALIBUT WITH PARSLEY SAUCE

Boil the halibut in salted and acidulated water. For the sauce boil a cupful of chopped parsley for five minutes in a cupful of water. Strain the water through a sieve, and thicken with a tablespoonful of butter blended with a tablespoonful of flour. Take from the fire, season with salt, pepper, and grated nutmeg, add the yolks of two eggs well beaten, a little minced parsley, two tablespoonfuls of butter, and a few drops of lemon-juice or vinegar. Strain over the fish and serve.

CARBONADE OF HALIBUT

Skin the halibut and cut into large cubes. Dip into melted butter, seasoned with salt, pepper, and onion-juice, then into beaten egg, then into crumbs. Put into a buttered baking-pan, spread with egg and butter, and cook in a hot oven for twelve minutes. Serve with Hollandaise Sauce.

FRIED HALIBUT—I

Cut into steaks, and sauté in butter in a frying-pan, or dip in egg and crumbs and fry in deep fat.

FRIED HALIBUT—II

Season halibut steaks with salt and pepper, dredge with flour, and sauté in salt pork fat. Serve the pork with the fish.

FRIED HALIBUT—III

Soak halibut steaks for an hour in a marinade of oil and vinegar. Drain, dredge with seasoned flour, dip in beaten egg, then in seasoned crumbs. Fry in deep fat.

FRIED HALIBUT WITH TOMATO SAUCE

Remove the skin and bones from small halibut steaks, dip in milk, roll in seasoned flour, and fry light brown. Serve with a sauce of stewed, strained, and seasoned tomatoes thickened with butter and flour, cooked together.

ESCALLOPED HALIBUT AU PARMESAN

Cut in thin slices four pounds of halibut meat. Put into a buttered pan with salt, pepper, grated nutmeg, and chopped onions to season. Cover, cook slowly, and then drain. Cook together two tablespoonfuls each of butter and flour, add a quart of milk and cook until thick, stirring constantly. Take from the fire, add the yolks of four eggs well beaten and half a cupful of grated cheese. Put into a buttered baking-dish a layer of fish, cover it with sauce, and repeat until the dish is full, having sauce on top. Sprinkle thickly with crumbs and grated cheese, dot with butter, and bake in a moderate oven.

BREADED HALIBUT STEAKS

Dip halibut steaks into egg and bread crumbs, and broil on a buttered gridiron, basting with melted butter or olive-oil.

HALIBUT TIMBALES

Chop fine a slice of raw halibut, and rub it through a sieve. Season one cupful of the pulp with salt, red pepper, and onion-juice, then add gradually the stiffly beaten whites of four eggs, and one cupful of whipped cream. Fill buttered timbale moulds, cover with buttered paper, and bake for fifteen minutes in a pan of hot water. Turn out and serve with any preferred sauce.

HALIBUT à LA POULETTE

Melt one fourth of a cupful of butter, and season it with salt, pepper, grated onion, and lemon-juice. Dip prepared fillets of halibut into it, roll up, and fasten with a wooden toothpick. Dredge with flour and bake, basting with melted butter. Arrange on a platter, pour over a Cream Sauce and sprinkle thickly with chopped hard-boiled eggs.

TWENTY-FIVE WAYS TO COOK HERRING

STEWED HERRING

Clean the fish and cut off the heads. Pack in layers in an earthen pot, and sprinkle salt and pepper over each layer. Chop together carrots and onions, enough to cover the fish, and fry in butter with parsley, a few peppercorns, and a minced clove of garlic. Pour over the vegetables enough white wine to cover the fish, and bring to the boil. Simmer for half an hour, then strain over the fish and cook over a slow fire until done.

MATELOTE OF HERRING

Cut off the heads and tails and divide each herring lengthwise into two fillets. Put a small amount of butter into a frying-pan and add enough flour to absorb nearly all of it, then add a little chopped parsley and a few chopped shallots. Lay the fish in the pan, add enough red wine to cover, and cook over a hot fire. Garnish with small onions fried in butter and sugar, and sautéd mushrooms.

BROILED HERRING

Clean and split the fish. Let stand for an hour in olive-oil, seasoned with minced parsley. Broil over a slow fire and serve with melted butter, lemon-juice and minced parsley.

BROILED HERRING WITH MUSTARD SAUCE

Clean and cut off the heads of the fish, but do not split. Dip in seasoned oil and let stand for an hour. Broil over a slow fire. Mix together one teaspoonful of flour and one tablespoonful of mustard. Add one cupful of white stock and bring to the boil. Add one tablespoonful of butter, a teaspoonful of minced parsley, and pepper and salt to taste. Pour over the fish and serve.

BROILED SMOKED HERRING

Put the cleaned herring into a bowl, cover with boiling water, let stand for ten minutes, skin, wipe dry, broil, and serve with melted butter.

BROILED HERRING WITH CREAM SAUCE

Soak for an hour in a marinade of oil and lemon-juice, seasoned with salt and pepper. Broil and serve with a Cream Sauce. Add to the sauce a teaspoonful of minced parsley, and a few drops of vinegar.

FRIED HERRING—I

Clean and cut up the fish, dip in milk, roll in flour and fry in hot fat. Serve with a Cream Sauce, to which four tablespoonfuls of prepared mustard have been added.

FRIED HERRING—II

Clean and cut up the fish, dredge with salt, pepper, and flour, and put into a frying-pan with hot lard.

FRIED HERRING—III

Remove the head and tail, clean, gash down to the bone, roll in corn-meal, and fry in salt pork fat. Garnish with lemon and parsley.

HERRING À LA NORMANDY

Chop a large onion fine and fry it. When brown, fry half a dozen prepared herrings in the same fat. When brown add salt, pepper, and two tablespoonfuls of vinegar. Bring to the boil and pour over the herring. Serve with mustard.

SMOKED HERRING À LA MARINE

Cut off the heads of smoked herrings and put the rest in a bowl. Cover with hot water and soak for two hours. Take them out, skin, bone, and soak for two weeks in enough oil to cover, with sliced onions, pepper-corns, and bay-leaves. Keep in a cool place.

BOILED HERRING

Clean the fish thoroughly, and rub with salt and vinegar. Skewer their tails in their mouths and boil for ten or twelve minutes. Drain and serve with melted butter and parsley.

HERRING RELISH

Soak six Holland herrings over night. Remove the backbones, cut up into inch pieces, and add three onions sliced thin. Cover with vinegar and serve the next day.

HERRING SALAD

Soak four salt herrings in water over night. Drain and chop fine. Mix with four boiled beets, three heads of celery boiled, four peeled sour apples, two onions, three pickles, and two pounds of lean roast veal. Chop very fine, season with salt and pepper, and pour over enough oil to moisten, and enough vinegar to suit the taste. Serve very cold with a garnish of hard-boiled eggs.

HERRING SALAD À LA BRENOISE

Peel and cut into dice a quart of cold boiled potatoes, four peeled and cored sour apples, the fillets of four salt herrings, a cucumber pickle and two boiled beets. Add salt, pepper, chopped onion, vinegar, mustard and Mayonnaise dressing. Sprinkle with minced parsley before serving.

SWEDISH HERRING SALAD

Soak two salted Holland herrings for twenty-four hours. Remove the bones and cut into dice. Add an equal amount of cooked meat cut into dice and half the quantity each of boiled potatoes, sour apples, and beets chopped fine. Chop one tablespoonful of capers and four hard-boiled eggs. Add to the salad with three tablespoonfuls of cream, two of olive-oil, two of vinegar, and pepper, sugar, and mustard to taste. Press in a mould, and serve on platter with a garnish of parsley. Serve with the same kind of dressing that was mixed with the salad.

SMOKED HERRING SALAD

Put the crisp leaves of a head of lettuce into a salad bowl. Skin and remove the bone from two smoked herrings, chop fine and mix with the lettuce. Pour over a French dressing to which a chopped hard-boiled egg has been added.

PICKLED HERRING

Soak in milk and water over night. Next day put the herring into a stone jar with alternate layers of sliced onion, a few slices of lemon, a few cloves, bay-leaves, and whole peppers, and enough mustard seed to season. Rub the roe through a sieve, add a tablespoonful of brown sugar and add it to the herring. Pour over enough vinegar to cover the fish and let stand three or four days before using.

HERRING BALLS

Parboil three red herrings, skin, and remove the bones. Add an equal quantity of baked potatoes, skinned and mashed. Make to a paste with cream and melted butter, season to taste, and shape into balls. Dip in egg and crumbs and fry in deep fat.

BAKED SMOKED HERRING

Wash thoroughly, wipe dry, wrap in clean wet manilla paper, and put into a quick oven for fifteen minutes. Served with sliced lemon.

BAKED FRESH HERRING

Clean a dozen fresh herrings, removing the head and tail. Butter a deep earthen dish, put in a layer of fish, two slices of lemon, and three or four slices of onion. Season with pepper and salt and repeat until the dish is full, cover with vinegar, tie a sheet of buttered brown paper over the dish, and bake in a slow oven for six hours. The bones will be dissolved.

MARINADE OF HERRING

Soak white salted herrings for two hours in milk to cover. Split, remove the bones, and cut each half into three pieces. Pack in layers in a deep jar, seasoning between the layers with minced shallot, pounded clove and white pepper. Add here and there a bit of bay-leaf and a slice of fresh lemon with half the rind taken off. Use the roe with the herring. Season the top layer, cover with vinegar, add three tablespoonfuls of olive-oil, and let stand for two days before using.

ESCALLOPED HERRING

Soak four or five Norway herrings over night. Divide the fish down the back, remove the skin and bones, and cut into eight squares. Arrange in a baking-pan with alternate layers of cold boiled potatoes, seasoning each layer with butter and red pepper. Have potatoes on top. Pour over three eggs beaten with three cupfuls of milk. Cover with crumbs, dot with butter, and bake for forty minutes.

GRILLED SMOKED HERRING

Soak over night and in the morning cover with hot water and let stand for half an hour. Put into cold water for ten minutes, then wipe dry and broil. Serve with hot corn bread.

GRILLED FRESH HERRING

Dip in seasoned melted butter, then in crumbs, and broil carefully, basting with melted butter if required. Serve with Maître d'Hôtel Sauce.

NINE WAYS TO COOK KINGFISH.

BOILED KINGFISH

Clean the fish and boil with enough fish stock to cover. Drain carefully, garnish with parsley, and serve with either Brown or White Sauce.

BOILED KINGFISH À LA HOLLANDAISE

Scale and clean two large kingfish, and boil in salted and acidulated water, with a bunch of parsley, a slice each of carrot and onion, and a pinch of powdered sweet herbs. Cover with buttered paper and simmer until done. Garnish with parsley and serve with Hollandaise Sauce.

FRIED KINGFISH—I

Cut the fish into fillets, remove the skin, season with salt and pepper, dredge with flour, dip in beaten egg, then in bread-crumbs, and fry in deep fat. Serve with any preferred sauce.

FRIED KING FISH—II

Prepare the fish according to directions given in the preceding recipe. Cook until firm in melted butter and lemon-juice. Drain, cool, dip in batter, and fry in deep fat. Serve with any preferred sauce.

FRIED KINGFISH—III

Clean and fillet the fish, dip in milk, roll in flour and fry. Drain, season, garnish with lemons, and serve with Tomato Sauce.

BROILED KING FISH

Clean thoroughly, wipe dry, and slit down the back; season with salt and pepper and baste with oil before and during the broiling. Serve with melted butter, minced parsley, and lemon-juice.

BAKED KING FISH

Clean four kingfish, cut off the fins and gash from head to tail on each side. Place on a buttered baking-dish, sprinkle with chopped shallots, parsley, and mushrooms. Sprinkle with salt and pepper and put small bits of butter in the incisions. Pour over two wine-glassfuls of white wine and baste with the liquid while baking. Thicken a cupful of beef stock with butter and browned flour, and pour over the fish when nearly done. Sprinkle with crumbs, dot with butter, and brown in the oven. Sprinkle with lemon-juice before serving.

BAKED KING FISH WITH WHITE SAUCE

Prepare the fish according to directions given in the recipe for Baked Kingfish, omitting the mushrooms and the seasoning. Pour over one cupful of white wine, and half a cupful of white stock. Baste with the liquid while baking. Take up the fish carefully, and add to the liquid remaining in the pan enough white stock to make the required quantity of sauce. Thicken with a tablespoonful each of butter and flour cooked together, take from the fire, add two tablespoonfuls of butter and a little lemon-juice. Strain over the fish and serve.

KINGFISH À LA MEUNIÈRE

Prepare and season eight small kingfish, dredge with flour, brown in butter, and finish cooking in the oven. When done, pour over two tablespoonfuls of butter which has been cooked brown, sprinkle with lemon-juice and minced parsley, and serve in the baking-dish.

SIXTY-FIVE WAYS TO COOK MACKEREL

BROILED SPANISH MACKEREL—I

Cut a fish down the middle, take out all the bones, and cut again in halves. Dry on a cloth and sprinkle with salt and pepper. Beat two eggs, add an equal quantity of olive-oil, dip the fish into this, then into bread-crumbs, and broil over a clear fire.

BROILED SPANISH MACKEREL—II

Split the mackerel down the back and broil carefully over a clear fire. Season with butter, pepper, and salt.

BROILED FRESH MACKEREL—I

Split two fresh mackerel, remove the backbone, season with salt and pepper, rub with olive-oil, and broil. Serve with melted butter, lemon-juice, and minced parsley.

BROILED MACKEREL—II

Draw and wash the mackerel, cut off the head, rub with olive-oil, and broil. Sprinkle with minced parsley, onions, and lemon-juice, and serve very hot.

BROILED MACKEREL—III

Split a mackerel down the back, take out the backbone, sprinkle with salt, and broil on a buttered gridiron. Serve with melted butter, lemon-juice, salt, and pepper. A little minced parsley may be added.

BROILED MACKEREL WITH ANCHOVY BUTTER

Split and broil a fresh mackerel and serve with melted butter, seasoned with anchovy paste.

BROILED MACKEREL AU BEURRE NOIR

Open the mackerel, remove the bones, sprinkle with pepper and salt, spread with butter, and broil. Cook a tablespoonful of butter until brown, take from the fire, add the juice of half a lemon, and pour over the fish. Garnish with parsley.

BROILED MACKEREL À LA LIVOURNAISE

Broil a Spanish mackerel, seasoning with salt and pepper, and basting with oil. Serve with a sauce made of eight pounded anchovies mixed with Mayonnaise and seasoned with pepper, grated nutmeg, and minced parsley. The sauce is served cold.

BROILED MACKEREL WITH NORMANDY SAUCE

Soak cleaned mackerel in oil with chopped onion and parsley to season. Leave the roe inside. Rub the inside with lemon-juice and butter, wrap in oiled paper, and broil over a slow fire for forty minutes. Prepare a Cream Sauce and add to it two tablespoonfuls each of mushroom catsup and fish stock, or boiling water in which a little anchovy paste has been dissolved. Bring to the boil, take from the fire, add the yolks of two eggs and the juice of half a lemon. Add one tablespoonful of butter, pour over the fish, and serve.

BROILED MACKEREL À LA FLEURETTE

Split a Spanish mackerel, remove the bones, and season with salt, pepper, and olive-oil, basting with oil as needed. For the sauce, cook in a saucepan, without browning, four chopped shallots, two tablespoonfuls of vinegar, a teaspoonful each of chopped chives and parsley, salt, pepper, and grated nutmeg to season, two tablespoonfuls of melted butter, and a tablespoonful of flour. Cook until smooth, stirring constantly, take from the fire, add two tablespoonfuls of butter and the juice of half a lemon, pour over the fish, and serve.

BROILED SALT MACKEREL—I

Soak the fish over night in cold water. In the morning drain, cover with boiling water, and let stand for an hour. Rinse in cold water, wipe dry, and soak for twenty minutes in oil and vinegar or lemon-juice. Broil and serve with melted butter, lemon-juice, and minced parsley.

BROILED SALT MACKEREL—II

Prepare the fish according to directions given in the preceding recipe. Take the fish from the hot water and cover for five minutes with cold water. Wipe dry, soak in olive-oil and lemon-juice for half an hour, drain, broil, and serve with Tartar Sauce.

BROILED SALT MACKEREL—III

Soak over night, drain, wipe, rub with butter, and broil. Pour over it a sauce made of a tablespoonful of butter, a teaspoonful of lemon-juice or vinegar, a tablespoonful of hot water, a pinch of pepper, and a chopped cucumber pickle. Bring to the boil and pour over the fish.

BROILED SALT MACKEREL WITH CREAM

Soak over night in cold water, drain, wipe dry, rub with oil, and broil. Serve on a hot platter and pour over half a cupful of hot cream. Sprinkle with minced parsley.

BROILED MACKEREL WITH TARRAGON SAUCE

Soak the cleaned fish for an hour in olive-oil, and broil. Serve with melted butter seasoned with pepper, salt, and tarragon vinegar.

BOILED MACKEREL—I

Boil in water or stock to cover, seasoning with onion, sweet herbs, pepper, salt, cloves, and vinegar. Strain the liquor, thicken it with butter and flour blended together, and add to it minced parsley and hard-boiled eggs, chopped fine. Pour over the fish and serve.

BOILED MACKEREL—II

Boil in salted water until done and drain. Serve with Egg Sauce.

BOILED MACKEREL-III

Boil a fresh mackerel in salted and acidulated water. Drain, and serve with a Cream Sauce.

BOILED MACKEREL—IV

Clean a fresh mackerel and split it down the back. Put it in a dripping-pan and pour over it two cupfuls of boiling water, two tablespoonfuls each of vinegar and lemon-juice, and a teaspoonful of salt. Add a sliced onion and boil for three quarters of an hour. Take up the fish, strain the liquid, add a teaspoonful of capers, bring to the boil, and pour over the fish.

BOILED MACKEREL WITH GOOSEBERRY SAUCE

Boil the mackerel in salted and acidulated water. Boil two cupfuls of gooseberries in water to cover until soft. Drain, rub through a sieve, and mix with an equal quantity of the fish broth, thickened with butter and flour. Add two tablespoonfuls of melted butter.

BOILED MACKEREL À LA PERSILLADE

Boil the fish according to directions given in the preceding recipe. Beat together with an egg-beater half a cupful of olive-oil, the juice of two lemons, two tablespoonfuls of minced parsley, one tablespoonful of mustard, and a little tarragon vinegar. Pour over the fish and serve.

FRESH BOILED MACKEREL

Clean the mackerel, sprinkle with vinegar, wrap in a floured cloth and baste closely. Boil for three-quarters of an hour in salted water, drain, and take off the cloth. Strain a cupful of the water in which the fish was boiled, and bring to the boil with a tablespoonful of walnut catsup, a teaspoonful of anchovy paste, and the juice of half a lemon. Thicken with butter and browned flour.

BOILED MACKEREL À LA BOLONAISE

Clean four fresh mackerel, remove the heads and tails and cut in halves crosswise. Put into a saucepan with sliced onions, a bunch of parsley, salt and pepper, a little white wine, and enough boiling water to cover. Cover with buttered paper and simmer for fifteen minutes. Take out the fish, strain the broth, and thicken a pint of it with two tablespoonfuls each of butter and flour cooked together. Add two tablespoonfuls of butter, a teaspoonful of chopped parsley, and a little tarragon vinegar. Pour over the fish and serve.

BOILED SALT MACKEREL—I

Soak the fish in cold water over night and in the morning rinse thoroughly. Wrap in a cloth and put to boil in cold water. Bring slowly to the boiling point and cook for thirty minutes. Unwrap carefully, take out the backbones, and pour over a little melted butter and cream, seasoning with pepper. Or, serve with a sauce made of a cupful of milk thickened with a teaspoonful of cornstarch, and season with butter, pepper, salt, and minced parsley. Take from the fire, add one egg well beaten, and pour over the fish. Garnish with lemon and parsley.

BOILED SALT MACKEREL—II

Soak over night in cold water and in the morning rinse thoroughly. Boil, drain, and pour over a cupful of hot cream in which a tablespoonful of butter has been melted.

BOILED SALT MACKEREL—III

Wash thoroughly, cover with cold water to which a chopped onion and a little black pepper have been added, and boil until the flesh loosens from the bone. Drain, and serve with melted butter and minced parsley.

BOILED SALT MACKEREL—IV

Soak the fish over night in cold water, and in the morning cover with hot water for half an hour. Drain and boil in acidulated water or in milk until done. Serve with a Cream Sauce to which chopped hard-boiled eggs have been added, or with Tomato Sauce.

BOILED SALT MACKEREL—V

Soak the fish over night in cold water, drain, and simmer for fifteen minutes in water to cover, adding a teaspoonful of vinegar, a bay-leaf, a slice of onion, and a sprig of parsley. When tender, place on a hot platter and pour over it a Cream Sauce.

BOILED SALT MACKEREL—VI

Prepare the fish according to directions given in the preceding recipe, and simmer for twenty minutes in acidulated water. Drain and pour over it a Cream Sauce.

BOILED SALT MACKEREL—VII

Prepare according to directions given in the preceding recipe. Pour over a sauce made of stewed and strained tomatoes, thickened with butter and browned flour, and seasoned with pepper, salt, sugar, and grated onion.

BAKED MACKEREL—I

Clean the mackerel, split down the back and cut each fish in four pieces. Put in a baking-dish in layers, seasoning each layer with bay-leaves, cloves, pepper-corns, and sliced onions or shallots. Cover with one cupful of stock, three tablespoonfuls each of white wine and vinegar, one tablespoonful each of anchovy sauce and mushroom catsup, and a teaspoonful of Worcestershire. Bake in a moderate oven. Take out the fish carefully, strain the sauce over them, and let cool.

BAKED MACKEREL—II

Split a fresh mackerel, take out the backbone, dry thoroughly, and sprinkle the inside with salt and pepper. Drain the liquor from a quart of oysters and put aside a dozen of the large ones. Chop the remaining oysters coarsely. Fry two chopped onions in butter, add the chopped oysters with three chopped hard-boiled eggs and a tablespoonful of minced parsley. Season with salt and pepper and cool. Mix with the yolks of two raw eggs and a tablespoonful of butter. Stuff the fish and sew up. Put into a baking-pan, cover with buttered paper, and bake for twenty minutes, basting as required. Add the oysters and bake for five minutes longer. Serve the fish on a warm platter with lemon-juice squeezed over it, and place the oysters around it on thin circles of toast spread with anchovy paste. Garnish with parsley and lemon and serve very hot.

BAKED MACKEREL—III

Gash two cleaned fresh mackerel, and put in a buttered baking-dish with two tablespoonfuls of white wine, three tablespoonfuls of mushroom liquor, a chopped shallot, and salt and pepper to season. Cover with buttered paper and bake for fifteen minutes in a moderate oven. Take up the fish and add to the gravy a little chopped onion, mushrooms, shallot, parsley, and garlic fried together, and enough white stock to make the required quantity of sauce. Thicken with butter and flour cooked together, take from the fire and add the yolks of three eggs well beaten. Add the juice of half a lemon and a tablespoonful of butter, and pour over the fish.

BAKED MACKEREL—IV

Soak a fresh cleaned fish for half an hour in olive-oil and lemon-juice. Lay in a baking-pan upon thin slices of fat salt pork, sprinkle with salt and pepper, and bake for twenty-five minutes. Serve with Tomato Sauce.

BAKED FILLET OF MACKEREL

Remove the head and backbone from a large fresh mackerel, and place the roe on top. Chop fine six shallots or three small onions, half a pound of mushrooms, and three or four sprigs of parsley. Add a teaspoonful of salt, and a pinch of pepper. Put half of this mixture in a buttered baking-pan, lay the fish upon it, and pour over six tablespoonfuls of white wine. Spread the remaining seasoning on top, sprinkle with crumbs, dot with butter, cover with buttered paper, and bake for thirty minutes. Pour over a little melted butter, garnish with lemon and parsley, and serve in the dish in which it is baked.

BAKED FILLETS OF MACKEREL

Butter an oval baking-dish and spread chopped oysters on the bottom. Arrange upon it the fillets of four fresh mackerel, skinned and seasoned with salt and pepper. Sprinkle with chopped onion, parsley, and mushrooms, cover with one cupful of beef stock thickened with browned flour, sprinkle with crumbs, dot with butter and bake for half an hour. Sprinkle with lemon-juice and serve in the same dish.

BAKED FILLETS OF MACKEREL

Clean and fillet the fish. Put in a buttered baking-dish, season with salt, pepper, and minced parsley, squeeze lemon juice over, pour on a little melted butter, cover with buttered paper, and bake. Drain, and serve with Maître d'Hôtel Sauce.

BAKED FILLETS OF MACKEREL WITH CREAM

Cook the prepared fillets in melted butter and drain. Thicken two cupfuls of white stock with butter and flour cooked together, add a wineglassful of white wine, take from the fire, and add the yolks of two eggs well beaten. Cover the fillets with the sauce, sprinkle with crumbs and grated cheese, dot with butter, and bake brown. Sprinkle with lemon-juice and serve in the same dish.

MACKEREL BAKED IN CREAM

Skin and bone a large fish. Cut it into four pieces, season it and fry in butter. Drain it and keep warm. Mix a cupful of white stock with two tablespoonfuls of Sherry and the yolk of an egg. Cook until it thickens, and pour over the fish, seasoning with minced parsley and onion. Sprinkle with crumbs and bake until brown.

BAKED FRESH MACKEREL WITH FINE HERBS

Split and clean the fish, remove the head and tail, put into a buttered dripping-pan, sprinkle with salt and pepper, dot with butter, and pour over two-thirds of a cupful of milk. Bake for twenty-five minutes in a hot oven.

BAKED SPANISH MACKEREL WITH FINE HERBS

Butter a baking-dish, sprinkle with chopped shallots, parsley and mushrooms, lay a cleaned mackerel upon it, sprinkle with more chopped shallots, parsley and mushrooms, season with salt, pepper, grated nutmeg, and dots of butter. Add two wineglassfuls of white wine and a cupful of white stock. Cover with a buttered paper and boil, basting frequently. Thicken the sauce with a tablespoonful of flour cooked in butter, pour over the fish, sprinkle with crumbs, dot with butter, and bake brown. Squeeze lemon-juice over the top and serve in the same dish.

BAKED MACKEREL WITH OYSTER STUFFING

Make a stuffing of a dozen chopped oysters, a cupful of bread crumbs, the chopped yolks of two hard-boiled eggs, a tablespoonful of butter, and onion-juice, minced parsley, salt, and pepper to season. Bind with the yolk of a raw egg and fill a cleaned fresh mackerel with the stuffing. Put the fish on a buttered baking-dish, dredge with flour and pour around it a cupful each of boiling water and stock. Bake until done, basting often with melted butter and the drippings. When done slide on to a hot platter and add to the remaining liquid sufficient warm water to make the required quantity of sauce. Thicken with browned flour, seasoned with tomato catsup and Worcestershire, pour over the fish, and serve.

BAKED SALT MACKEREL

Soak over night in cold water. In the morning drain, cover with boiling water, and let stand for five minutes. Drain and put into a baking-pan. Rub with butter, season with pepper, and pour over half a cupful of cream or milk. Bake until brown.

BAKED SALT MACKEREL WITH CREAM SAUCE

Soak a salt mackerel over night. In the morning drain, rinse, and put into a baking-pan with a pint of milk. Bake for twenty minutes, take up the fish, and thicken the milk with a tablespoonful each of butter and flour cooked together. Season with salt and pepper, pour over the fish, and serve.

FRIED MACKEREL

Fry three slices of salt pork, and add to the fat a teaspoonful of Worcestershire Sauce. Fry in this fresh mackerel, dredged with flour. Season with melted butter. The mackerel may be dipped in beaten egg before it is dipped in flour.

FRIED SALT MACKEREL

Soak all day in cold water, changing the water every two hours. In the morning drain, wipe dry, roll in flour and fry in melted butter. Serve with melted butter and parsley.

MACKEREL À LA HAVRAISE

Clean the fish, take out the backbone and put into a baking-pan. To each mackerel add four tablespoonfuls of butter, two tablespoonfuls of chopped shallots, and salt, pepper, and grated nutmeg to season. Add two cupfuls of white wine, cover and cook slowly for thirty minutes. Take up the fish, thicken the sauce with a tablespoonful each of butter and flour cooked together, and boil, for five minutes. Take from the fire, add the yolks of three eggs beaten with a cupful of cream, season with lemon-juice and minced parsley, pour over the fish, and serve.

SPANISH MACKEREL À LA CASTILLANE

Open a Spanish mackerel, take out most of the backbone, season with salt and pepper, and stuff with seasoned crumbs. Put into a buttered baking-dish with two sliced onions, a bunch of parsley, half a cupful of Sherry, and two cupfuls of white stock. Cover with a buttered paper and cook for half an hour in the oven, basting as needed. Take up the fish, strain the sauce and thicken with butter and flour cooked together. Season with lemon-juice and anchovy paste, add a tablespoonful of butter, pour over the fish, and serve.

SPANISH MACKEREL À L'ESPAGNOLE

Put a cleaned Spanish mackerel in a buttered pan with one cupful each of wine and white stock. Season with salt, pepper, and grated nutmeg, add a bunch of parsley, and a clove of garlic, cover with buttered paper, and simmer for forty minutes. Take up the fish, thicken the sauce with browned flour, season with lemon-juice and melted butter, pour over the fish, and serve.

SPANISH MACKEREL À LA NASSAU

Clean and gash a large mackerel. Put in a buttered dish with salt, pepper, half a dozen peeled and sliced tomatoes, two wineglassfuls of white wine and half a cupful of water. Add two sliced and parboiled onions, a tablespoonful of minced parsley, and half a cupful of mushrooms. Add two tablespoonfuls of butter, cover with buttered paper, and bake for half an hour, basting as needed. Take out the fish and add enough stock to make the required quantity of sauce. Thicken with a tablespoonful each of butter and flour cooked together, pour over the fish, cover with crumbs, dot with butter, and bake brown. Squeeze lemon-juice over and serve.

SPANISH MACKEREL À LA VÉNITIENNE

Put the cleaned mackerel into a baking-pan with salt, pepper, grated onion, grated nutmeg, minced parsley, a tablespoonful of butter and half a cupful each of white wine and white stock. Cover with a buttered paper and cook for forty minutes, basting as needed. Take out the fish and add two cupfuls of white stock to the sauce. Bring to the boil, take from the fire, thicken with the yolks of four eggs and add two tablespoonfuls of butter, two tablespoonfuls of minced parsley, and the juice of a lemon. Pour over the fish and serve.

MACKEREL À LA TYROL

Wash and dry two fresh fish, and put into a saucepan with salt, pepper, grated nutmeg, chopped parsley and onion, and two tablespoonfuls of cider. Cover and cook for half an hour, then add one cupful of white stock thickened with flour and butter, the yolk of an egg, and a tablespoonful of tarragon vinegar. Strain the sauce over the fish, cover with crumbs, dot with butter, and brown in the oven. Serve in the same dish.

FILLETS OF MACKEREL À LA HORLY

Clean and fillet the fish, remove the skin and bones and soak for an hour in oil and lemon-juice, seasoned with chopped onion, parsley, salt, pepper, and sweet herbs. Drain, dredge with flour, dip in beaten eggs, roll in crumbs, fry in deep fat, and serve with Tomato Sauce.

FILLETS OF MACKEREL À L'INDIENNE

Fillet two large fresh mackerel, cut in two and remove the skin. Simmer for fifteen minutes with two tablespoonfuls each of melted butter and curry powder mixed with two wineglassfuls of white wine. Season with salt and pepper. Prepare a Cream Sauce and add to it two tablespoonfuls of butter and the juice of a lemon. Pour over the fish and serve with a border of plain boiled rice.

MACKEREL À LA BRETONNE

Wash and split a large mackerel, wipe dry, dredge with flour, and fry brown in butter. Sprinkle with salt, pepper, and lemon-juice.

SALT MACKEREL À LA BRETONNE

Soak the fish for twelve hours and prepare according to directions given above. Serve with melted butter.

SCOTCH MACKEREL PIE

Make a forcemeat of the roe and some parsley, onion, butter, bread crumbs, thyme, sweet marjoram, and the yolk of an egg. Cut the fish into strips, spread with the filling, and roll. Arrange in a deep dish, pour in half a cupful of stock, and cover with a layer of mashed potatoes. Bake for three quarters of an hour and serve.

TOASTED SALT MACKEREL

Soak over night in cold water, and hang up for a day or two until perfectly dry. Put in a dry tin and set into the oven for ten minutes.

MACKEREL EN PAPILLOTES

Oil a sheet of paper a little larger than the fish. Lay a slice of cooked ham on each piece of paper, and spread with chopped onion, carrot, parsley, and green pepper fried together in butter. Lay a mackerel on the ham, spread with the fried vegetables, cover with another slice of ham, and fold the paper over, twisting the ends. Bake for fifteen minutes in a moderate oven. Serve in the paper.

POTTED MACKEREL

Pound together an ounce of black pepper and six blades of mace. Mix with two ounces of salt and half an ounce of grated nutmeg. Rub thoroughly into pieces of fresh mackerel, and fry in oil. Drain, and put the fish in a stone jar. Fill with vinegar, and put two tablespoonfuls of oil on top. Cover closely and let stand for two days before using.

FILLETS OF MACKEREL WITH RAVIGOTE SAUCE

Cook the fillets of four fish in a buttered dish with salt, pepper, grated nutmeg, and half a cupful of white wine. For the sauce chop fine four shallots and put into a saucepan with two tablespoonfuls of butter and four tablespoonfuls of tarragon vinegar. Reduce half by boiling and add a pint of white stock thickened with a tablespoonful each of butter and flour cooked together. Add two tablespoonfuls of butter, pour over the fish, and serve.

MACKEREL WITH WHITE WINE SAUCE

Cook three fresh mackerel in a cupful of white wine, with butter, salt, pepper, grated nutmeg, minced onion, and parsley to season. Take out the fish, and add two cupfuls of white stock to the gravy. Thicken with two tablespoonfuls each of butter and flour cooked together, take from the fire, and add the yolks of three eggs well beaten. Pour the sauce over the fish, sprinkle with crumbs, dot with butter, and bake brown. Sprinkle with lemon-juice and serve in a baking-dish.

SPANISH MACKEREL SALAD

Drain the oil from a can of pickled Spanish mackerel, and cut the fish in slices. Boil a bunch of red beets for half an hour in water to cover, then drain and bake for half an hour in a hot oven. Peel, slice thin, and cool thoroughly. Mix with the mackerel, add a small bunch of radishes sliced thin, and half a dozen sliced pickles. Surround with lettuce leaves and pour over a French dressing.

STUFFED MACKEREL WITH ANCHOVY SAUCE

Stuff the prepared fish with seasoned crumbs mixed with chopped shallots, parsley, and mushrooms. Sew up and bake, basting with oil. Serve with Cream Sauce, seasoned with anchovy essence.

GERMAN PICKLED MACKEREL

Skin, bone, and cut into pieces four pounds of fresh mackerel, and put it in layers into a stone jar, sprinkling each layer with pepper, salt, bay-leaves, and sweet herbs. Cover with vinegar, seal firmly, and bake for six hours in a moderate oven.

FIVE WAYS TO COOK MULLET

BROILED MULLET

Soak the cleaned fish for an hour in salted and acidulated water. Drain, wipe dry, split, rub with seasoned butter, and broil.

BROILED MULLETS WITH MELTED BUTTER

Rub prepared mullets with seasoned flour and broil, basting with olive-oil as required. Serve with melted butter and minced parsley.

MULLET À LA MAÎTRE D'HÔTEL

Clean four mullets and soak in olive-oil to cover for thirty minutes, with a bunch of parsley, a sliced onion, and salt and pepper to season. Drain, broil, and serve with Maître d'Hôtel Sauce.

BAKED MULLET

Clean the fish and soak for an hour in salted and acidulated water. Drain, wipe dry, stuff with seasoned crumbs, sew up, rub with butter and put into a baking-pan, adding enough hot water to keep from burning. Baste as required and serve with any preferred sauce.

FRIED MULLET

Cut the cleaned fish in convenient pieces for serving and sauté in pork fat, or dip in egg and seasoned crumbs and fry in deep fat.

FIFTEEN WAYS TO COOK PERCH

FRIED PERCH—I

Clean the fish, dip in flour, then in beaten egg, then in crumbs, and fry in plenty of fat. Drain and garnish with lemon and parsley.

FRIED PERCH—II

Dip the cleaned perch in flour and fry brown in salt pork fat.

FRIED PERCH—III

Prepare and clean the fish, season with salt and pepper, dip in egg and corn-meal, and fry in deep fat.

BROILED PERCH

Rub the prepared fish with butter, season with salt and pepper, and broil. Garnish with fried parsley and lemon.

BOILED PERCH

Boil the cleaned fish with parsley, a tablespoonful of butter, and salt and pepper to season. Drain, strain the liquid, thicken with butter and flour, season to taste, pour over the fish, and serve.

BOILED PERCH WITH OYSTER SAUCE

Prepare and clean the fish and simmer until done in salted and acidulated water. Drain and serve with Oyster Sauce.

PERCH À L'ALLEMANDE

Put two large cleaned perch into a saucepan with two chopped carrots, a sprig of parsley, a celery root, a sliced onion and a pinch of salt. Cover with white wine and simmer for twenty minutes. Drain and keep warm. Take out the onion, parsley and celery root, add half a cupful of chopped mushrooms, and cook for five minutes. Cook with a tablespoonful each of butter and flour thickened together, take from the fire, add a tablespoonful of butter and the juice of two lemons. Pour over the fish and serve.

STEWED PERCH À LA BATELIÈRE

Put four pounds of cleaned perch into a saucepan with salt and pepper to season, two sliced onions, a bunch of parsley, and Claret and water in equal parts to cover. Simmer for half an hour, drain, remove the parsley and thicken the sauce with two tablespoonfuls each of butter and flour cooked together. Add a tablespoonful of anchovy essence, the juice of half a lemon, and two tablespoonfuls of butter. Pour over the fish and serve.

PERCH À LA FRANÇAISE

Boil the perch in white wine, and when cooked, skin and arrange on a serving-dish. Pour over a Cream Sauce to which has been added chopped cooked carrots and mushrooms and a tablespoonful of minced parsley. Add also to the sauce a tablespoonful of butter and grated nutmeg and lemon-juice to season.

PERCH À LA MAÎTRE D'HÔTEL

Prepare according to directions given for Mullet à la Maître d'Hôtel.

PERCH À LA NORMANDY

Prepare and clean the fish and put into a stewpan with a chopped onion, a bunch of parsley, a pinch of salt, and enough white wine to cover. Simmer for fifteen minutes, take up the fish, and strain the liquid. Add one cupful of oyster liquor and boil the liquid until reduced half. Take from the fire, add one tablespoonful of butter and two of flour, cooked together, stir until smooth, return to the fire, and cook until thick, stirring constantly. Take from the fire and add slowly the yolks of three eggs well beaten. Bring to the boil, pour over the fish, and serve.

PERCH À LA SICILY

Cook three or four large perch for twenty minutes with a bunch of parsley in salted and acidulated water. Put into a saucepan one tablespoonful of malt vinegar, one tablespoonful of tarragon vinegar, a teaspoonful of minced parsley, a small chopped onion, a bay-leaf, and four pepper-corns. Boil for ten minutes, strain, and cool. Cook together four tablespoonfuls of butter and two of flour. When brown, add a pint of beef stock and cook until thick, stirring constantly. Take from the fire, add the strained vinegar, the beaten yolks of six eggs, and two tablespoonfuls of grated horseradish. Bring to the boil, pour over the fish, and serve.

PERCH À LA STANLEY

Clean four large perch, put into a saucepan with a tablespoonful of butter, a small bunch of parsley, a pint of Rhine wine, a pint of white stock, and salt and pepper to season. Simmer slowly until done, drain, and keep warm. Thicken the sauce with two tablespoonfuls each of butter and flour cooked together, take from the fire, add the yolks of four eggs beaten with the juice of a lemon and three tablespoonfuls of butter. Bring to the boil, add a dozen parboiled oysters, pour over the fish, and serve.

BAKED PERCH

Prepare and clean the fish, stuff with seasoned crumbs, and sew up. Bake with a little white wine and melted butter.

PERCH SALAD

Clean and boil the fish, drain, and cool. Serve very cold on lettuce with Mayonnaise.

TEN WAYS TO COOK PICKEREL

BROILED PICKEREL À LA MAÎTRE D'HÔTEL

Prepare and clean the fish and cut into pieces suitable for serving. Dip in seasoned oil, broil, and serve with Maître d'Hôtel Sauce.

FRIED PICKEREL.—I

Prepare and clean the fish and cut into pieces suitable for serving. Dip in beaten egg and cracker dust and fry in deep fat.

FRIED PICKEREL—II

Prepare and clean the fish and cut into steaks. Dip in corn-meal and fry in hot fat. Add one cupful of cream to the fat remaining in the pan and thicken with one tablespoonful each of butter and flour cooked together. Season with salt and pepper, add a tablespoonful of minced parsley, pour over the fish and serve.

FRIED PICKEREL WITH TOMATO SAUCE

Prepare and clean the fish and cut into pieces of a suitable size for serving. Dip in milk, roll in flour, and fry brown in plenty of hot lard. Drain and serve with Tomato Sauce.

FRIED PICKEREL À LA CRÈME

Clean the fish and cut into pieces suitable for serving. Roll in flour, and fry diced salt pork crisp. Strain the fat, fry the fish in it, take up and keep warm. Add a tablespoonful of butter and a tablespoonful of flour to the fat remaining in the pan. When cooked, add enough cream to make the required quantity of sauce, and a pinch of soda. Cook until thick, stirring constantly, add the salt pork fat and pour over the fish.

BAKED PICKEREL—I

Lay the cleaned fish in a baking-pan, spread with butter, season with salt and pepper, and sprinkle with flour. Bake as usual, basting with a cupful of hot water to which has been added a tablespoonful of butter and the juice of half a lemon. Serve with any preferred sauce.

BAKED PICKEREL—II

Clean the fish, remove the backbone, and soak for an hour in a marinade of oil and lemon-juice. Cover the bottom of a baking-dish with thin slices of salt pork, lay the fish upon the pork, rub the fish with butter, cover and bake for forty minutes. Serve with Hollandaise or Tartar Sauce.

BAKED PICKEREL WITH OYSTER SAUCE

Lay the fish in a buttered baking-pan, spread with butter, season with salt and pepper and dredge with flour. Bake in a hot oven, basting with a cupful of hot water to which a tablespoonful of butter and the juice of a lemon have been added. Serve with Oyster Sauce.

BAKED PICKEREL WITH EGG SAUCE

Put the prepared fish in a buttered baking-pan, and bake slowly, basting with melted butter and hot water. Serve with Egg Sauce.

STUFFED PICKEREL

Prepare, clean, and split the fish. Remove the backbone and stuff with crumbs, seasoned with salt, pepper, sweet herbs, and melted butter. Mix with a beaten egg, stuff the fish, sew up, and bake, basting with melted butter as required.

PICKEREL À LA BABETTE

Butter a kettle and cover the bottom with sliced celery and onion. Lay the prepared and cleaned fish upon it, add a bunch of parsley and a tablespoonful of butter. Season with salt and white pepper, add a dozen peppercorns, a sliced lemon, a dozen pounded almonds, and cold water to cover. Simmer slowly until done. Take up the fish, beat the yolks of three eggs with a tablespoonful of cold water, take out the parsley, thicken the sauce, pour over the fish, sprinkle with parsley and serve.

TWENTY WAYS TO COOK PIKE.

FRIED PIKE—I

Prepare and clean the fish, and cut into pieces suitable for serving. Fry brown in butter, add to the butter a teaspoonful of anchovy essence, a bit of ginger root, a grating of nutmeg, salt and pepper to season, and enough Claret to cover. Simmer until tender, add the juice of an orange and a teaspoonful of butter. Serve with sauce poured over the fish.

FRIED PIKE—II

Clean the fish and cut it into pieces suitable for serving. Dip in egg and crumbs and fry in oil.

FRIED PIKE À LA HOLLANDAISE

Clean the fish and cut it into steaks. Soak for two hours in a marinade of oil and lemon-juice, seasoning with pepper, salt, minced parsley, and grated nutmeg. Drain, dip in flour, fry in lard, and serve with Hollandaise Sauce.

BOILED PIKE WITH MELTED BUTTER

Boil the fish with a bunch of parsley in salted and acidulated water to cover. Serve with melted butter, seasoned with salt, pepper, grated nutmeg, and lemon-juice.

BOILED PIKE WITH CAPER SAUCE

Prepare and clean a fish, put into a fish-kettle, and simmer for forty minutes in court-bouillon to cover. Serve with Caper Sauce.

BOILED PIKE WITH HORSERADISH SAUCE

Boil a large fish in salted and acidulated water with a bunch of parsley. Cook together two tablespoonfuls each of butter and flour, add three cupfuls of cream, and cook until thick, stirring constantly. Season with salt and pepper, add two tablespoonfuls of butter and three tablespoonfuls of freshly grated horseradish. Pour over the fish, and serve.

BOILED PIKE WITH EGG SAUCE

Put the cleaned fish into a fish-kettle and cover with cold water. Add half a cupful of vinegar, a teaspoonful each of cloves and pepper-corns, a bay-leaf, half a lemon sliced, and a tablespoonful of salt. Boil until the fins pull off easily, take up and skin the fish carefully. Pour over an Egg Sauce made with a portion of the liquid in which the fish was cooked.

BOILED PIKE À LA DUBOIS

Prepare and clean the fish and cook it in equal parts of white wine and water, adding minced carrots and celery, sweet herbs and parsley, half a dozen pepper-corns, and salt to season. Cook together one tablespoonful each of butter and flour, add two cupfuls of the liquid and cook until thick, stirring constantly. Add a teaspoonful of Worcestershire Sauce and two tablespoonfuls of butter. Pour over the fish and serve.

BAKED PIKE—I

Clean a four-pound pike and put into a buttered baking-pan with enough hot water to keep from burning. Score the upper side deeply, cover with chopped salt pork, sprinkle with salt and pepper and dredge with flour. Bake for half an hour, basting as required. Serve with any preferred sauce.

BAKED PIKE—II

Put the cleaned fish into a buttered baking-dish with two onions sliced, two bay-leaves, pepper and salt to season, and one cupful of sour cream. Rub the fish with butter, sprinkle thickly with bread crumbs and grated Parmesan cheese, and bake until brown. Pour the liquid remaining in the pan around the fish and serve.

BAKED PIKE À LA FRANÇAISE

Marinate the prepared fish for two hours in oil and lemon-juice, seasoning with salt, pepper, chopped onion, and minced parsley. Put into the oven in the marinade, adding one cupful of stock and a wineglassful of white wine. Bake slowly, basting as required. Take up the fish, strain the sauce, thicken with a tablespoonful each of butter and flour cooked together, season with anchovy essence, add two tablespoonfuls of butter and two tablespoonfuls of capers. Pour over the fish and serve.

STUFFED AND BAKED PIKE

Clean and draw the fish, stuff with seasoned crumbs, sew up and put into a buttered baking-dish in the form of a circle. Score the fish deeply, sprinkle with pepper and salt, minced parsley, chopped onion, and chopped mushrooms. Add a cupful of Sherry and a cupful of beef stock, cover, and bake, basting frequently with the liquid. Take up the fish carefully, and add to the liquid enough stock to make the required quantity of sauce. Thicken with two tablespoonfuls of flour cooked brown in butter, add two tablespoonfuls of butter, lemon-juice, red pepper, and anchovy essence to season. Pour over the fish, and serve.

PIKE BAKED IN SOUR CREAM.

Clean a four-pound pike, cut into steaks, and free from skin and bone. Put into a buttered baking-dish with two small onions chopped and two bay-leaves.

Season with salt and cayenne, add one cupful of sour cream and bake. Put on a serving-dish, cover with crumbs and dots of butter and brown in the oven. Add enough stock to the liquid to make the required quantity of sauce, thicken with butter and flour, season, add a dash of lemon-juice, pour around the fish, sprinkle with minced parsley and serve.

PIKE SALAD

Flake cold cooked pike with a silver fork, mix with Mayonnaise and chopped capers, and serve very cold on lettuce leaves.

ROASTED PIKE

Prepare a large fish, stuff with seasoned crumbs, and sew up. Spread with butter, sprinkle with chopped onion, minced parsley, minced pickle, and pounded anchovies. Sprinkle with salt and pepper, put in a buttered baking-dish, and bake slowly for an hour, basting with melted butter as required. Add half a cupful of white wine and one cupful of white stock to the drippings. Thicken with a tablespoonful each of butter and flour cooked together, take from the fire, add two tablespoonfuls of butter and the yolks of three eggs beaten with the juice of a lemon. Bring to the boil, pour over the fish and serve.

PIKE À L'ALLEMANDE

Prepare according to directions given for Carp à l'Allemande.

CRIMPED PIKE À LA HOLLANDAISE

Prepare and clean the fish and cut into steaks. Soak in ice-water for two hours. Boil until tender in salted and acidulated water to cover and serve with Hollandaise Sauce.

PIKE À LA FRANÇAISE

Cut a cleaned and prepared pike into thick steaks, and marinate for two hours in oil and lemon-juice, seasoned with salt, pepper, minced onion and parsley, and a pinch of sweet herbs. Drain, dip in crumbs, and broil. Serve with any preferred sauce.

PIKE À LA NORMANDY

Clean and draw a large fish and tie in a circle. Put into a fish-kettle with sliced onion, a bay-leaf, a pinch of thyme, a sprig of parsley, and salt and pepper to season. Add two cupfuls each of white wine and white stock and enough water to cover. Add a tablespoonful of butter, cover and simmer for forty minutes. Take up the fish, strain the sauce and thicken with two tablespoonfuls each of butter and flour cooked together. Take from the fire, add the yolks of four eggs beaten with the juice of a lemon, and two tablespoonfuls of butter. Strain over the fish and serve.

PICKLED PIKE

Draw and clean a pike, put into a fish-kettle, cover with Claret, add three bay-leaves, and simmer until tender. Let cool in the liquor. Serve with French dressing, Mayonnaise, or Tartar Sauce.

TEN WAYS TO COOK POMPANO

BROILED POMPANO—I

Clean and split the fish, sprinkle with salt and pepper, rub with butter, and broil. Squeeze lemon-juice over it and serve.

BROILED POMPANO—II

Split the fish, remove the backbone, season with salt and pepper, and put on a tin sheet. Rub with butter and broil under the gas flame.

BROILED POMPANO—III

Clean and split the fish, rub with oil, sprinkle with salt and pepper, roll in crumbs, and broil.

BROILED POMPANO À LA MAÎTRE D'HÔTEL

Clean and split the fish, rub with salt, pepper, and olive-oil, and broil. Serve with Maître d'Hôtel Sauce.

FRIED POMPANO—I

Cut the cleaned fish into slices, dredge with flour, and fry brown in butter. Serve with any preferred sauce.

FRIED POMPANO—II

Cut the cleaned fish into strips, season with salt, pepper, and nutmeg, dip in egg and crumbs and fry in fat to cover.

FILLETS OF POMPANO

Cut a prepared and cleaned pompano into strips. Marinate for an hour in oil and vinegar, seasoned with salt and pepper. Drain, dip in crumbs, then in egg, then in crumbs, and put in a buttered paper and bake until done. Serve with Tomato Sauce.

FILLETS OF POMPANO À LA DUCHESSE

Cut a cleaned pompano into strips, sprinkle with salt, pepper, and onion-juice, and put into a small baking-pan. Steam until done, take up carefully and spread each one with seasoned mashed potato mixed with well-beaten egg. Bake in the oven until puffed and brown and serve immediately.

FILLETS OF POMPANO AU GRATIN

Split the fish in two lengthwise, and remove the bone and skin. Cut into strips, season with salt, pepper, and butter, roll up, and tie or fasten with toothpicks or skewers. Simmer slowly until done in equal parts of white wine and water, adding a little Maître d'Hôtel Sauce.

POMPANO À LA CARDINAL

Butter a baking-dish and lay upon it a large cleaned and split pompano. Open a can of sweet Spanish peppers, drain, and cover the fish with them. Sprinkle with chopped onion, minced parsley, chopped mushrooms, crumbs, and dots of butter. Add one cupful of stock, and a wineglassful of Port wine. Bake for twenty minutes, basting as required, take up carefully, and serve with fried sweet potatoes.

THIRTEEN WAYS TO COOK RED SNAPPER

FRIED RED SNAPPER

Clean the fish, skin, and remove the backbone. Slice lengthwise in long thin strips, roll up and fasten with a toothpick or skewer. Dip in egg, then in cracker dust, and fry in deep fat. Serve with Tartar Sauce.

BOILED RED SNAPPER—I

Clean and draw the fish and boil slowly in salted and acidulated water to cover. Drain and serve with any preferred sauce.

BOILED RED SNAPPER—II

Clean a red snapper, sew it up in mosquito netting, and boil it in salted and acidulated water. Drain carefully, unwrap, and serve with Tomato Sauce.

BAKED RED SNAPPER—I

Prepare and clean the fish, stuff with seasoned crumbs and chopped oysters. Put on a buttered tin sheet and lay into a baking-pan. Sprinkle with salt, pepper, and flour and bake for an hour, basting with melted butter and hot water as required. Serve with any preferred sauce.

BAKED RED SNAPPER—II

Clean and season the fish, rub with vinegar, and put into a baking-pan. Dot with butter, sprinkle with parsley, and bake, basting with melted butter and hot water as required. Serve with Tomato Sauce.

BAKED RED SNAPPER—III

Clean the fish, leaving the head on, and stuff with seasoned crumbs, cover with sliced tomatoes and sliced lemon, and bake, basting occasionally with melted butter and hot water.

BAKED RED SNAPPER WITH TOMATO SAUCE

Season four pounds of prepared and cleaned red snapper with salt and pepper. Cover with thin slices of bacon, dredge with flour, and put into a buttered baking-pan with two cupfuls of boiling water. Bake slowly. While it is baking fry brown two slices of chopped bacon, add a chopped onion, a pepper pod, a can of tomatoes, and salt and black pepper to taste. Cook until it thickens, pour over the fish, and finish baking. Take up carefully.

BAKED RED SNAPPER À LA CRÉOLE

Clean, split, and bone a large red snapper, lay it together again, sprinkle with salt and pepper, and put into a buttered baking-pan. Fry in butter a chopped onion, half a dozen sliced mushrooms, two fresh tomatoes, and one green pepper chopped. Add a cupful of stock, spread over the fish and bake for twenty minutes, basting with melted butter and hot water as required. Take up carefully, sprinkle with minced parsley, and serve.

STUFFED RED SNAPPER

Make a stuffing of one cupful of chopped oysters, half a cupful of cracker crumbs, one egg well beaten, a teaspoonful of chopped onion, a tablespoonful of butter, a tablespoonful of minced parsley, and salt, pepper, and paprika to season. Add cream or oyster liquor to make soft, fill the fish, and sew up. Put a layer of salt pork, sliced tomato, and sliced onion into a baking-pan, lay the fish upon it, cover with chopped salt pork, sprinkle with salt, pepper, and flour, add two cupfuls of stock and bake for an hour, basting as required. Take up the fish carefully, rub the tomatoes and liquid through a purée sieve, thicken with butter and flour cooked together, pour around the fish, and serve.

STUFFED RED SNAPPER À LA CRÉOLE

Cook together a can of tomatoes, six chopped onions, a cupful of dry bread crumbs, a tablespoonful of Worcestershire Sauce, three tablespoonfuls of butter, and salt, red and black pepper to season. Stuff the prepared and cleaned red snapper with the mixture, sew up, spread with the remaining dressing, dot with butter, and bake for an hour. Take up carefully.

STEAMED RED SNAPPER

Lay a cleaned red snapper in a steamer on a bed of sliced tomatoes and chopped onion. Steam slowly for an hour or more, turning once. Serve with Oyster or Tartar Sauce.

RED SNAPPER À LA BABETTE

Clean the fish and rub with salt and pepper inside and out. Boil in salted water to which has been added a small bunch of parsley, a celery root, two sliced onions, a chopped carrot, and a blade of mace. When done, take up, sprinkle with crumbs, dot with butter, and brown in the oven. Strain the liquid, thicken with butter and flour cooked together, pour around the fish, and serve.

RED SNAPPER À LA BEAUFORT

Put the prepared and cleaned fish into a fish-kettle with a pint each of white wine, white stock, and water, adding salt and sweet herbs to season, and half a cupful of mixed vegetables cut fine. Simmer for an hour, drain, skin, and put on a serving-dish. Strain the liquid, thicken with two tablespoonfuls each of butter and flour cooked together, add a teaspoonful of beef extract, salt and cayenne pepper to season, take from the fire, add the yolks of four eggs, beaten with the juice of a lemon and two tablespoonfuls of butter, pour over the fish, and serve.

ONE HUNDRED AND THIRTY WAYS TO COOK SALMON

BROILED SALMON—I

Marinate slices of salmon in olive-oil with salt and pepper, minced parsley, bay-leaves, and mixed herbs to season. Soak in the marinade for an hour or more and broil, basting with the marinade. Serve with Caper Sauce.

BROILED SALMON—II

Take a young fish weighing from four to six pounds, clean, split, remove the backbone and broil. Sprinkle with lemon-juice and red pepper.

BROILED SALMON—III

Take three pounds of the tail part of the salmon, let it stand for six hours in a marinade of oil and lemon-juice, with minced parsley, two bay-leaves and a sprig of thyme. Drain and broil. Serve with Maître d'Hôtel Sauce to which a teaspoonful of chopped chives has been added.

SALMON BROILED IN PAPER

Season salmon steaks with pepper and salt, wrap in buttered paper, twisting the ends, broil and serve with Anchovy or Caper Sauce.

BROILED SALMON STEAKS—I

Season with pepper and salt, broil carefully on a buttered gridiron, pour over melted butter, garnish with parsley, and serve.

BROILED SALMON STEAKS—II

Sprinkle with pepper and salt, dredge with flour, and broil, basting with melted butter as required. Spread with melted butter, or with Maître d'Hôtel Sauce.

BROILED SALMON STEAKS—III

Marinate the steaks for an hour in oil and lemon-juice, seasoning with salt and pepper. Broil carefully and serve with any preferred sauce.

BROILED SALMON À LA RAVIGOTE

Marinate salmon steaks in seasoned oil and lemon-juice, and broil quickly. Serve with Ravigote Sauce.

SALMON CUTLETS IN PAPILLOTES

Butter large sheets of white paper, sprinkle with crumbs, and fold tightly over small cutlets of salmon. Broil carefully over a slow fire and serve in the papers.

SALMON CUTLETS WITH CAPER SAUCE

Marinate for two hours slices of salmon in oil with minced parsley and onion. Dip large pieces of paper in oil and wrap carefully around each slice, fastening firmly. Broil carefully and serve with a Cream Sauce to which capers have been added.

SALMON STEAKS WITH PARSLEY SAUCE

Season salmon steaks, dip in melted butter, then in corn-meal, and broil. Cook together two tablespoonfuls each of butter and flour, add two cupfuls of cold water, and cook until thick, stirring constantly. Take from the fire, season with salt and pepper, add the juice of half a lemon and a tablespoonful of minced parsley, and pour over the fish.

BOILED SALMON—I

Wash and wipe a small salmon, wrap in a cloth, tie securely and put into the fish-kettle. Cover with cold water, add a handful of salt, and boil slowly until done. Cook together one tablespoonful each of butter and of flour, add two cupfuls of boiling cream and a tablespoonful of the water in which the fish is cooked. Cook until thick, stirring constantly, season with salt and minced parsley, pour over the fish, and serve.

BOILED SALMON—II

Chop together a carrot, an onion and a stalk of celery. Fry in butter, add half a cupful of vinegar, four cloves, four pepper-corns, a bay-leaf, a sprig of parsley, and six cupfuls of boiling water. Boil for an hour, strain, cool, and boil the salmon in it. Serve with any preferred sauce.

BOILED SALMON WITH EGG SAUCE

Tie a large chunk of salmon in mosquito netting and simmer until done in salted and acidulated water. Drain, skin, and, if possible, remove the bone. Serve with Drawn-Butter Sauce to which chopped hard-boiled eggs have been added.

BOILED SALMON WITH GREEN SAUCE

Boil a small salmon in salted and acidulated water. Take up carefully and reduce the liquid by rapid boiling to two cupfuls. Cook together two tablespoonfuls each of butter and flour, add the reduced liquid, and cook until thick, stirring constantly. Take from the fire, add two tablespoonfuls of chopped capers, one tablespoonful of chopped parsley, the juice of a lemon, and one tablespoonful of butter. Pour over the fish and serve.

BOILED SALMON STEAKS—I

Wrap each steak separately in mosquito netting. Put into boiling water to which has been added a slice of onion, a bay-leaf, a blade of mace, four tablespoonfuls of tarragon vinegar, and a teaspoonful of salt. Simmer for twenty minutes, remove carefully, drain, and serve with any preferred sauce.

BOILED SALMON STEAKS—II

Boil the steaks slowly in salted and acidulated water to cover or in court-bouillon seasoned with wine. Serve with Hollandaise Sauce.

BOILED SALMON STEAKS—III

Cook the steaks in water to cover and add a celery root, a small bunch of parsley, salt and pepper to season, and a tablespoonful of vinegar. Strain the liquid, thicken with a tablespoonful each of butter and flour cooked together, pour over the fish, and serve.

BOILED SALMON À LA PIQUANT

Boil slices of salmon in court-bouillon seasoned with wine. Drain, garnish with parsley, and serve with Piquant Sauce.

BOILED SALMON À LA WALDORF

Boil a large piece of salmon in salted and acidulated water, seasoned with herbs and spice. Drain and keep warm. Add two cupfuls of the liquid in which the fish was cooked, one wineglassful of white wine, and two anchovies rubbed to a paste. Boil for fifteen minutes, then add in small bits a tablespoonful of butter. Serve the sauce separately.

SALMON WITH OYSTER SAUCE

Boil two pounds of fresh salmon in salted and acidulated water to cover, with a chopped onion, two cloves, eight pepper-corns, and a small bunch of parsley. Drain, and serve with Oyster Sauce.

SALMON CUTLETS WITH OYSTER SAUCE

Boil large slices of salmon in salted water until done. Fry a small onion, chopped, in oil, add four dozen oysters, cut small, two tablespoonfuls of flour, the liquor drained from the oysters, two teaspoonfuls of sugar, and pepper, salt, and anchovy essence to season. When thick, take from the fire, add the beaten yolks of four eggs, and reheat but do not boil. Pour the sauce into a platter, and cool. Lay the slices of salmon on the sauce, brush with egg, sprinkle with crumbs and brown in the oven.

SALMON À LA SUPRÊME

Boil a salmon in court-bouillon with wine, drain, cool, skin, and serve with Tartar Sauce.

MAYONNAISE OF SALMON

Cook fresh salmon in a court-bouillon, drain, cool, skin, and serve with Mayonnaise.

SALMON PUDDING

Flake the fish, add half the quantity of bread crumbs, a tablespoonful of melted butter, a teaspoonful of onion juice, and pepper and salt to season. Beat two eggs light with two tablespoonfuls of cream, mix with the fish, put into a buttered mould and boil for an hour and a half. Serve with a Cream Sauce seasoned with lemon-juice and anchovy paste.

BAKED SALMON—I

Put four salmon steaks into a buttered saucepan with two cupfuls each of white wine and white stock. Season with salt, pepper, grated nutmeg, minced parsley, and a pinch of allspice. Add a heaping teaspoonful of butter and flour cooked together. Take from the fire, add the yolks of four eggs well beaten and a little minced parsley. Arrange a mound of seasoned mashed potatoes in a deep platter. Take the skin from the steaks and arrange them around it. Pour the sauce over, sprinkle with crumbs, dot with butter, and brown in the oven.

BAKED SALMON—II

Wash and wipe a small fish. Rub with pepper and salt and sprinkle with paprika and powdered mace. Bake carefully, basting with melted butter and its own dripping. Take up the fish carefully and add to the gravy enough stock or water to make the required quantity of sauce. Thicken with butter and flour cooked together, season with tomato catsup and lemon-juice. Pour around the fish and serve.

BAKED SALMON—III

Rub a small cleaned salmon with olive-oil, sprinkle with salt and pepper, put into a buttered baking-pan, and add one cupful of boiling water and two tablespoonfuls of butter. Baste every ten minutes until done. Take up the fish and keep it warm. Thicken the gravy with a teaspoonful or more of cornstarch mixed with a little cold water. Season with grated onion, lemon-juice, and tomato catsup.

BAKED SALMON WITH CREAM SAUCE

Wrap a large middle cut of salmon in buttered paper and fasten firmly. Bake in a buttered baking-pan, basting with butter melted in hot water. Take from the oven at the end of an hour, remove the paper carefully, and keep warm. Bring to the boil one cupful of cream and add one tablespoonful of corn-starch rubbed smooth with a little cold cream. Add one tablespoonful each of butter and minced parsley, and pepper and salt to season. Pour the sauce over the fish or serve separately.

SALMON BAKED IN PAPER

Season a large piece of salmon with salt, pepper, and lemon-juice, wrap in a large piece of buttered paper and pin firmly. Put into a buttered baking-pan, cover and bake for an hour, basting frequently with hot water and melted butter. Take off the paper and serve with any preferred sauce.

BAKED SALMON STEAKS

Put the steaks in a buttered baking-dish. Lay bits of butter upon them, seasoning with salt, pepper, minced parsley, and grated onion. Bake carefully, basting as required, and serve with Caper or Tomato Sauce.

BAKED SALMON CUTLETS

Put salmon steaks into a buttered baking-pan with half a cupful of hot water and half a cupful of white wine. Sprinkle with salt, paprika, and grated nutmeg. Cover with raw oysters and crumbs fried in butter. Bake for twenty minutes. Take up the fish carefully. Cook together one tablespoonful each of butter and flour, add the liquor from the pan and a teaspoonful of anchovy paste. Cook until thick, stirring constantly, pour around the fish, and serve.

SALMON À LA WINDSOR

Season salmon steaks with salt and pepper, dip in egg and crumbs, put into a buttered baking-pan, and bake quickly. Serve with any preferred sauce.

STUFFED SALMON

Clean, bone, and parboil a small salmon. Rub the inside with salt, pepper, and grated nutmeg. Stuff with chopped oysters, minced parsley, and seasoned crumbs. Fold together, put into a buttered baking-dish, and bake for half an hour, basting with its own dripping.

SALMON STEAKS À LA FLAMANDE

Sprinkle a buttered dripping-pan with chopped onion, and season with pepper and salt. Lay salmon steaks on top, brush with the yolk of a beaten egg, cover with a layer of chopped onion and parsley, season with salt, red pepper, lemon-juice, and dots of butter, and bake for half an hour.

SALMON EN PAPILLOTES

Use six small salmon steaks. Season with salt and pepper. Butter sheets of white paper a little larger than the steaks and lay on each one a thin slice of lean boiled ham. Cook together in butter a chopped onion, a handful of chopped mushrooms, a minced bean of garlic, and a tablespoonful of minced parsley.

Spread a thin layer on the ham, lay a slice of salmon upon it, spread with the cooked vegetables, cover with another slice of ham, put another piece of oiled paper over, and fold carefully at the edges. Bake in a moderate oven for fifteen or twenty minutes, and serve in the papers.

FILLETS OF SALMON EN PAPILLOTES

Cut salmon steaks into fillets, dip into melted butter and lemon-juice, fold in buttered paper, and bake for half an hour in a slow oven. Serve in the papers and pass Hollandaise Sauce.

SALMON CUTLETS EN PAPILLOTES

Cut slices of salmon into cutlets. Beat together three tablespoonfuls of olive-oil, the yolk of an egg, a teaspoonful of minced onion and a tablespoonful of chopped parsley. Sprinkle the fish with salt and pepper, spread the mixture over, fold each piece in buttered paper, fastening securely, and bake for half an hour. Serve in the papers.

FRIED SALMON—I

Cut slices of salmon into small pieces and put into a saucepan with pepper, salt, minced parsley, and lemon-juice to season. Add sufficient butter and fry carefully. Serve with Ravigote or any preferred sauce.

FRIED SALMON—II

Wrap slices of salmon in oiled paper, fastening firmly, and fry in deep fat. Drain carefully and serve in the paper.

FRIED SALMON—III

Sprinkle salmon steaks with salt and flour, brush with the beaten yolk of an egg and fry in hot olive-oil. Drain, garnish with fried parsley, and serve.

FRIED SALMON STEAKS

Dredge the steaks with seasoned flour or dip into egg and seasoned crumbs and fry.

FRIED SALMON CUTLETS—I

Steam salmon steaks, cool, cut into fillets, dip in egg and crumbs, fry in deep fat, and serve with Tartar or Hollandaise Sauce.

FRIED SALMON CUTLETS—II

Prepare very thick Cream Sauce and mix with it cold cooked salmon cut fine. Season with red pepper, salt, and lemon-juice and let cool. Shape into cutlets, dip into beaten egg, then in crumbs, and fry in deep fat.

FRIED SALMON CUTLETS—III

Rub cold boiled salmon smooth with one-third the quantity of mashed potatoes. Season with salt, pepper, and pounded mace. Shape into cutlets, dip in egg and crumbs and fry in deep fat. Serve with any preferred sauce.

SALMON CUTLETS À L'ANGLAISE

Cut slices of salmon in the shape of cutlets, season with salt and pepper and fry in butter. Drain and serve with Ravigote Sauce.

SALMON À LA LYONS

Fry slices of salmon in butter with pepper and salt to season. Serve with a Hollandaise Sauce to which cooked oysters, cooked shrimps, and minced parsley have been added.

SALMON CUTLETS WITH MILANAISE SAUCE

Cut slices of salmon into small pieces, dip into white wine and wrap in buttered paper, fastening securely. Fry carefully in butter, remove the papers, garnish with parsley, and serve with Milanaise Sauce.

FILLETS OF SALMON À L'ORLY

Cut fresh salmon into small pieces, remove the skin, and marinate for an hour in lemon-juice seasoned with salt and pepper. Drain, dip in egg and crumbs, fry in deep fat, and serve with Tomato Sauce.

SALMON À L'ALLEMANDE

Put a large middle cut of salmon into a saucepan, with a sliced carrot, a large onion, a bunch of parsley, salt and pepper to season, half a cupful of butter, two cupfuls of Claret, and enough stock to cover. Cover with buttered paper and cook slowly for an hour. Take up the fish carefully and keep warm. Strain the liquid, skim the fat, and thicken with butter and flour cooked together until brown. Add a tablespoonful of butter, seasoned with lemon-juice and anchovy essence, pour over the fish, and serve.

SALMON À L'ADMIRAL

Fry in butter two chopped onions, two parsley roots, a bunch of chopped parsley with a sprig of thyme, a broken bay-leaf, a clove, and three small chopped carrots. Add one cupful of white wine, put a small cleaned salmon into a buttered baking-dish, spread the vegetables over, cover, and cook until tender, basting with the drippings or with hot water if needed. Take out the fish, strain the liquid, add to it a cupful of cream and thicken with a tablespoonful each of butter and flour cooked together. Pour it around the fish and garnish with lemon and parsley.

SALMON À LA BORDEAUX

Clean a small salmon, stuff with seasoned crumbs and oysters, and put into a fish-kettle with two tablespoonfuls of butter, two onions sliced, a bunch of parsley, and salt, pepper, and grated nutmeg to season. Add two cupfuls each of stock, water, and white wine. Cover the fish with buttered paper and simmer for an hour. Drain the fish and keep warm. Prepare a sauce according to directions given in the recipe for Salmon à la Genoise, using the liquid strained from the fish.

SALMON À LA CANDACE

Put a large cut of salmon on the drainer in a fish-kettle and cover it with a small slice of raw ham. Add two cupfuls of Rhine wine, a quart of stock, and a bunch of parsley. Cover with buttered paper, simmer for an hour, drain, and remove the skin. Strain the liquid, thicken with flour cooked brown in butter, add a tablespoonful of butter, cayenne, and lemon-juice to season. Bring to the boil, pour over the fish, and serve.

SALMON À LA CHAMBORD

Put a large middle cut of salmon into a saucepan with sliced carrots and onions, a bunch of parsley, two tablespoonfuls of butter and two cupfuls each of white wine and white stock. Season with salt and pepper-corns, cover, and simmer slowly for an hour. Take up the fish carefully and keep warm. Strain the liquid and thicken with flour cooked brown in butter. Add half a cupful of stewed and strained tomatoes, the juice of a lemon, two tablespoonfuls of butter, and a teaspoonful of anchovy essence. Pour over the fish and serve.

SALMON À L'ESPAGNOLE

Cut fresh salmon in small pieces suitable for serving, and fry in butter. Drain and keep warm. Add two tablespoonfuls of flour to the butter, in which the fish is cooked, and brown. Add two cupfuls of stock and cook until thick, stirring constantly. Take from the fire, add a tablespoonful of butter, a teaspoonful of minced parsley, and the juice of a lemon. Pour over the fish and serve.

SALMON À LA GENOISE

Boil a small fresh salmon in salted and acidulated water to cover, drain, and skin. Arrange on a serving-dish and keep warm. Chop fine a small slice of ham, a slice of carrot, a small stalk of celery, an onion, a parsley root, and three or four shallots. Add a sprig of thyme, a bay-leaf, a blade of mace, and two cloves. Fry in butter, add two tablespoonfuls of flour and cook until brown. Add two cupfuls of Claret and cook until thick, stirring constantly. Add half a cupful of beef stock, bring to the boil, and strain through a sieve. Reheat, add a tablespoonful of butter, and minced parsley, lemon-juice, grated nutmeg, and anchovy essence to season. Pour around the fish and serve.

SALMON À L'ITALIENNE

Flake cold salmon fine with a silver fork and mix with an equal quantity of cold cooked spaghetti cut fine. Reheat in a Cream Sauce, add a few capers and serve very hot.

SALMON STEAKS À LA MARINIÈRE

Marinate salmon steaks in seasoned oil, drain, and broil. Cover with small boiled onions and cooked oysters. Pour over a sauce made according to directions given in the recipe for Salmon à la Genoise, and serve.

SALMON À LA MARSEILLES

Boil a small salmon in salted and acidulated water. Skin and put on a serving-dish. Spread over it some very thick Cream Sauce, sprinkle with crumbs, brush with beaten egg, cover with crumbs again, sprinkle with salt, pepper, and grated nutmeg, and brown in the oven. Serve with a sauce made of equal parts of white wine and stock, thickened with butter and flour cooked together.

SALMON À LA MARYLAND

Prepare and clean a small salmon and simmer in salted water until done. Prepare a Drawn-Butter Sauce and add to it half a cupful of butter. When the butter is melted, take from the fire and add quickly two eggs beaten with the juice of half a lemon. Pour the sauce over the fish and serve.

SALMON À LA NAPLES

Fry salmon steaks in butter, seasoning with salt, pepper, and grated nutmeg. When half cooked, add half a cupful of white wine to the butter, cover, and simmer slowly until done. Cover the salmon with cooked oysters, pour the liquid remaining in the pan over the fish, and serve.

SALMON À LA PROVENCE

Season four salmon steaks and cook with a tablespoonful of butter and the juice of a lemon. Add a dozen oysters, half a dozen small shrimps, and one cupful of white stock thickened with flour and butter cooked together. Simmer until the oysters are cooked, take from the fire, add the yolk of an egg beaten smooth with a tablespoonful of Sherry, and serve with triangles of fried bread.

SALMON À LA PROVENÇALE

Put a large cut of salmon into a saucepan and cover with salted and acidulated water. Add a sliced onion, a carrot, a bunch of parsley, and salt, pepper, sweet herbs, and a pinch of allspice to season. Cover the fish with buttered paper and cook slowly for an hour. Chop together a small onion, a clove of garlic, and a few sprigs of parsley. Fry in olive-oil, add two tablespoonfuls of flour, and cook until the flour is brown. Add two cupfuls of brown stock and one cupful of stewed and strained tomato. Cook until thick, stirring constantly, seasoning with red and white pepper and lemon-juice. Remove the skin from the fish, pour the hot sauce over it, and serve.

FILLETS OF SALMON À LA VÉNITIENNE

Put salmon steaks into a buttered baking-pan with fine match-like strips of larding pork laid on each side. Season with salt, pepper, and lemon-juice, add one cupful of white wine and cover with a sheet of buttered paper, having a small hole in the centre. Bake for forty minutes, basting often. Cook together one tablespoonful each of butter and flour, add one cupful of stock, and cook until thick, stirring constantly. Add a tablespoonful each of butter and lemon-juice and a teaspoonful of minced parsley. Pour around the fish and serve.

SALMON À LA WALDORF

Marinate salmon steaks for an hour in lemon-juice. Cover with stock, add pepper, salt and minced parsley to season, and simmer slowly until done. Drain, thicken the sauce, add a tablespoonful of butter, and serve separately.

SALMON MOUSSE

Rub half a pound of raw salmon to a smooth paste with water, adding gradually a dozen chopped raw oysters, half a cupful of Tomato Sauce and the yolks of three eggs. When smooth, fold in the stiffly beaten whites, season with salt and pepper, and press through a purée sieve into small buttered moulds. Put into a baking-pan, surround with hot water, and bake for fifteen or twenty minutes in a moderate oven. Unmould and serve with any preferred sauce.

SALMON MOUSSE À LA MARTINOT

Pound to a pulp with a little water, half a pound of raw salmon, and add the well-beaten whites of two eggs. Cook together one tablespoonful each of butter and flour, add a cupful of milk, and cook until thick, stirring constantly. Season with salt, red and white pepper, grated onion, and mushroom essence. Take from the fire, and add the yolks of three eggs beaten smooth with two tablespoonfuls of cream. Cool the sauce, and when cold mix it with the fish. Fold in carefully one cupful of whipped cream and fill a buttered mould with the fish. Put the mould in a pan of hot water and bake in a moderate oven for half an hour.

For the sauce, cook together for ten minutes a tablespoonful each of butter and flour, a teaspoonful each of chopped onion, salt, and sugar, and half a can of tomatoes. Rub through a sieve, and add the yolks of four eggs beaten smooth with a tablespoonful of cream and a grating of nutmeg. Take from the fire and add two tablespoonfuls of butter in small bits. Return to the fire, and add a little lemon-juice or tarragon vinegar. Strain, and add a little whipped cream.

SALMON STEAKS WITH CLARET SAUCE

Put four steaks into a buttered saucepan with salt, pepper, and grated nutmeg to season, add a bunch of parsley, a teaspoonful of mixed sweet herbs, a chopped onion, and two cupfuls of Claret. Cover with a buttered paper, simmer until done, and drain. Strain the sauce, thicken with flour cooked brown in butter, skim, add two tablespoonfuls of butter and the juice of a lemon; pour over the fish and serve.

SALMON MAYONNAISE WITH CUCUMBERS

Steam salmon steaks until tender, remove the skin, and cool. Cover with thinly sliced cucumbers, mask with Mayonnaise, and serve with a border of lettuce leaves and sliced hard-boiled eggs.

CREAMED SALMON ON TOAST

Reheat a cupful of cold flaked salmon, either fresh or canned, in Cream Sauce. Take from the fire, add one egg beaten smooth with half a cupful of cream, pour over buttered toast, and serve.

CURRIED SALMON

Chop a Spanish onion, fry it in butter, and add a tablespoonful of curry powder mixed with a teaspoonful of flour. Add two cupfuls of stock and cook until thick, stirring constantly. Add cold cooked salmon, cut into small pieces, and reheat. Serve in a border of boiled rice.

CHARTREUSE OF SALMON

Wash a cupful of rice in several waters, drain and parboil for five minutes in salted water at a galloping boil. Drain in a colander, return to the saucepan, add a pinch of salt and three cupfuls of milk or stock. Steam until tender, then add three tablespoonfuls of butter melted and mixed with one tablespoonful of curry powder and two tablespoonfuls of lemon-juice. Mix thoroughly and line a two-quart buttered mould with the rice. Fill the center with flaked cooked salmon, seasoned with salt, pepper and lemon-juice, cover with rice, steam for half an hour and serve with Egg Sauce.

FRICASSEE OF SALMON

Cut two pounds of salmon steaks into strips. Put into a saucepan with half a cupful of water, salt and pepper to season, a clove, a blade of mace, a tablespoonful of sugar, a chopped onion, and a heaping teaspoonful of mustard mixed with half a cupful of vinegar. Bring to the boil, add six tomatoes peeled and sliced, a teaspoonful of minced parsley, and a wineglassful of Sherry. Simmer for forty-five minutes and serve either hot or cold.

SALMON WITH EGGS

Steam salmon steaks until tender, cool, and lay upon a platter covered with lettuce leaves. Season with salt, pepper, and lemon-juice and surround with slices of hard-boiled eggs. Mix together a tablespoonful of melted butter, a teaspoonful of made mustard, and salt and pepper to season. Spread over the egg slices and serve.

JELLIED SALMON—I

Simmer salmon steaks in court-bouillon until done. Drain and arrange on a platter. Spread with Mayonnaise, tinted green with spinach juice to which a little dissolved gelatine has been added. Serve cold.

JELLIED SALMON—II

Mix two cupfuls of cold boiled salmon with one tablespoonful of lemon-juice, one teaspoonful of minced parsley, two drops of tabasco sauce and one tablespoonful of granulated gelatine dissolved in cold water. Add it to half a cupful of cooked salad dressing. Wet in cold water one large mould or several small ones, fill with the salmon and put on ice until thoroughly chilled. Serve with sliced cucumbers and Tartar Sauce.

SALMON PIE

Butter a baking-dish and line the sides with a rich biscuit crust. Fill the pan with fresh or canned salmon, seasoned with salt and pepper, lemon-juice, a pinch of mace, and a teaspoonful of onion juice. Spread over the salmon a cupful of boiled lobster which has been seasoned with melted butter and Worcestershire Sauce. Cover with biscuit crust, slit diagonally down the centre, and bake for an hour in a moderate oven.

COLD SALMON PATTIES

Season chopped salmon highly with salt and pepper, grated nutmeg and melted butter. Add the beaten yolk of an egg to bind. Line patty-tins with puff paste or rich pastry, fill with the salmon mixture, cover with the paste, and bake.

PICKLED SALMON—I

Boil large fresh pieces of salmon in salted and acidulated water to cover. Bring to the boil one quart of vinegar, six blades of mace, half a dozen white peppers, half a dozen cloves, a teaspoonful of made mustard, two tablespoonfuls of sugar, and a cupful of water in which the fish was boiled. Let the fish cool in the water, then put it in an earthen jar, pour the boiling liquid over, and let stand for a day or two before using.

PICKLED SALMON—II

Cut the fish into large pieces and cook until done in salted and acidulated water. Drain, cool, and skin. Put into a preserving-kettle two quarts of vinegar, one cupful of boiling water, four blades of mace, two tablespoonfuls of sugar, a dozen cloves, two tablespoonfuls of mustard seed, an onion sliced, a dozen pepper-corns, one small red pepper, two bay-leaves, and a teaspoonful of celery seed. Bring to the boil, put in the fish, boil up once and cool. Let stand for two or three days before using.

PICKLED SALMON—III

Boil large pieces of salmon in salted and acidulated water, drain, and cool. Add one quart of the water in which the fish was cooked, two quarts of vinegar, a tablespoonful of pepper-corns, grated nutmeg and a dozen blades of mace. Boil for half an hour and cool. Pour over the salmon, add a tablespoonful of olive-oil, cover, and keep in a cool place for two or three days before using.

SPICED SALMON

Mix half a cupful of vinegar, the juice of half a lemon, two cloves, a bay-leaf, an inch of stick cinnamon, a teaspoonful of salt and a pinch of black pepper. Bring to the boil and pour over salmon steaks which have been boiled, drained, and cooled. Let stand for two or three hours before serving.

SALMON SOUFFLÉ

Cook together one tablespoonful each of butter and flour, add one cupful of milk, and cook until thick, stirring constantly. Add half a cupful of stale bread crumbs, a teaspoonful of grated onion, a tablespoonful of Worcestershire Sauce, a teaspoonful of minced parsley, and the yolks of three eggs, well-beaten. Add one cupful of flaked salmon, mix thoroughly, and fold in the salmon, and bake in a pan of hot water in a moderate oven for forty-five minutes. Serve with any preferred sauce.

SALMON ON TOAST

Reheat two cupfuls of cold salmon steaks in a cupful of Drawn-Butter Sauce, seasoning with salt and red pepper. Take from the fire and add one egg beaten light with three tablespoonfuls of cream. Pour over slices of fried bread, sprinkle with minced parsley, and serve.

SALMON TIMBALES

Flake a pound of cooked salmon and rub to a paste. Season with salt, pepper, and grated onion, add a tablespoonful of chopped almonds and the unbeaten whites of three eggs. Mix thoroughly and stir in one cupful of cream whipped solid. Put into small buttered moulds, set into boiling water, and bake for twenty minutes. Turn out and serve with Hollandaise Sauce.

SALMON TURBOT—I

Cook together two tablespoonfuls of butter and three of flour. Add two cupfuls of milk and cook until thick, stirring constantly. Take from the fire, add two eggs, well beaten, a teaspoonful of minced parsley and the juice of half a lemon. Put into a baking-pan alternate layers of the sauce and cold flaked salmon, cover with crumbs, dot with butter, and brown in the oven.

SALMON TURBOT—II

Cook together one tablespoonful each of butter and flour, add two cupfuls of milk and cook until thick, stirring constantly. Take from the fire, add two tablespoonfuls of butter, and salt and pepper to season. Put a layer of flaked salmon into a buttered baking-dish, spread with the sauce, and repeat until the dish is full, having crumbs and butter on top. Bake for half an hour.

SALMON BOX

Line a square tin mould with hot boiled rice, fill the centre with cold boiled salmon flaked and seasoned with salt, pepper, and grated nutmeg. Cover with rice, steam for an hour, turn out on a platter, and serve with Egg Sauce.

SALMON WITH CUCUMBER SAUCE

Put a large cut of salmon into a buttered saucepan with salt, pepper, a bunch of parsley, a chopped onion, and sweet herbs. Add half a cupful of white wine and enough stock to cover. Simmer until the fish is done and drain carefully. Strain the liquid and thicken with flour cooked in butter. Peel and slice three small cucumbers, parboil in salted water, drain, and fry in butter with a little sugar. Add to the sauce with a tablespoonful of butter and the juice of a lemon. Pour over the fish and serve.

SALMON CROQUETTES—I

Cook together one tablespoonful of butter and two tablespoonfuls of flour, add one cupful of cream, and cook until thick, stirring constantly. Take from the fire, add one egg well beaten, and one pound of cold cooked salmon flaked. Let cool, shape into croquettes, dip into egg and crumbs, and fry in deep fat. Serve with any preferred sauce.

SALMON CROQUETTES—II

Cook together one tablespoonful of butter and three tablespoonfuls of flour. Add one cupful of cream, and cook until thick, stirring constantly. Season with salt, red pepper, and minced parsley, take from the fire, add the juice of a lemon and a can of flaked salmon. Mix thoroughly and cool. Shape into croquettes, dip in egg and crumbs, and fry in deep fat.

SALMON CROQUETTES—III

Cook together one tablespoonful of flour and two of butter, add a cupful of cream or milk, and cook until thick, stirring constantly. Take from the fire, add an egg well beaten, half a cupful of crumbs, a small can of flaked salmon, and salt, red pepper, and powdered mace to season. Mix thoroughly, cool, shape into croquettes, dip into egg and crumbs, and fry in deep fat.

SALMON CROQUETTES—IV

Cook together two tablespoonfuls each of butter and flour and add one cupful of cream in which the yolks of two eggs have been beaten. Cook until very thick, stirring constantly. Take from the fire, add a pound can of salmon, flaked, salt and pepper to season, and a teaspoonful of minced parsley. Stir in the beaten whites of the eggs and cool. Shape into croquettes, dip in egg and crumbs, fry in deep fat, and serve with Tomato Sauce.

SALMON CROQUETTES—V

Cook together two tablespoonfuls of butter and one of flour. Add one cupful of milk and cook until thick, stirring constantly. Add a small can of flaked salmon, pepper and salt to season, and three eggs well beaten. Reheat, but do not boil. When it thickens, take from the fire, and cool. When cold, shape into croquettes, dip in egg and crumbs, and fry in deep fat.

SALMON CROQUETTES—VI

Cook together one tablespoonful of butter and two of flour. Add one cupful of milk and cook until very thick, stirring constantly. Season with salt, pepper, and celery salt. Add two cupfuls of canned salmon freed from skin, fat, and bone and chopped fine. Mix thoroughly and spread on a platter to cool. Shape into croquettes, dip in crumbs, then in beaten egg, then in crumbs, and fry in deep fat. Serve with green peas.

SWEDISH SALMON CROQUETTES

Cook one cupful of white stock with a tablespoonful of butter, the yolks of two eggs, and parsley, pepper and salt, and grated onion to season. Add a can of flaked salmon and cook until thick, stirring constantly. Cool, shape into croquettes, dip in egg and crumbs, and fry in deep fat. Serve with Tartar Sauce.

SALMON CUTLETS

Cook together one tablespoonful of butter and three of flour. Add one cupful of cream and cook until thick, stirring constantly. Add a can of salmon, chopped, the juice of half a lemon, a tablespoonful of minced parsley, and salt and red pepper to season. Mix thoroughly, and cool. Shape into cutlets, dip in egg and crumbs and fry in deep fat.

SALMON CHOPS

Prepare according to directions given for Salmon Croquettes, shape into chops, dip into egg and crumbs, fry in deep fat, and serve with Tartar Sauce.

BAKED SALMON LOAF—I

Put a cupful of milk into a double-boiler and add enough bread crumbs to make a smooth paste. Cook until thick, stirring constantly. Add a can of salmon, chopped, half a cupful of cream, salt and red pepper to season and three eggs beaten separately, folding in the stiffly beaten whites last. Mix thoroughly, pour into a buttered mould, set into a pan of hot water, and bake until firm in a moderate oven.

SALMON LOAF—II

Mash a can of salmon, add the juice of a lemon, and half a cupful of fresh bread-crumbs, three tablespoonfuls of minced parsley, four tablespoonfuls of melted butter and four eggs beaten separately, folding in the stiffly beaten whites last. Put into a buttered mould and steam for an hour. Add to the oil drained from the salmon one cupful of boiling milk, one tablespoonful of cornstarch rubbed smooth in a little cold milk, and a tablespoonful of butter. Cook until thick, stirring constantly, take from the fire, add one egg well beaten, a teaspoonful of tomato catsup and mace and pepper to season. Turn the mould out on a platter and pour the sauce around it.

SALMON LOAF—III

Flake a can of salmon and mix it with the pounded yolks of two hard-boiled eggs, a tablespoonful of capers, and pepper, salt, mace, and parsley to season. Dissolve a teaspoonful of anchovy paste in a cupful of boiling water, add a tablespoonful of lemon-juice and a tablespoonful of soaked gelatine. Heat until the gelatine is dissolved and mix with the fish. Butter a mould and arrange upon it the rings of the hard-boiled eggs. Put the fish into it and put on ice until perfectly cold and firm. Turn out on a platter and serve with Mayonnaise.

SALMON LOAF—IV

Drain the oil from a can of salmon, remove skin, fat, and bone, and flake the fish with a silver fork. Add the yolks of four eggs, well beaten, half a cupful of bread crumbs, four tablespoonfuls of melted butter, and pepper, salt, and minced parsley to season. Fold in the stiffly beaten whites of the eggs, put into a buttered pan, and bake for half an hour. Add to the drained oil one cupful of milk. Thicken it with a tablespoonful each of butter and flour cooked together, take from the fire, and add one egg well beaten.

FRICASSEED SALMON

Reheat a can of flaked salmon in a cupful of Drawn-Butter Sauce, adding half a cupful of cream, and salt, red and white pepper to season. Take from the fire, add one egg, well beaten, pour over buttered toast, and sprinkle with parsley.

CURRIED SALMON—I

Chop a small onion fine, and fry brown in butter. Add to it the liquor drained from a can of salmon, and a tablespoonful of flour. When the flour is smooth, add half a cupful of water, a teaspoonful each of curry powder and lemon-juice, and salt and pepper to taste. Add a can of salmon flaked, reheat, and serve.

CURRIED SALMON—II

Fry a chopped onion in olive-oil, and when the onion is brown add a tablespoonful of flour mixed with a teaspoonful of curry powder. Add one cupful of boiling water and cook until thick, stirring constantly. Reheat flaked canned salmon in the sauce and serve with a garnish of sliced lemon.

CURRIED SALMON—III

Fry a chopped onion brown in olive-oil. add two teaspoonfuls of curry powder and a tablespoonful of flour. When the flour is cooked, add two cupfuls of hot water and cook until thick, stirring constantly. Add a tablespoonful of tomato catsup or Chutney Sauce and salt and pepper to season. Add a can of salmon flaked. Reheat and serve.

CREAMED SALMON

Bring to the boil one cupful of cream and half a cupful of milk. Add a teaspoonful of butter and two teaspoonfuls of corn-starch rubbed smooth with a little cold milk. Cook until thick, stirring constantly, and add one can of flaked salmon. Fill ramekins with the mixture, sprinkle with crumbs, dot with butter, and brown in the oven.

CREAMED SALMON ON TOAST

Prepare the fish according to directions given for Baked Creamed Salmon. Pour over slices of buttered toast, sprinkle with minced parsley, and serve.

BAKED CREAMED SALMON

Cook together two tablespoonfuls of butter and two of flour, add two cupfuls of milk or cream, and cook until thick, stirring constantly. Add salt, pepper and minced parsley to season, and a can of flaked salmon. Reheat and arrange in a baking-dish with alternate layers of crumbs and butter, having crumbs and butter on top. Bake in the oven until brown.

SALMON PATTIES

Prepare Creamed Salmon according to directions given in the recipe for Baked Creamed Salmon. Fill patty-shells and serve.

ESCALLOPED SALMON—I

Prepare Creamed Salmon according to directions given for Baked Creamed Salmon. Put into a buttered baking-dish, cover with crumbs, dot with butter, and brown in the oven.

ESCALLOPED SALMON—II

Cook together two tablespoonfuls of butter and one of flour. Add a cupful of water, the juice of a lemon, a small onion chopped, the yolks of three boiled eggs mashed smooth, and pepper and salt to season. Cook until thick, stirring constantly. Add a can of flaked salmon, reheat, and serve.

COQUILLES OF SALMON

Prepare Creamed Salmon according to directions given in the recipe for Baked Creamed Salmon, seasoning with salt, pepper and lemon-juice. Put into buttered shells or individual dishes with alternate layers of cooked mushrooms. Sprinkle with crumbs and grated cheese, dot with butter and brown in the oven.

DEVILLED SALMON

Prepare Creamed Salmon according to directions given for Baked Creamed Salmon, adding half a cupful of Worcestershire Sauce and the juice of a lemon. Fill individual dishes or a large baking-dish, sprinkle with crumbs, dot with butter, and brown in the oven.

BANKED SALMON

Reheat a can of salmon in a Cream Sauce. Arrange on a platter and put around it a border of mashed potatoes. Sprinkle with crumbs, dot with butter, and brown in the oven.

PRESSED SALMON

Mix together two beaten eggs, a tablespoonful of butter, two cupfuls of bread crumbs, a can of salmon, flaked, and salt and pepper to season, turn into a buttered mould, steam for half an hour, and serve cold with Mayonnaise or Tartar Sauce.

MOULDED SALMON

Free a pint can of salmon from fat, skin, and bone and flake the fish with a silver fork. Add salt and pepper to season, half a cupful of cracker crumbs, two tablespoonfuls of butter melted, and three eggs beaten separately, mix thoroughly, put into a buttered mould and steam for an hour. Serve with Drawn-Butter Sauce to which chopped olives and capers have been added.

SALMON IN GREEN PEPPERS

Prepare Creamed Salmon according to directions given for Baked Creamed Salmon. Cut slices from the tops of sweet green peppers, remove the seeds and fibre, fill with the prepared salmon, sprinkle with crumbs, dot with butter, put into a pan of hot water and bake for twenty or thirty minutes.

SALMON EN CASSEROLE

Chop a large onion and fry it in butter. Add a cupful of bread crumbs and one and one half cupfuls of milk. Bring to the boil, add salt and pepper to season, a flaked can of salmon, and two eggs well beaten. Pour into a buttered casserole, dot with butter, and bake brown. Sprinkle with minced parsley and serve.

BROILED SMOKED SALMON—I

Soak for twelve hours, changing the water three times. Drain, wipe dry, dip in olive-oil and vinegar, and broil. Serve with a garnish of lemon and parsley.

BROILED SMOKED SALMON—II

Cut into narrow strips, parboil for ten minutes, drain, cover with cold water, let stand for fifteen minutes, wipe dry, and broil. Season with red pepper and lemon-juice and serve with buttered toast.

BROILED SMOKED SALMON—III

Cut smoked salmon into strips and broil carefully. Pour over it melted butter and lemon-juice, sprinkle with minced parsley, and serve.

BROILED SMOKED SALMON—IV

Parboil slices of smoked salmon for twenty minutes, drain, cool, rub with flour, broil carefully, and serve with any preferred sauce.

BROILED SMOKED SALMON—V

Wash thoroughly and soak for a few hours very salt. Cover with warm water, simmer for fifteen or twenty minutes, drain, wipe dry, rub with butter, and broil.

BROILED SALMON À LA MAÎTRE D'HÔTEL

Soak the smoked salmon for an hour in cold water, then drain and wipe dry. Brush with melted butter and broil carefully. Serve with Maître d'Hôtel Sauce.

SMOKED SALMON

Cut it into thin slices, warm it up in a little olive-oil, strain the oil when it is warmed, add to it lemon-juice and minced parsley, pour over the fish, and serve.

BROILED KIPPERED SALMON

Cut the salmon into strips, wrap in buttered paper, and broil carefully over a clear fire. Remove the paper and serve.

FRIED KIPPERED SALMON

Soak slices of kippered salmon in olive-oil for several hours. Drain off the oil and fry the salmon slices in it. Serve with melted butter and lemon-juice.

BROILED SALT SALMON

Soak the fish for thirty-six hours in cold water, changing the water often. Drain, wipe dry, rub with melted butter, broil, and serve with Egg Sauce.

BOILED SALT SALMON

Soak the fish over night, drain, rinse, and simmer for fifteen or twenty minutes. Season with pepper and butter and garnish with parsley.

PICKLED SALT SALMON

Prepare according to directions given for Pickled Salmon, soaking the salt fish for twelve hours before cooking.

SALT SALMON IN PAPILLOTES

Cut the fish into strips, soak for an hour in cold water, drain, and dry. Season with pepper and wrap each piece in tough, well-buttered paper, twisting the ends. Broil carefully over clear coals, unwrap and serve with any preferred sauce.

P.S. This is an insignificant fraction of what we really know about salmon. We are saving the rest for a Piscatorial Encyclopedia.

FOURTEEN WAYS TO COOK SALMON-TROUT

FRIED SALMON-TROUT CUTLETS

Cut cutlets from a large salmon-trout, dip in seasoned crumbs, and sauté in hot fat. Serve with Cream Sauce.

BOILED SALMON-TROUT—I

Wrap the prepared and cleaned fish in mosquito netting, tie firmly, cover with cold salted water, bring to the boil and boil slowly until done. Serve with any preferred sauce.

BOILED SALMON-TROUT—II

Prepare and clean a salmon-trout, stuff with seasoned crumbs, and put on the grate in a fish-kettle. Sprinkle with salt, pepper, and grated nutmeg, add a bunch of sweet herbs, a clove of garlic and two tablespoonfuls of butter. Add enough Claret to cover and simmer until done. Drain the fish, strain the liquid, thicken if desired, and serve the sauce separately.

BOILED SALMON-TROUT—III

Wrap a small cleaned fish in mosquito netting, sew up, and simmer in salted and acidulated water until tender. Take up carefully, remove the netting, garnish with lemon and parsley, and serve with Egg or Cream Sauce.

BOILED SALMON-TROUT—IV

Clean a salmon-trout, stuff with seasoned crumbs, and put into a fish-kettle with equal parts of white wine and stock or water to cover. Add a carrot, an onion, a bay-leaf, and two or three beans of garlic. Cook the fish slowly, drain, and reduce the liquid by rapid boiling to one pint. Thicken with butter and flour, pour over the fish, and serve.

BAKED SALMON-TROUT—I

Clean a salmon-trout, stuff it with seasoned crumbs, and sew up. Put into a fish-kettle with a quart of white wine, half a cupful of butter, a chopped onion, two tablespoonfuls of chopped parsley, a can of button mushrooms, and salt, pepper, and grated nutmeg to season. Cover and cook in a moderate oven for an hour. Take up carefully, skin the fish, cover with crumbs, dot with butter, and brown in the oven. Reduce the gravy by rapid boiling, thicken with butter and flour cooked together, and serve in a gravy-boat.

BAKED SALMON-TROUT—II

Prepare and clean the fish and put into a buttered baking-pan with enough water to keep from burning. Bake slowly, basting as required with melted butter and hot water. Cook together one tablespoonful each of butter and flour, add a cupful of cream, and half a cupful of boiling water in which a bit of soda has been dissolved. Cook until thick, stirring constantly, and add two tablespoonfuls of melted butter and a teaspoonful of minced parsley. Pour the sauce around the fish and serve.

BAKED SALMON-TROUT—III

Have a large salmon-trout cleaned and larded. Put into a buttered baking-pan, rub the fish with salt and pepper, and pour over a wineglassful of Madeira. Cover with buttered paper and bake, basting every ten or fifteen minutes with the liquid. Serve with any preferred sauce.

SALMON-TROUT À LA GENOISE

Prepare and clean a salmon-trout, remove the backbone, stuff with seasoned crumbs, and put into a buttered pan with half a cupful of Sherry, two cupfuls of stock, a bunch of parsley, a sliced onion, and salt, pepper, and sweet herbs to season. Cover with a buttered paper and cook slowly, basting often. Take up the fish, strain the liquid, and add enough stock to make the required quantity of sauce. Thicken with flour cooked in butter, add two tablespoonfuls of butter, and lemon-juice and anchovy essence to season. Serve the sauce separately,

SALMON-TROUT À LA HOLLANDAISE

Prepare and clean the salmon-trout and cook in salted and acidulated water, seasoning with salt, pepper, and parsley. Drain, and serve with a Hollandaise Sauce to which chopped cooked oysters have been added.

SALMON-TROUT À LA MAÎTRE D'HÔTEL

Prepare and clean a salmon-trout, split and broil, basting with oil if required. Serve with Maître d'Hôtel Sauce.

SALMON-TROUT À LA RICHELIEU

Put a cleaned salmon-trout into a baking-dish, with two tablespoonfuls of butter, salt, pepper, and grated nutmeg to season, and enough white wine to keep from burning. Cover with a buttered paper and bake, basting frequently with the liquid. Drain the fish and add enough white stock or oyster liquid to make the required quantity of sauce. Thicken with flour cooked in butter. Take from the fire, add the yolks of four eggs beaten with the juice of a lemon, reheat, pour over the fish, and serve.

PICKLED SALMON-TROUT

Clean the fish thoroughly and cut into strips. Cover the bottom of a baking-dish with sliced onion, sprinkle with salt and pepper, cover with pieces of fish, add more onions, and cover with cold water, made very acid with good vinegar.

Add a few cloves, a bit of ginger root, and a pinch of allspice. Bake slowly until the fish is tender and serve cold.

SALMON-TROUT WITH SHRIMP SAUCE

Prepare and clean a salmon-trout and cook in salted and acidulated water to cover, adding a bunch of parsley. Drain and serve with Shrimp Sauce.

TWENTY WAYS TO COOK SARDINES.

BROILED SARDINES—I

Broil a dozen large sardines on a double broiler. Lay on fingers of toast, garnish with lemon, and serve with Maître d'Hôtel Sauce.

BROILED SARDINES—II

Drain the fish and broil quickly on a double-broiler. Serve on toast and garnish with lemon and parsley.

BROILED SARDINES—III

Drain large sardines, broil, lay on fingers of hot buttered toast, sprinkle with grated Parmesan cheese, and brown in the oven.

BROILED SARDINES ON TOAST

Drain large sardines, skin carefully, broil on a double-broiler, arrange on fingers of hot buttered toast, and pour over a tablespoonful of melted butter and a cupful of canned tomatoes. Boil slowly until tender, take up carefully, rub the sauce through a coarse sieve, bring to the boil, and add a cupful of cream beaten smooth with a tablespoonful of flour. Cook until thick, stirring constantly; take from the fire, add a teaspoonful of minced parsley, pour over the fish, and serve.

BAKED SARDINES—I

Skin a dozen sardines and heat in the oven. Drain the oil from them, bring to the boil, add one cupful of water, a teaspoonful of Worcestershire Sauce, and salt and pepper to season. Take from the fire, add the yolk of an egg beaten with a teaspoonful each of vinegar and made mustard, bring to the boil, pour over the fish, and serve with toasted crackers.

BAKED SARDINES—II

Drain the oil from large sardines, roll in cracker dust, season with pepper and lemon-juice, and brown in the oven. Serve with toasted crackers.

BAKED SARDINES—III

Drain and skin a dozen large sardines, put in the oven, and keep warm. Bring the oil to a boil, add a teaspoonful of Worcestershire Sauce and a teaspoonful of tomato catsup. Arrange the fish on fingers of buttered toast, pour over the fish, and serve.

BAKED SARDINES—IV

Marinate drained sardines in lemon-juice, then drain, sprinkle with cracker crumbs, and put into a hot oven for ten minutes. Cook together a heaping teaspoonful each of butter and flour, add one cupful of tomato-juice, and cook until thick, stirring constantly. Season with salt, pepper, grated onion, and sugar. Arrange the sardines on toasted strips of brown bread, pour the sauce over, and serve.

FRIED SARDINES

Drain large sardines, dip in egg and crumbs, fry, and serve on toast.

CURRIED SARDINES—I

Rub to a paste one tablespoonful of butter, one teaspoonful each of French mustard and curry powder, using lemon-juice to make smooth. Drain and skin large sardines, spread with the paste, broil, and serve on toast with a border of broiled tomatoes.

CURRIED SARDINES—II

Mix together a teaspoonful each of sugar and curry powder, add a cupful of cream and the juice of half a lemon, bring to the boiling point, add a dozen sardines, and heat thoroughly. Serve on toast with fried apple and sliced fried onion.

DEVILLED SARDINES

Skin, split and bone a dozen sardines. Season with salt, pepper, lemon-juice, and made mustard. Let stand for an hour in the seasoning. Broil and serve on toast, garnishing with lemon and parsley.

SARDINES À LA MAÎTRE D'HÔTEL

Skin large sardines, arrange on fingers of buttered toast, and heat in the oven. Add to one cupful of Cream Sauce a tablespoonful of grated onion, a teaspoonful of minced parsley, salt and pepper to season, and a tablespoonful of vinegar. Pour over the fish and serve.

SARDINES À LA PIEDMONT

Skin a dozen sardines and put in the oven to heat. Put into a saucepan the yolks of four eggs well beaten with one teaspoonful each of malt vinegar, tarragon vinegar, and made mustard. Add a pinch of salt, and a tablespoonful of butter. Stir until thick, but do not boil. Put the sardines on circles of fried or toasted bread, pour the sauce over, and serve.

STUFFED SARDINES

Drain the oil from large sardines, skin and bone them, and stuff with chopped mushrooms, fine herbs, and bread crumbs made smooth with brown stock. Wrap in buttered paper, heat thoroughly in the oven, unwrap carefully, and serve on a hot dish.

SARDINE SALAD

Drain a dozen large sardines, remove the skin and bone, and lay upon a bed of lettuce leaves. Sprinkle with hard-boiled eggs, chopped fine, pour over a French dressing and serve with toasted crackers.

SARDINES IN CRUSTS

Scoop out the crumbs from stale French rolls and toast or fry in deep fat. Cook together a tablespoonful each of butter and flour, add a little boiling water, and cook until thick, stirring constantly. Season with anchovy paste and Worcestershire Sauce, and add drained and flaked sardines. Reheat, fill the shells, fit on the covers, and serve with quarters of lemon.

SARDINE CANAPES

Skin, bone, and mash sardines. Rub to a smooth paste, using melted butter and lemon-juice, and seasoning with salt and Tabasco Sauce. Toast small triangles of crustless bread, butter them, spread with the sardine mixture, heat thoroughly in the oven, and serve piping hot as a first course at dinner or luncheon.

SARDINE IN EGG CUPS

Cut hard-boiled eggs in halves crosswise and take out the yolks. Cut a thin slice off the bottom of each cup. Rub the yolks to a smooth paste with olive-oil and add half a dozen sardines skinned, boned, and mashed. Season with salt, pepper, mustard and lemon-juice, fill the egg cups, and serve on lettuce leaves with French or Mayonnaise dressing.

SARDINE EGG CUPS À LA BEARNAISE

Prepare according to directions given in the preceding recipe. Heat in a double-boiler, or in the oven, being careful to keep dry. Pour over a Bearnaise Sauce and serve hot.

SARDINES À LA CAMBRIDGE

Boil and chop a peck of spinach. Add one cupful of fresh bread crumbs and four tablespoonfuls of melted butter. Mix thoroughly and add a dozen skinned and boned sardines pounded to a paste. Heat thoroughly, adding stock or water if needed. Put on a platter, shape into a mound, lay sardines on top and garnish with sliced hard-boiled eggs and lemon.

SARDINE RAREBIT

Toast strips of bread, lay a broiled sardine on each, and keep warm. Melt one tablespoonful of butter, add two tablespoonfuls of grated cheese, and gradually, as the cheese melts, the yolk of an egg beaten smooth with one fourth of a cupful of cream. When smooth and thick, season with salt and Tabasco Sauce; pour over the sardines and serve. Garnish with lemon and parsley.

NINETY-FIVE WAYS TO COOK SHAD

BROILED SHAD—I

Prepare and clean the fish, split, and remove the backbone. Season with salt and pepper, dip in oil, broil carefully, and serve with Maître d'Hôtel Sauce.

BROILED SHAD—II

Marinate the prepared fish for an hour in olive-oil, seasoned with salt, pepper, minced onion, and parsley. Drain and broil, basting with the oil as required. Serve with Maître d'Hôtel Sauce. The onion and parsley may be omitted from the seasoning.

BROILED SHAD—III

Clean the shad, split, remove the backbone and marinate for an hour in oil and lemon-juice, seasoning with salt and pepper. Drain, sprinkle with crumbs, and broil carefully. Serve with Fine Herbs Sauce.

BROILED SHAD—IV

Prepare, clean, and split the fish. Put on a platter skin side down and sprinkle with sugar, pepper, and salt. Let stand over night, broil, and serve with melted butter.

BROILED SHAD—V

Clean, split, season with salt and pepper, broil on a buttered gridiron, and serve with plenty of melted butter.

BROILED SALT SHAD

Soak for twelve hours in tepid water, drain and put into ice-cold water for half an hour. Drain, wipe dry, sprinkle with pepper, and broil on a buttered gridiron, skin side up. Serve with plenty of melted butter.

FRIED SHAD—I

Prepare and clean the fish and cut into suitable pieces for serving. Roll in seasoned flour and sauté in hot fat. Serve with any preferred sauce.

FRIED SHAD—II

Clean, split, and take out the backbone, cut into strips, season to taste, and fry in hot lard until brown. Serve with any preferred sauce.

BONED FRIED SHAD

Remove the head and tail, then take out the back and side bones. Cut into convenient pieces for serving, season with salt and pepper, dip in egg and crumbs, and fry in deep fat. Serve with any preferred sauce.

SHAD CUTLETS

Cut the cleaned fish into convenient pieces for serving, dip into egg and crumbs and fry in fat to cover. Serve on a bed of spinach and garnish with hard-boiled eggs.

BOILED SHAD

Boil the fish in salted and acidulated water or in court-bouillon. Drain carefully, garnish with lemon and parsley and serve with Maître d'Hôtel or Hollandaise Sauce.

BOILED SHAD WITH EGG SAUCE

Sew the cleaned fish in mosquito netting, and boil slowly in salted and acidulated water. Drain, remove the netting, and serve with Egg Sauce.

BOILED ROE SHAD

Clean the fish and do not break the roe. Sprinkle with salt and pepper, wrap in separate squares of mosquito netting, tie firmly and put into a fish-kettle, side by side. Cover with salted water and simmer until done. Drain, remove the cloth carefully, and serve with Egg or Hollandaise Sauce.

BOILED SHAD WITH HOLLANDAISE SAUCE

Cook the prepared fish slowly in salted and acidulated water, drain, and serve with Hollandaise Sauce.

SHAD IN COURT-BOUILLON

Put the prepared and cleaned fish on a perforated sheet in a fish-kettle. Add two tablespoonfuls of butter, two sliced onions, and salt, pepper, mace, and parsley to season. Add enough Claret to cover and simmer slowly until done. Drain, strain the liquid and thicken with flour cooked in butter. Take from the fire, add two tablespoonfuls of butter, the juice of half a lemon, and red pepper to season. Pour over the fish and serve.

COLD BOILED SHAD

Boil a cleaned shad in salted and acidulated water or in court-bouillon. Serve very cold with Tartar Sauce.

BOILED SHAD À LA VIRGINIA

Chop together an onion, a carrot, and a stalk of celery. Fry in butter. Cover a prepared shad with boiling salted and acidulated water, and add the cooked vegetables to it. Add also two tablespoonfuls of white wine, a blade of mace, half a dozen peppercorns, two cloves, and a bay-leaf. Simmer slowly until the fish is done, drain, and serve with a Drawn-Butter Sauce, using the strained cooking liquor for liquid.

BOILED SALT SHAD

Soak the fish all day in warm water, changing the water frequently, wipe off the salt, and plunge into ice-water for an hour. Put into a fish-kettle with boiling water to cover, and simmer until done. Season with pepper and serve with plenty of melted butter.

BAKED SHAD—I

Bake a shad in a buttered baking-pan, adding enough boiling water to keep from burning. Baste while baking with melted butter and lemon-juice, seasoning with pepper and salt. Cook together a tablespoonful each of butter and flour until brown. Add slowly a cupful of stock and cook until thick, stirring constantly. Take from the fire and add the yolks of two eggs beaten with the juice of half a lemon. Pour over the fish and serve.

BAKED SHAD—II

Clean a large fish and stuff with seasoned crumbs mixed with minced parsley, adding enough melted butter to make a smooth paste. Score one side of the fish deeply and lay a small strip of salt pork in each gash. Put the fish in a buttered baking-dish, sprinkle with salt, pepper, and flour, and add enough boiling water to keep from burning. Baste as required with the drippings, adding more boiling water if necessary. Serve with Hollandaise Sauce or Drawn-Butter Sauce to which the mashed roe has been added.

BAKED SHAD—III

Stuff a fish with seasoned crumbs made smooth with melted butter. Season the fish with salt and pepper and cover with thin slices of breakfast bacon. Bake until well done, basting with melted butter and hot water. Add a teaspoonful each of lemon-juice and anchovy essence to the gravy remaining in the pan and thicken with flour browned in butter. Serve the sauce separately.

BAKED SHAD—IV

Stuff a large fish with seasoned crumbs, adding chopped onion and melted butter to taste. Sew up the fish and put into a buttered baking-pan with a cupful of salted boiling water and two tablespoonfuls of butter. Dredge with flour, and bake, basting with the drippings. Take up the fish carefully and thicken the gravy with two tablespoonfuls of flour browned in butter and made smooth with a little cold water. Add a cupful of stock or water, the juice of a lemon, and Worcestershire Sauce and kitchen bouquet to season. Strain through a sieve and serve with the fish.

BAKED SHAD—V

Stuff the cleaned fish with seasoned crumbs made very rich with melted butter. Wrap in a large sheet of buttered paper, fastening it securely, and bake in a moderate oven. Remove the paper carefully and serve with any preferred sauce.

BAKED SHAD—VI

Leave the head on. Make a stuffing of bread-crumbs, cold ham or bacon minced fine, sweet marjoram, pepper, salt, mace or ground cloves and a raw egg, or two if necessary, to bind. Put the fish into a deep buttered baking-pan fastening its tail in its mouth; put into the pan enough water to cover, add half a cupful of Port or Claret, and a tablespoonful of butter rolled in flour. Baste frequently with the gravy and bake until done. Pour the gravy over and serve.

BAKED SHAD—VII

Prepare a stuffing of two cupfuls of bread-crumbs, the beaten yolk of an egg, a tablespoonful of powdered sweet herbs, a tablespoonful of chopped onion, a teaspoonful of lemon-juice and salt, pepper, Worcestershire and powdered cloves to season. Stuff and sew up a prepared shad, lay on a buttered baking-pan, cover with slices of salt pork, dredge with flour, season with salt and pepper and bake, basting with hot water and melted butter as required. Serve with Hollandaise Sauce.

BAKED SHAD—VIII

Clean a shad and stuff with seasoned crumbs mixed with beaten eggs. Cover a buttered baking-dish with sliced raw potatoes, lay the shad upon it, add enough stock or water to keep from burning and bake. Serve with any preferred sauce.

BAKED SHAD—IX

Stuff the fish with cracker crumbs, mixed with minced parsley, capers, and lemon-juice, seasoning with salt and pepper, and adding enough melted butter to make a smooth paste. Put the fish in a buttered baking-pan, rub with butter, dredge with flour, and add enough boiling water to keep from burning. Baste every ten minutes with the gravy in the pan and melted butter, dredging lightly after each basting with seasoned flour. Serve with Brown Sauce.

BAKED SHAD—X

Trim and clean a small shad, put it into a buttered baking-dish, seasoning with salt, pepper, minced onion and half a cupful of white wine. Add water or stock, if necessary, to keep from burning. Cover with buttered paper and bake for half an hour. Prepare a cupful of Allemande Sauce and add to it the liquid drained from the fish and a little chopped cooked spinach. Strain over the fish and serve.

SHAD BAKED IN MILK

Clean a large roe shad, saving the roe and removing the back-bone. Soak stale bread in cold water and squeeze dry. Chop a large onion fine and fry in butter. Add the bread, and salt, pepper, parsley, and sage to season. Cook thoroughly, take from the fire and add the yolks of two eggs well beaten. Stuff the fish, sew up, rub with salt and put in a buttered baking-pan with thin slices of salt pork or bacon to cover the top. Fill the pan with sweet milk, leaving only the pork exposed. Bake slowly, basting often. Take up the fish carefully, strain the liquor, thicken with butter and flour, and serve separately. Fry the roe in butter, cut in slices, and garnish the fish with it.

BAKED SHAD À LA VIRGINIA

Clean the fish and stuff with seasoned crumbs made very rich with melted butter. Put in a baking-pan with enough boiling water to keep it from burning, and bake until done, basting with melted butter and the liquid in the pan. Take up the fish carefully and keep warm. Thicken the gravy with a tablespoonful of flour browned in butter, and mix smooth with cold water. Season with catsup, lemon-juice, Sherry or Madeira. Serve the sauce separately.

BAKED SHAD À LA CAROLINA

Clean a large roe shad, leaving the head on, take out the backbone and stuff with the boiled roe chopped, six chopped hard-boiled eggs, half a cupful of bread-crumbs, a chopped onion, a tablespoonful of butter, and salt, pepper, and minced parsley to season. Stuff the fish, sew up and put in a buttered baking-pan, adding enough hot water to keep from burning, three or four slices of bacon, and salt and pepper to season. Baste often and serve with Tartar Sauce.

BAKED SHAD WITH FINE HERBS

Sprinkle a buttered baking-dish with chopped onion and parsley, lay the prepared fish upon it and sprinkle with onion and parsley, seasoning with salt, pepper, and dots of butter. Add half a cupful of white wine and a cupful of white stock. Cover with a buttered paper and bake in a moderate oven. Take up the fish carefully and thicken the gravy with flour cooked in butter. Pour the sauce over the fish, sprinkle with crumbs, dot with butter, and brown in the oven. Squeeze the juice of a lemon over and serve.

BAKED SHAD STUFFED WITH OYSTERS

Rub a large cleaned fish with salt inside and out. Stuff with oysters and seasoned crumbs made very rich with melted butter, and bake, basting with melted butter and hot water. Thicken the gravy with flour browned in butter, adding a little hot water or stock if necessary, season with lemon-juice and catsup and serve the sauce separately.

STUFFED SHAD—I

Make a stuffing of two cupfuls of bread-crumbs, half a cupful of tomatoes, an onion chopped fine, half a cupful of melted butter, and salt and pepper to season. Stuff the fish, sew up, rub with butter, season with salt and pepper, dredge with flour, and bake for an hour, basting often with melted butter and hot water. Serve with Tomato Sauce.

STUFFED SHAD—II

Season a cupful of cracker crumbs with grated onion, minced capers and parsley, add a heaping tablespoonful of butter, and salt and pepper to season. Or, fry a small chopped onion in butter, add a cupful of crumbs, season with salt, pepper and lemon-juice, take from the fire and add the yolk of an egg beaten smooth with a little milk. Stuff the cleaned shad and sew up. Cover the bottom of a baking-dish with thin slices of salt pork, lay the fish upon it, cover with more pork, add enough boiling water to keep from burning, and bake, basting frequently. For the sauce, melt half a cupful of butter and add to it the juice of half a lemon and three tablespoonfuls of Claret. Serve the sauce separately.

STUFFED SHAD—III

Prepare a shad as for boiling and stuff with seasoned crumbs, adding the beaten yolk of an egg to bind. Fill the fish and sew up; put into a baking-pan enough water or stock to keep from burning and two tablespoonfuls of butter. Bake carefully, basting as required. Take up the fish and add to the liquid enough stock to make the required quantity of sauce. Thicken with flour browned in butter, season with lemon-juice, catsup, and Sherry or Madeira. Pour around the fish and serve.

ROASTED SHAD

Marinate the cleaned fish for an hour in oil and lemon-juice, seasoning with salt, pepper, minced parsley, and thyme. Drain, wrap in oiled paper, fastening securely, and bake carefully. Take up the fish and serve with Ravigote Sauce.

TOASTED SHAD

Put into a baking-pan a tablespoonful of butter and lay a cleaned and split shad upon it, skin-side up. Place it under a gas flame until the skin is puffed and blistered. Turn out on a hot platter; season with salt and pepper, dot with butter, and serve garnished with lemon and parsley.

PLANKED SHAD—I

Prepare the fish as for boiling, butter the plank, and tack the fish upon it, skin-side down. Season the fish with salt, pepper, and butter and bake in the oven. Serve on the plank.

PLANKED SHAD—II

Split the shad as for broiling and tack it on a buttered fish plank, skin-side down. Rub with melted butter and cook under a gas flame or in the oven. Season with salt, pepper, and melted butter, surround with a border of mashed potatoes, garnish with lemon and parsley and serve on the plank.

PLANKED SHAD—III

Tack the split fish on a buttered board, flesh-side up. Put into the oven and bake until brown, basting with melted butter seasoned with walnut catsup. Serve with a garnish of pickled walnuts.

PLANKED SHAD—IV

Tack a large split shad skin-side down on a buttered plank. Spread with butter, season with salt and pepper, and pour over a tablespoonful of walnut catsup or white wine. Cook under a gas flame, sprinkle with minced parsley, and serve with any preferred sauce.

PANNED SHAD

Split the fish down the back, remove the backbone, and put into a buttered baking-pan, flesh-side up. Rub with butter, sprinkle with salt and pepper, and bake in the oven. Garnish with lemon and parsley and serve with any preferred sauce.

STEWED SHAD

Prepare and clean a small shad and soak it for two or three hours in a marinade of oil and lemon-juice seasoned with onion and parsley. Put it in a buttered stewpan with half a wineglassful of white wine, three tablespoonfuls of mushroom liquor, four sprigs of parsley, a sprig of celery, a bay-leaf, a sprig of thyme, and two cloves. Add two handfuls of picked and washed sorrel or spinach, chopped fine. Season with salt and pepper and simmer slowly for two hours. Take up the fish, thicken the gravy with butter and flour cooked together, pour over the fish and serve.

PICKLED SHAD—I

Boil a shad in salted water to cover, drain and cool. Add to the water in which it was boiled half as much vinegar and a red pepper pod, whole cloves, allspice, and mace to season. Boil for an hour. Cut the fish into large pieces, put into an earthen jar and pour the boiling spiced liquid over the fish. Cover and let stand for two days before using.

PICKLED SHAD—II

Cut a large shad into pieces, put a layer in the bottom of an earthen crock, sprinkle with salt, and add a few whole cloves, allspice, peppers, and bay-leaves.

Cover with fish, add more spices, and pour on strong vinegar to cover. Cover the dish, bake for four hours in a moderate oven, and let stand for three or four days before using. Serve cold.

CREAMED SHAD

Cook together a tablespoonful each of butter and flour, add two cupfuls of milk and cook until thick, stirring constantly. Add a teaspoonful of grated onion, take from the fire and add the beaten yolks of two eggs, and salt, pepper, and minced parsley to season. Add two cupfuls of cold cooked shad flaked fine, put into a buttered baking-dish, sprinkle with crumbs and brown in the oven.

SHAD VERT-PRÉ

Prepare and clean a small shad and put into a buttered baking-dish with salt and pepper to season, two finely chopped shallots and half a wineglassful of white wine. Cover with buttered paper and bake in a moderate oven. Take up the fish, add the juice to a cupful of Allemande Sauce and tint green with minced parsley and spinach juice. Pour over the fish and serve.

BROILED SHAD ROE—I

Soak two shad roes for twenty minutes in seasoned olive-oil, drain and broil. Serve with Maître d'Hôtel Sauce.

BROILED SHAD ROE—II

Wash and dry the roe and broil on a well-greased broiler, rubbing with butter while broiling. Serve with Maître d'Hôtel Sauce.

BROILED SHAD ROE—III

Parboil a large shad roe, drain, rub with melted butter, and broil. Serve with Maître d'Hôtel Sauce.

BROILED SHAD ROE—IV

Parboil the roe for ten minutes in salted water, drain, and plunge into ice-water for ten minutes. Wipe dry and put on ice for half an hour. Rub with oil and lemon-juice, broil, and serve with Maître d'Hôtel Sauce.

BROILED SHAD ROE—V

Wash a shad's roe in cold water, wipe it dry, rub with butter, and broil. Garnish with lemon and parsley.

BROILED SHAD ROE WITH BACON

Marinate the roe in seasoned oil, broil carefully, surround with slices of broiled bacon, and serve with Maître d'Hôtel Sauce.

FRIED SHAD ROE—I

Sauté in hot lard, turning carefully. Garnish with lemon and parsley.

FRIED SHAD ROE—II

Season the roes with salt and pepper, dredge with flour, dip in beaten egg, then in crumbs, and fry in fat to cover. Drain, and serve with Tomato Sauce.

FRIED SHAD ROE—III

Parboil the roe in salted water, drain, plunge into cold water, and let stand for ten minutes. Drain, wipe dry, cut in half-inch slices, dip in seasoned lemon-juice, then in beaten egg, then in crumbs, and fry in fat to cover.

FRIED SHAD ROE—IV

Parboil the roe, drain, and cool. Dredge with seasoned flour and sauté in butter.

FRIED SHAD ROE—V

Parboil the roe for ten minutes in salted and acidulated water. Drain, plunge into cold water, and cool. Drain, dip in beaten egg, then in seasoned crumbs, and fry brown in deep fat. Serve with any preferred sauce.

FRIED SHAD ROE—VI

Season the roe, dip it in corn-meal and sauté in butter or lard. Or, parboil, cool, season, dip in beaten egg, then in cracker crumbs and sauté in butter or lard.

FRIED SHAD ROE—VII

Parboil the shad roes in salted water to which a slice of lemon and a sprig of parsley have been added. Cool in the liquid, drain, wipe dry, dip in beaten egg, then in cracker crumbs, and fry brown in butter. Take up, strain the cooking liquid into the frying-pan, add a teaspoonful each of Worcestershire and catsup, and bring to the boil. Thicken with a tablespoonful of flour browned in butter and made smooth with a little Sherry or Madeira. Bring to the boil, pour over the roes and serve.

SHAD ROE SAUTÉ

Plunge a large shad roe into boiling water, then into cold water, drain, and sauté until brown in butter. Add a tablespoonful of butter to a cupful of cream, bring to the boil, season with salt and pepper, pour over the fish and serve.

BAKED SHAD ROE—I

Butter a baking-dish and sprinkle thickly with chopped onion, parsley, and mushrooms. Lay the roes upon it, sprinkle with more onion, parsley, and mushrooms, season with salt and pepper and dot with butter. Add half a cupful of white wine and one cupful of white stock. Bake carefully, basting as required. Drain, thicken the gravy with flour cooked in butter, pour over the roes, sprinkle with crumbs, dot with butter, and brown in the oven. Squeeze lemon-juice over and serve.

BAKED SHAD ROE—II

Boil the shad roe slowly until done. Drain and put into a buttered baking-dish. Season with salt and pepper, spread with butter, and dredge thickly with flour. Bake in a moderate oven, basting frequently with melted butter and hot water.

BAKED SHAD ROE—III

Cover the roe from a large shad with boiling water and drain. Put into a buttered baking-pan with two tablespoonfuls of butter, one cupful of stock and salt and paprika to season. Bake slowly until done, strain the liquid and thicken with the yolks of three eggs beaten with one cupful of cream. Pour over the sauce, and serve with thin slices of broiled bacon.

BAKED SHAD ROE—IV

Lay the roe in a buttered baking-pan, season, add a little milk, and bake about fifteen minutes, basting often. Take up, sprinkle with lemon-juice, salt, cayenne, and minced parsley, and pour over a Cream Sauce, to which the yolks of two well-beaten eggs have been added.

BAKED SHAD ROE—V

Butter a baking-dish, put in two shad roes, season with salt and pepper, and add half a cupful of white wine. Bake carefully, basting as required. Chop an onion, two sprigs of parsley, and ten mushrooms. Fry in butter, add the liquid drained from the fish, and thicken with a little flour rubbed smooth in cold water. Spread the paste upon the roe, cover with large fresh mushrooms, sprinkle with crumbs, dot with butter, and brown in the oven. Serve immediately in the same dish.

BAKED SHAD ROE—VI

Butter an earthen dish and sprinkle with chopped onion, parsley, mushrooms, and bread-crumbs. Lay two skinned shad roes upon it, cover with crumbs, mushrooms, minced onion, and parsley, and pour over one cupful of white stock mixed with a tablespoonful of Sherry. Bake for half an hour, drain off the sauce, strain it and thicken with flour and butter, cooked together. Pour over the fish, cover with crumbs, dot with butter, sprinkle with lemon-juice, and brown in the oven.

SHAD ROE BAKED WITH BACON

Cover the bottom of a baking-pan with thin slices of bacon, lay the shad roes upon it, cover with bacon, and bake in a very hot oven. Squeeze lemon-juice over and serve with bacon as a garnish.

SHAD ROE BAKED IN TOMATO SAUCE

Boil the roe, drain, cool, and skin. Cook together for ten minutes one cupful of canned tomatoes, one cupful of stock or water, a slice of onion, and salt and pepper to season. Cook together two tablespoonfuls of butter and one of flour, add the tomato, and cook until thick, stirring constantly. Rub the sauce through a strainer. Put the roe on a buttered baking-dish, season with salt and pepper, cover with the sauce and bake. Serve in the dish in which it was baked.

SHAD ROE BAKED WITH CREAM SAUCE

Brown two tablespoonfuls of flour in butter, add two cupfuls of milk, and cook until thick, stirring constantly. Season with salt and pepper and continue according to directions given for Shad Roe Baked in Tomato Sauce.

ESCALLOPED SHAD ROE—I

Boil the roes in salted and acidulated water, drain, and flake with a fork. Spread a layer of the roe in a shallow buttered baking-dish, sprinkle with chopped hard-boiled eggs, season with minced parsley and lemon-juice, add a thin layer of Cream Sauce and repeat. Cover with buttered crumbs and bake brown.

ESCALLOPED SHAD ROE—II

Prepare according to directions given above, sprinkling crumbs on each layer of Cream Sauce, and adding grated cheese to the crumbs on top.

ESCALLOPED SHAD ROE—III

Boil the roes in salted and acidulated water, plunge into cold water, cool, drain, wipe dry, and mash. Add the chopped yolks of three hard-boiled eggs to a cupful of well seasoned Drawn-Butter Sauce. Mix the sauce with the roes. Butter a baking-dish, sprinkle with seasoned crumbs, add the roe mixture, cover with crumbs, dot with butter, and brown in the oven.

ESCALLOPED SHAD ROE—IV

Parboil in salted water the roes of two shad, drain, plunge into ice-water for ten minutes, drain, wipe dry, and flake with a fork. Add the yolks of three hard-boiled eggs rubbed smooth with a teaspoonful of anchovy paste and the juice of half a lemon. Add also one cupful of bread-crumbs, salt, cayenne, and minced parsley to season, and one cupful of Drawn-Butter Sauce. Butter a baking-pan, sprinkle with crumbs, fill with the mixture, cover with crumbs, dot with butter, and brown in the oven.

SHAD ROE CROQUETTES—I

Boil the roe for fifteen minutes in salted water, drain, and mash. Cook together two tablespoonfuls each of butter and corn-starch, add two cupfuls of hot cream, and cook until thick, stirring constantly. Take from the fire, add the mashed roe, and salt, cayenne, grated nutmeg, and lemon-juice to season. Cool, shape into croquettes, dip in egg and crumbs, and fry in deep fat. Serve with any preferred sauce.

SHAD ROE CROQUETTES—II

Simmer shad roes in salted boiling water for fifteen minutes, drain, and plunge into cold water. When cold, drain, dry, cut into slices two inches thick, season with salt, pepper, and lemon-juice, dip in egg, roll in crumbs, fry in deep fat, and serve with Tartar Sauce.

SHAD ROE CROQUETTES—III

Boil the roe, cool, skin, and mash fine. Cook together one tablespoonful of butter and two of flour, and add one-half cupful of cream and one-half cupful of stock. Cook until thick, stirring constantly. Take from the fire, add the yolks of two well-beaten eggs, and the mashed roe, and cool. Season with salt, pepper, lemon-juice, and minced parsley, shape into croquettes, dip in egg and crumbs, and fry in deep fat. Serve with Hollandaise Sauce.

SHAD ROE CROQUETTES—IV

Parboil two shad roes, drain, cool, skin, and mash. Cook together one tablespoonful of butter and two of flour, add one cupful of boiling cream or milk, and cook until thick, stirring constantly. Take from the fire, add the beaten yolks of two eggs, and minced parsley, lemon-juice, grated nutmeg, salt, pepper, and cayenne to taste. Reheat, stir until thick, add the mashed shad roe, mix thoroughly, and cool. Shape into croquettes, dip in egg and crumbs, fry in deep fat, and serve with Tartar Sauce.

SHAD ROE CROQUETTES—V

Cook the roe in boiling salted and acidulated water for fifteen minutes, drain, and mash. Beat together one-fourth cupful each of corn-starch and butter, add one and one half cupfuls of hot cream, and cook for ten minutes, stirring constantly. Take from the fire, add the juice of half a lemon, a grating of nutmeg, salt and paprika to season, the mashed roe, and a few chopped mushrooms fried. Cool, shape into croquettes, dip in egg and crumbs, and fry in deep fat. Serve with any preferred sauce.

SHAD ROE CROQUETTES—VI

Simmer two shad roes in salted boiling water for fifteen minutes. Take from the fire, drain, skin, and mash. Cook together one tablespoonful of butter and two of flour, add gradually one cupful of boiling cream, and cook until thick, stirring constantly. Take from the fire, add the yolks of two eggs, the mashed roe, one tablespoonful each of lemon-juice and minced parsley, and salt, pepper, cayenne, and grated nutmeg to season. Cool, shape into croquettes, dip in egg and crumbs, and put into the ice-box for an hour. Fry in deep fat and serve with Tartar Sauce.

SHAD ROE CROQUETTES—VII

Boil the roe of a large shad until done, drain, mash, and mix with half a cupful of bread-crumbs, a beaten egg, two tablespoonfuls of melted butter, and salt and paprika to season. Shape into small flat cakes and sauté in melted butter, or dip in egg and crumbs and fry in deep fat. Serve with any preferred sauce.

SHAD ROE CROQUETTES—VIII

Parboil the roes in salted and acidulated water, drain, and plunge into ice-water to cool. Drain and flake with a fork. Cook together two tablespoonfuls each of butter and flour, add a cupful of milk and cook until thick, stirring constantly. Take from the fire, season with salt and pepper, add the mashed roes and two eggs well-beaten. Season with lemon-juice and anchovy paste, reheat, but do not boil. Cool, shape into croquettes, dip in egg and cracker crumbs and let stand for an hour before frying in deep fat.

SHAD ROE À LA BALTIMORE

Put two or three roes into a well-buttered baking-dish, sprinkle with salt and pepper, add a cupful and a half of stock, and two tablespoonfuls of butter. Cover and cook in the oven for fifteen minutes. Take up the roe and add slowly to the liquid the yolks of three eggs beaten smooth with one cupful of cream. Cook over hot water until thick, adding two tablespoonfuls of butter and salt and pepper to season. Pour over the fish, garnish with broiled bacon and serve.

SHAD ROE À LA BROOKE

Parboil two shad roes, drain, cool, and skin. Put into a saucepan, cover with white wine, add a clove, a blade of mace, and salt to season. Simmer for half an hour. Wash and drain two cupfuls of scallops, put into a saucepan and cover with salted boiling water, adding a bit of bay-leaf, four whole allspice, and two cloves. Cover the dish and boil for half an hour. Cook together one tablespoonful each of butter and flour, add a cupful of the water in which the scallops were boiled, and cook until thick, stirring constantly. Season with salt and pepper, add a teaspoonful of minced garlic, and gradually three tablespoonfuls of butter in small bits. Take from the fire and add the yolks of three eggs well-beaten. Put the roe into a serving-dish, cover with the scallops, and freshly grated horseradish. Pour the sauce over, reheat, and serve.

SHAD ROE À LA MAÎTRE D'HÔTEL

Marinate the roes for an hour in oil and lemon-juice, seasoning with salt and pepper. Drain, broil, and serve with a Maître d'Hôtel Sauce to which chopped onion has been added.

SHAD ROE À LA MARYLAND

Put two or three roes in a well-buttered baking-pan, season with salt and pepper, add half a cupful each of stock and Sherry, spread the roe with butter, cover, and bake for fifteen minutes. Take up carefully and thicken the liquid with the yolks of three eggs beaten smooth with a cupful of cream. Take from the fire, add a tablespoonful of butter, pour over the roe, garnish with fried bacon, and serve.

PANNED SHAD ROE

Boil a shad roe for fifteen minutes in salted water, drain, and break up with a fork. Melt two tablespoonfuls of butter, add the shad roe with the yolks of two hard-boiled eggs mashed fine, a small cupful of bread-crumbs, and pepper, salt, and minced parsley to season. Reheat and serve very hot.

SHAD ROES EN BROCHETTE

Parboil shad roes for fifteen minutes, drain, and plunge into cold water. When cool, cut into small pieces and roll in flour. String on slender skewers with alternate squares of bacon cut very thin and broil over a clear fire or cook in the oven until the bacon is crisp. The flour may be omitted. Serve with melted butter or Maître d'Hôtel Sauce.

SHAD ROE KROMESKIES

Parboil a shad roe, drain, cool, skin, and cut into small pieces. Season with salt and pepper, wrap a thin slice of bacon around each piece, and fasten with a toothpick. Fry in deep fat and serve with any preferred sauce.

SHAD ROES WITH BROWN BUTTER SAUCE

Boil the roes slowly in salted and acidulated water, drain, and pour over half a cupful of butter melted and browned, and mixed with a tablespoonful of vinegar.

SHAD ROE WITH MUSHROOMS

Boil a shad roe, flake with a fork, and add an equal quantity of fresh or canned mushrooms cut in small pieces. Cook together a tablespoonful each of butter and flour and add half a cupful of cream mixed with the beaten yolks of two eggs. Mix with the mushrooms and roe. Fill ramekins, sprinkle with crumbs, dot with butter, and brown in the oven.

CREAMED SHAD ROE WITH MUSHROOMS

Parboil a shad roe, plunge into cold water, drain, cool, cut into squares, and sauté in butter until brown. Season with salt and pepper and add half a cupful of cooked mushrooms and one cupful of boiling cream. Thicken with a teaspoonful of flour rubbed smooth with a little cold cream, season with salt and red pepper, and serve very hot.

SHAD ROE WITH EGGS

Boil a shad roe and flake fine with a fork. Beat three eggs, season with salt and pepper, add the roe, and cook in a chafing-dish or frying-pan with plenty of melted butter.

SHAD ROE WITH OYSTERS

Fry the shad roe according to directions previously given and serve with fried oysters and broiled bacon.

SHAD ROE WITH BROWN SAUCE

Soak a shad roe in water for half an hour, scald, drain, cool, and cut in slices. Sauté in butter and drain, Cook a tablespoonful of flour in the butter, add one cupful of stock, and cook until thick, stirring constantly. Season with salt, paprika, Worcestershire, and curry powder; pour over the fish and serve.

SIXTEEN WAYS TO COOK SHEEPSHEAD

BOILED SHEEPSHEAD

Clean and salt the fish and soak in cold water for an hour. Drain, wipe dry, and cut several deep gashes across both sides. Put the fish on the drainer of the fish-kettle, pour the juice of a lemon over it, and cover with equal parts of milk and water. Add salt and pepper and minced parsley to season and simmer gently until the fish is done. Drain carefully and serve the sauce separately, thickening if desired.

BOILED SHEEPSHEAD WITH OYSTER SAUCE

Boil a prepared and cleaned fish in salted and acidulated water with a bunch of parsley, a sliced onion, and some sweet herbs. Drain, garnish with parsley, and serve with a Holandaise Sauce to which cooked oysters have been added.

BROILED SHEEPSHEAD

Prepare and clean a large sheepshead, score the sides deeply, and broil, seasoning with salt and pepper, and basting with oil. Melt half a cupful of butter and add to it the juice of a lemon and two tablespoonfuls of anchovy essence. Pour over the fish and serve.

FRIED FILLETS OF SHEEPSHEAD

Prepare and clean the fish and cut in fillets. Dip into salted milk, then in flour, then in beaten egg, then in seasoned crumbs, and fry in deep fat. Serve with any preferred sauce.

SHEEPSHEAD WITH CAPER SAUCE

Boil according to directions previously given and serve with Caper Sauce.

SHEEPSHEAD WITH DRAWN BUTTER

Clean a medium sized fish, rub with salt and pepper, steam for an hour, take up carefully, garnish with parsley and lemon, and serve with Drawn-Butter Sauce.

SHEEPSHEAD WITH PARSLEY SAUCE

Cook the prepared and cleaned fish in salted and acidulated water to cover, drain, and serve with Parsley Sauce.

SHEEP SHEAD À LA BAHAMA

Prepare and clean a large sheepshead and remove the fins. Score deeply to the bone on both sides and put into a buttered fish-pan with a chopped onion, a small bunch of parsley, four sliced tomatoes, and four chopped chilli peppers. Add salt and pepper to season, one cupful of Catawba wine, and enough white stock to cover. Cover with a buttered paper and boil until done. Drain, strain the liquid through a coarse sieve, and add enough stock to make the required quantity of sauce. Thicken with flour cooked in butter, take from the fire, add two tablespoonfuls of butter, a teaspoonful of minced parsley, and the juice of half a lemon. Cover the fish with broiled tomatoes, pour the sauce around, and serve.

SHEEPSHEAD À LA BIRMINGHAM

Prepare and clean a large sheepshead and put into a buttered fish-pan with four tablespoonfuls of butter, a bunch of parsley, a shredded green pepper, a chopped onion, six peeled and sliced tomatoes, two cupfuls each of white wine and water, and salt and paprika to season. Simmer until the fish is done, drain, and keep warm. Strain the liquid and thicken with flour browned in butter. Pour over the fish and serve with rice and baked green peppers.

SHEEPSHEAD À LA CAROLINE

Clean a sheepshead, cut off the fins and score to the bone on each side. Put into a buttered baking-pan with two tablespoonfuls of butter, a bunch of parsley, a small chopped onion, a shredded green pepper, and salt and pepper to season. Add one cupful of white wine and two cupfuls of water or white stock. Cover with buttered paper and bake in a moderate oven, basting often with the liquid. Take up the fish, strain the liquid, thicken with flour cooked in butter, take from the fire, add two tablespoonfuls of butter, the juice of a lemon and a teaspoonful of minced parsley. Pour over the fish and serve.

SHEEPSHEAD À LA CRÉOLE

Chop together an onion, a green pepper, a tomato, four mushrooms, a clove of garlic and a bunch of sweet herbs. Fry in olive-oil, add a tablespoonful of flour and cook until the flour is brown. Add one cupful of beef stock and cook until thick, stirring constantly. Put six slices of sheepshead into a buttered baking-pan, spread with the sauce, and bake slowly for an hour.

SHEEPSHEAD À LA HOLLANDAISE

Prepare and clean a sheepshead, cover with salted and acidulated water, and simmer until done. Drain and serve with Hollandaise Sauce.

SHEEP SHEAD À L'INDIENNE

Cook a large sheepshead in a fish-boiler with two cupfuls each of water and white wine, two tablespoonfuls of butter, two chopped onions, a chopped green pepper, a bunch of parsley, and salt, pepper, and sweet herbs to season. Cover with buttered paper, boil until done and drain. Cook three tablespoonfuls of butter with two tablespoonfuls each of flour and curry powder, add the liquid drained from the fish, and enough stock to make the required quantity of sauce. Cook until thick, stirring constantly, and skim off the fat. Add two tablespoonfuls each of butter and chutney sauce, take from the fire, add the juice of a lemon, pour over the fish, and serve with plain boiled rice.

SHEEPSHEAD À LA LOUISIANNE

Prepare and clean a large sheepshead and put into a buttered baking-dish with two sliced onions, a chopped green pepper, a cupful of stewed and strained tomatoes, two cupfuls of white wine, a bunch of parsley, a tablespoonful of butter, and salt and white pepper to season. Cover with buttered paper and bake for forty minutes, basting as necessary. When done, drain the fish and keep it warm. Strain the liquid and add enough brown stock to make the required quantity of sauce. Thicken with flour browned in butter, add the juice of a lemon and a little minced parsley. Pour over the fish and serve with a border of plain boiled rice.

SHEEPSHEAD À LA MAJESTIC

Butter a baking-pan and line it with sliced onions and tomatoes, sprinkled with salt, pepper, and minced parsley. Lay upon it a cleaned sheepshead weighing three pounds. Sprinkle with salt, pepper, and flour, and add enough stock and white wine to keep from burning. Baste as required and serve with the onions and tomatoes around the platter.

SHEEPSHEAD À LA MOBILE

Prepare and clean a large fish and cut it into thin slices. Put into a buttered saucepan with half a dozen sliced tomatoes, two sliced onions, a bunch of parsley, two bruised beans of garlic, and salt, paprika, and sweet herbs to season. Add equal parts of Claret and white stock to cover. Cover with buttered paper, bring to the boil, and simmer for forty minutes. Drain, strain the sauce, thicken with flour browned in butter, take from the fire, add a tablespoonful of butter and the juice of a lemon, pour over the fish and serve.

NINE WAYS TO COOK SKATE

FRIED SKATE

Prepare and clean the fish and cut into suitable pieces for serving. Dip in flour, then in egg, then in crumbs, and fry in deep fat. Serve with any preferred sauce.

BOILED SKATE

Prepare and clean a small skate and cut into convenient pieces for serving. Put into a kettle an onion and a carrot sliced, a bunch of parsley, a sprig of thyme, two bay-leaves, a tablespoonful each of salt and pepper-corns, and half a cupful of vinegar. Put the fish on this, add cold water to cover, and boil slowly for forty-five minutes. Drain and serve with any preferred sauce.

BOILED SKATE WITH BLACK BUTTER

Boil the skate until tender in salted and acidulated water to cover, with onion, thyme, parsley, bay-leaves, and pepper to season. Drain the fish and pour over half a cupful of browned butter to which a tablespoonful of vinegar has been added.

BOILED SKATE WITH CAPER SAUCE

Cook the fish in salted and acidulated water to cover, adding a sliced onion, two bay-leaves, and a bunch of parsley to the water, with salt and pepper to season. Drain, place on a hot dish, and serve with Caper Sauce.

BOILED SKATE WITH OYSTER SAUCE

Boil the fish in salted and acidulated water to cover, drain, and serve with Oyster Sauce.

BAKED SKATE

Skin the fish and cut into suitable pieces for serving. Put into a buttered saucepan with the juice of half a lemon and a bunch of sweet herbs. Sprinkle with salt and pepper, dredge with flour, and pour in two cupfuls of milk. When nearly tender, drain, brown in the oven, thicken the sauce with butter and flour cooked together, pour around the fish and serve.

SKATE WITH FINE HERBS

Butter a baking-dish and put into it pieces of prepared skate. Sprinkle with chopped mushrooms, onion, and parsley, season with salt and pepper, add two wineglassfuls of Sherry and half a cupful of stock. Sprinkle with crumbs and bake. Take up the fish carefully and add to the liquid enough brown stock to make the required quantity of sauce. Thicken with butter and flour cooked together, add a tablespoonful of butter, a teaspoonful of anchovy essence, and the juice of half a lemon. Pour around the fish and serve.

SKATE À L'ITALIENNE

Put the prepared fish into a buttered saucepan with a bean of garlic, one bay-leaf, two sprigs of thyme, a tablespoonful of butter, three cloves, and salt and pepper to season. Sprinkle with flour, cover the fish with milk, and simmer gently until done, then drain. Put into a serving-dish, sprinkle with grated cheese, and garnish with boiled button onions and triangles of fried bread. Strain the sauce over and serve.

SKATE À LA ROYALE

Parboil small pieces of skate, drain, cool, and marinate in oil and vinegar, seasoning with salt and pepper. Drain, dip in batter, and fry. Serve with any preferred sauce.

THIRTY-FIVE WAYS TO COOK SMELTS

BROILED SMELTS—I

Dip prepared smelts in lemon-juice and seasoned melted butter, then in flour; broil in a double-broiler, and serve with Remoulade Sauce.

BROILED SMELTS—II

Draw and clean large smelts, dip in oil, season with salt and pepper, and broil on a double-broiler. Serve with Maître d'Hôtel Sauce.

BROILED SMELTS—III

Split and bone large smelts, rub with seasoned oil, and broil. Serve with Bearnaise Sauce.

BROILED SMELTS—IV

Soak the prepared fish for an hour in seasoned olive-oil, drain, broil carefully, and serve with Maître d'Hôtel Sauce.

BROILED SMELTS—V

Take off the heads, split the fish, remove the back-bone, and broil for five minutes on a buttered broiler. Garnish with lemon and parsley and serve with melted butter, made very hot with red pepper.

BROILED BONED SMELTS À LA BEARNAISE

Split a dozen good-sized smelts, take out the back-bone, rub with seasoned oil, and broil on a double-broiler. Pour Bearnaise Sauce into the platter, lay the smelts upon it, and serve.

BROILED SMELTS WITH ONION SAUCE

Clean six or seven large smelts, dip in beaten egg, then into seasoned crumbs, and string on skewers by the heads. Broil, basting with melted butter as required. Fry two teaspoonfuls of chopped onion in butter, but do not brown. Take from the fire, add a teaspoonful of vinegar, and an equal quantity of minced parsley. Pour into a bowl and put on ice until cool. When ready to serve, mix a tablespoonful and a half of fresh butter with the sauce and make it into small balls. Serve one ball of the butter with each fish.

BAKED SMELTS—I

Remove the heads, split, dip in melted butter, then in flour. Put into a buttered baking-pan, bake for ten minutes, sprinkle with cayenne and lemon-juice, and serve.

BAKED SMELTS—II

Put prepared smelts into a buttered baking-dish, sprinkle with chopped parsley and mushrooms, and salt, pepper, and grated nutmeg to season. Pour over half a cupful of white wine, cover with a Cream Sauce, sprinkle with crumbs, dot with butter, and bake in the oven. Squeeze lemon-juice over and serve in the baking-dish.

BAKED SMELTS—III

Clean eighteen or twenty smelts and put into a baking-dish with one tablespoonful each of chopped onion and celery, a wineglassful of white wine, and salt and pepper to season. Cover with large fresh mushrooms and a cupful of Spanish Sauce. Sprinkle with crumbs, dot with butter, and bake in a hot oven. Sprinkle with parsley, squeeze lemon-juice over, and serve.

BAKED SMELTS À LA DUXELLES

Put a dozen cleaned and prepared smelts into a buttered baking-dish and sprinkle with chopped onion, parsley, mushrooms, salt, pepper, and grated nutmeg, cover with Drawn-Butter Sauce to which a wineglassful of white wine has been added. Sprinkle with crumbs, dot with butter, and bake for thirty minutes. Squeeze lemon-juice over and serve.

BAKED SMELTS À LA MANTON

Prepare according to directions given for Baked Smelts a la Duxelles, omitting the chopped onion and the wine from the sauce. Sprinkle with crumbs and grated Parmesan cheese, dot with butter, and brown in the oven. Squeeze the juice of a lemon over and serve.

FRIED SMELTS—I

Dip the prepared fish into seasoned, melted butter, then into corn-meal, and fry in deep fat. Or, dip in beaten egg and corn-meal.

FRIED SMELTS—II

Clean the fish, season with salt and pepper, and sauté in hot fat. Or, dip in egg and crumbs and fry in deep fat.

FRIED SMELTS—III

Dredge the cleaned fish with flour, dip in egg and crumbs, and sauté in a frying-pan with butter, or fry in deep fat.

FRIED SMELTS—IV

Dip the cleaned smelts in cream, then in seasoned flour, and fry in fat to cover. Serve with Tartar Sauce.

FRIED SMELTS—V

Clean small smelts, season with salt and pepper, dip in egg and crumbs, and string on skewers, piercing the head with a skewer. Fry in deep fat and serve with Mayonnaise or Tartar Sauce.

FRIED SMELTS—VI

Clean the smelts, trim off the tails, and remove the back-bone. Sprinkle with salt and pepper inside and out and skewer into circles with tooth-picks. Dip in egg and crumbs, fry in deep fat, and serve with Tartar Sauce.

FRIED SMELTS À L'ANGLAISE

Dip the cleaned fish into cracker crumbs, then in beaten eggs, then in cracker crumbs, and fry brown in deep fat. Serve with Tartar Sauce.

FRIED SMELTS AU BEURRE NOIR

Clean the smelts, season with salt and pepper, dip in corn-meal, then in beaten egg and crumbs, and fry in deep fat. Drain and serve with Brown Butter Sauce. If desired, the fish may be skewered in circles before frying.

FRIED SMELTS À LA PARISIENNE

Wash the smelts, remove the bone, wipe dry, dredge with flour, put their tails in their mouths, fasten with a tooth-pick, and fry in very hot fat. Garnish with hard-boiled eggs and serve with Tartar Sauce.

FRIED SMELTS WITH SALT PORK

Clean the smelts, leaving them whole. Dip into fine crumbs or corn-meal. Cut half a pound of fat salt pork into dice, and fry until crisp. Take up the pork, fry the fish in the fat, and drain on brown paper. Make a Cream Sauce, using the pork fat instead of butter, add to it the diced pork, pour around the fish and serve.

STUFFED SMELTS—I

Stuff the cleaned fish with bread-crumbs mixed with tomato and melted butter, seasoning with salt and pepper. Bake in a buttered pan and serve with any preferred sauce.

STUFFED SMELTS—II

Stuff cleaned smelts with chopped oysters and seasoned crumbs. Roll in melted butter, then in crumbs, and bake for fifteen minutes, basting with melted butter; the breading may be omitted if a more simple dish is desired. Serve with Bearnaise Sauce.

STUFFED SMELTS—III

Cook to a paste one cupful of crumbs and one cupful of milk. Beat smooth, add one egg well-beaten, a teaspoonful each of minced parsley, lemon-juice, and chopped olives, and one cupful of chopped oysters. Stuff large smelts, lay them in a pan lined with buttered paper, skewer the head and tail together, and fill the circles with stuffing. Steam for fifteen minutes or sprinkle with crumbs and butter and bake.

STUFFED SMELTS À L'ITALIENNE

Prepare, clean, and split the smelts, stuff with seasoned crumbs, and arrange in a buttered baking-dish, cover with Italian Sauce, and bake. Squeeze lemon-juice over and serve. Chopped oysters or cooked fish may be used with, or instead of, the crumbs.

STUFFED SMELTS AU GRATIN

Chop half a pound of raw fish, either sea-bass or salmon, and pound in a mortar to make very fine. Add two tablespoonfuls of bread-crumbs which have been soaked in hot milk and squeezed dry. Add the yolks of two eggs and the white of one, two tablespoonfuls of cream, and salt and pepper to season. Rub until very smooth and fold in lastly two tablespoonfuls of whipped cream. Let cool thoroughly.

Fry two tablespoonfuls of chopped onion in butter with two tablespoonfuls of minced parsley and a quarter of a pound of chopped fresh mushrooms. Season with salt and pepper and set aside. Stuff the smelts with the fish paste. Butter a silver platter and spread it thinly with the fried onions and mushrooms. Add two tablespoonfuls of white wine and lay the fish upon it. Sprinkle with salt and pepper, spread with the rest of the onion and mushrooms, cover with crumbs, dot with butter, and brown in the oven. Serve in the Same dish.

SMELTS AU GRATIN

Clean and dry eighteen smelts. Fry together in butter a chopped onion, two shallots, twice the quantity of mushrooms, a minced bean of garlic, and a tablespoonful of minced parsley. Butter a baking-dish, spread the cooked vegetables upon it, and lay upon it the prepared fish. Season with salt and pepper, moisten with half a glassful of white wine, cover with large fresh mushrooms, pour over a cupful of Spanish Sauce, sprinkle with crumbs, dot with butter, and bake in the oven. Sprinkle with lemon-juice and minced parsley and serve. The smelts may be boned if desired.

SMELTS AU BEURRE NOIR

Roll the cleaned smelts in flour, sauté in butter, and arrange on fingers of buttered toast. Brown half a cupful of butter, add a tablespoonful of vinegar, pour over the fish, and serve.

SMELTS À LA BOULANGER

Clean and dry the fish, dip into cream, then into flour, and fry in deep fat.

SMELTS À LA DAVIS

Prepare and clean the fish, remove the bone, dip in milk, season with salt and pepper, dip in flour, and brown in butter. Melt two tablespoonfuls of peanut butter, add to it the juice of a lemon, pour over the fish and serve, garnishing with lemon and parsley.

SMELTS À LA TOULOUSE

Clean and bone a dozen large smelts. Cook in a saucepan with white wine and mushroom liquor or stock, seasoning with salt and pepper. Drain, and add the remaining liquid to a cupful of Allemande Sauce. Add a few button mushrooms and a tablespoonful of butter to the sauce. Pour over the smelts and serve.

SMELTS À LA DRESDEN

Clean and remove the bone from large smelts and stuff them with seasoned crumbs, chopped oysters, and mushrooms rubbed to a paste with melted butter. Butter a serving-dish, lay the prepared fish upon it, cover with chopped onion, and squeeze over the juice of a lemon. Add a tablespoonful of butter and a cupful of white stock and bake half an hour. Serve with any preferred sauce.

BOILED SMELTS

Cook smelts in salted and acidulated water, or in court bouillon, drain and serve with Tartar Sauce.

SMELTS WITH MAYONNAISE

Dip the cleaned fish into beaten egg, then into crumbs, and fry in deep fat. Serve cold with Mayonnaise.

STEWED SMELTS

Clean the fish and remove the heads. Put into a buttered china baking-dish. Add enough fish or veal stock to cover, and chopped onions, capers, parsley, thyme, pepper and salt, and white wine to season. Bring to the boil, pour over the fish and bake for ten or fifteen minutes. Serve in the same dish.

SMELTS WITH FINE HERBS

Chop together chives and parsley, and sprinkle a buttered baking-dish. Season with salt and pepper, lay prepared smelts upon it, sprinkle with chopped onions and seasoning, add half a cupful of white wine, cover with buttered paper and bake for ten minutes. Take up carefully, thicken the liquid with butter and flour cooked together, and serve with the fish.

SMELT CROQUETTES

Clean and split smelts and remove the backbone. Pound fine a pound of cooked halibut, seasoning with salt, white pepper, and Sherry. Add enough very thick Cream Sauce to make a stiff paste, and cool. Shape into croquettes and roll a smelt around each one, fastening it by sticking the tail through the head. Dip in egg and crumbs and fry in hot lard to cover. Serve with Tartar Sauce.

SMELTS IN MATELOTE

Chop together an onion, a sprig of parsley, three mushrooms, and a bean of garlic. Fry in oil and season with salt and pepper. Put the cleaned smelts into the pan, add enough white wine to cover, and simmer until done. Strain the liquid, thicken it with butter and flour cooked together, pour over the fish, and serve with a garnish of lemon and parsley.

FIFTY-FIVE WAYS TO COOK SOLES

NOTE:—If the imported sole is not readily obtainable, flounder or pompano makes a very acceptable substitute.

BOILED SOLES

Trim the soles, rub with lemon-juice and boil in salted water. Drain, and serve with any preferred sauce.

BROILED SOLE—I

Marinate for an hour in oil and lemon-juice seasoned with salt and pepper. Broil on a double-broiler and serve with Maître d'Hôtel Sauce.

BROILED SOLE—II

Clean and skin a sole, dip in melted butter and lemon-juice, then in seasoned crumbs, and broil. Remove the bone from an anchovy and rub it to a paste with a small lump of butter. Add a wineglassful of white wine and the juice of half a lemon and keep the sauce warm. Place the sole on a hot dish, pour the sauce over and serve.

BAKED FILLETS OF SOLE—I

Butter a baking-pan, sprinkle with chopped onions and parsley, lay fillets of sole upon it, spread with butter, season with salt and pepper, add a wineglassful of white wine, and bake in the oven, basting frequently. Take up the fish carefully, add to the liquid a dozen chopped mushrooms, a tablespoonful of fresh bread-crumbs and minced parsley to season. Lay the fillets on a baking-dish, spread with the paste, cover with large fresh mushrooms, sprinkle with crumbs, dot with butter, and brown in the oven. Serve very hot in the same dish.

BAKED FILLETS OF SOLE—II

Put the prepared fillets in a buttered baking-dish, sprinkling with chopped onion, parsley, and mushrooms, and seasoning with salt and pepper. Add a tablespoonful of butter and enough white wine and white stock in equal parts to keep from burning. Bake, basting frequently. Cook together one tablespoonful each of butter and flour, add a cupful of brown stock and cook until thick, stirring constantly. Take up the fish, drain the liquor from the pan into the sauce, and reheat. Spread the sauce over the fish, sprinkle with crumbs, dot with butter, and brown in the oven.

FILLETS OF SOLE BAKED IN WHITE WINE

Butter a baking-dish and put into it six fillets of sole. Add half a cupful of hot water and a tablespoonful of lemon-juice. Cook together one tablespoonful each of butter and flour, seasoning with minced parsley, grated onion, salt, cayenne, and powdered mace. Add one cupful of white wine and cook until thick, stirring constantly. Drain the fish, pour the sauce over, and serve.

BAKED SOLE WITH WINE SAUCE

Clean a large sole, trimming off the gills and dark skin and scraping the white side. Make a deep cut on each side of the back-bone and take off the fins. Put into a buttered baking-pan with salt and pepper to season and two cupfuls of white wine. Bake for twenty minutes. Cook together one tablespoonful of butter and two of flour, add a cupful of cold water and cook until thick, stirring constantly. Strain the liquor from the fish into the sauce, bring to the boil, add one tablespoonful each of butter and minced parsley, pour over the fish and serve.

FRIED SOLE—I

Remove the skin, dip in beaten egg, then in crumbs, and fry in deep fat. Serve with any preferred sauce.

FRIED SOLE—II

Skin and clean a pair of soles and marinate for an hour in oil and lemon-juice. Dip in egg and crumbs and fry in deep fat. Cool, trim, dip into melted butter, then into the beaten yolks of eggs, then into seasoned crumbs. Sprinkle with grated Parmesan cheese and broil slowly, basting with melted butter if needed. Serve with Maître d'Hôtel Sauce.

FRIED FILLETS OF SOLE—I

Marinate a sole for an hour in white wine, seasoned with salt, pepper, and sweet herbs. Drain, cut into fillets, dip in milk, dredge with flour, and fry in hot lard.

FRIED FILLETS OF SOLE—II

Sprinkle the prepared fillets with salt, pepper, and lemon-juice, dip in egg and crumbs, repeat, fry in fat to cover, and serve with Tartar Sauce.

FRIED FILLETS OF SOLE À L'ORLY

Soak the prepared fillets for an hour in lemon-juice seasoned with grated onion, minced parsley, salt and pepper. Drain, dry, dredge with flour or dip in batter. Fry in deep fat and serve with Tomato Sauce.

FRIED SOLE À L'ANGLAISE

Dredge the prepared fish with flour, brush with the beaten yolk of an egg, cover with crumbs, and fry in deep fat.

FRIED SOLE À LA COLBERT—I

Cut the fish into fillets, dip in milk, then in flour, and fry brown. Serve with melted butter and garnish with lemon and parsley.

FRIED SOLE À LA COLBERT—II

Select six small soles, cut off their heads, and make an incision down the back-bone. Season with salt, pepper, and lemon-juice, dip in egg and crumbs, fry in hot fat, drain, and serve with Colbert Sauce.

FRIED SOLES WITH SHRIMP SAUCE

Fillet the fish, dip in flour, then into egg and crumbs, fry in deep fat, and serve with Shrimp Sauce.

SOLE À L'AURORE

Butter a shallow platter, lay a sole upon it, cover with buttered paper and put into the oven for ten minutes. Take it out and remove the back-bone, filling its place with chopped onions and parsley. Replace the upper side of the fish, cover with a cupful of Cream Sauce and put in the oven for ten or fifteen minutes. Rub the yolks of hard-boiled eggs through a sieve over the fish, and garnish with the whites in rings, sliced lemon, and parsley.

FILLETS OF SOLE À LA BERCY

Cook some fillets of sole in butter, seasoning with salt, pepper, and minced onion. Take up the fish, add two tablespoonfuls of butter, a teaspoonful of minced parsley, and the juice of a lemon. Pour over the fish and serve.

FILLETS OF SOLE À LA BORDEAUX

Season the prepared fillets with salt and pepper, dip in melted butter, then into flour, then into beaten eggs, then into bread-crumbs. Fry brown in deep fat, garnish with lemon and parsley, and serve with Tomato Sauce.

SOLES À LA COLBERT

Skin and trim the soles and boil in salted water until done. Chop fine a head of endive and fry it in butter. Add two cupfuls of stock, bring to the boil, take from the fire, and add the yolk of an egg beaten smooth with a little cream. Place the soles on a hot dish, pour over the sauce, and serve.

FILLETS OF SOLE À LA CRÈME

Simmer the prepared fillets in salted and acidulated water to cover, seasoning with salt and pepper, sliced onion, cloves, and parsley. Cook together a tablespoonful each of butter and flour and add one cupful of cream and half a cupful of stock. Cook until thick, stirring constantly. Take from the fire, season with salt and pepper, and add the yolks of two eggs beaten smooth with a teaspoonful of lemon-juice and a tablespoonful of melted butter. Pour the sauce over the fillets and serve.

SOLE À LA DIEPPOISE

Butter a baking-dish, sprinkle with chopped shallot, and lay upon it the fillets of three soles. Add half a wineglassful of white wine and three tablespoonfuls of mushroom liquor. Cook for six minutes, take up, and reduce the liquid half by rapid boiling. Add to it one cupful of Allemande Sauce, a dozen cooked mussels or oysters, and half a dozen small cooked mushrooms. Take from the fire, add a tablespoonful of butter and the juice of half a lemon. Pour over the fish and serve.

FILLETS OF SOLE À LA FRANÇAISE

Fry the fillets with a chopped onion and a tablespoonful of chopped parsley in seasoned butter. Serve with Italian Sauce.

FILLETS OF SOLE À L'ITALIENNE

Arrange the prepared fillets in a buttered saucepan, with salt, pepper, chopped onion, and half a cupful of white wine. Cook for ten minutes and drain carefully, reserving the liquid. Add four tablespoonfuls of chopped mushrooms, and two cupfuls of Spanish Sauce. Add a tablespoonful of butter, a teaspoonful of minced parsley, and the juice of half a lemon. Pour over the fish and serve.

FILLETS OF SOLE À LA JOINVILLE

Season the prepared fillets with salt, pepper, and grated nutmeg, and put into a buttered baking-pan with a tablespoonful of butter and half a cupful of white wine. Cover, cook for ten minutes, and drain, reserving the liquid. Arrange on a serving-dish and cover with cooked mushrooms, oysters, and lobster. Cook together two tablespoonfuls each of butter and flour, add the fish gravy and two cupfuls of white stock, and cook until thick, stirring constantly. Take from the fire, add the yolks of four eggs beaten with the juice of half a lemon, two tablespoonfuls of butter, a pinch of red pepper, and enough pounded lobster coral to tint. Pour the sauce over the fish and serve.

FILLETS OF SOLE À LA JOINVILLE—II

Butter a flat baking-dish and arrange in it, crown-shaped, the prepared and cleaned fillets of three soles. Add half a wineglassful of white wine, three tablespoonfuls of mushroom liquor, and salt and pepper to season. Cook for six minutes, take up the fish, and put on a hot dish. Cover with Allemande Sauce, garnish with broiled mushrooms and serve.

SOLE À LA MAÎTRE D'HÔTEL

Simmer fillets of sole for six minutes in salted and acidulated water to cover. Drain and serve with Maître d'Hôtel Sauce.

FILLETS OF SOLE À LA MAÎTRE D'HÔTEL

Put the fillets into a buttered baking-tin, sprinkle with salt and lemon-juice, cover with buttered paper, and cook in a hot oven for six minutes. Put the bones and trimmings of the fish into a saucepan with cold water to cover and simmer slowly. Cook together one tablespoonful of butter and two of flour, add the strained fish stock, and cook until thick, stirring constantly. Add one-fourth cupful of cream, reheat, take from the fire, add a tablespoonful of minced parsley, a dash of lemon-juice, and salt and pepper to season. Arrange the fillets on a hot platter, drain the liquid from the pan into the sauce, pour over the fish, and serve.

FILLETS OF SOLE À LA MARÉCHALE

Season the prepared fillets with salt, pepper, and lemon-juice, and cover with a thin coating of Béchamel Sauce. Put on ice for an hour, dip in crumbs, then in beaten egg, then in crumbs, and sauté in clarified butter, drain, and serve with Béchamel Sauce.

SOLE À LA NORMANDY—I

Make a stuffing of bread-crumbs, sweet herbs, oysters, mushrooms, truffles, and a quarter of a pound of ham, all chopped very fine and mixed to a paste with stock. Stuff the fish with this, sprinkle with lemon-juice, dot with butter, sprinkle with crumbs, minced parsley, and salt and pepper to season. Add half a cupful of white stock and bake slowly, basting frequently and adding more stock if required.

SOLE À LA NORMANDY—II

Butter a baking-dish and cover with sliced onions, parboiled. Lay the sale upon them, seasoning with salt, pepper, grated nutmeg, and minced parsley. Add the juice of a lemon and white wine to cover. Bake in a slow oven, basting with the gravy, and adding melted butter if necessary. Serve with a sauce made by adding half a cupful of cream to the gravy and thickening with a tablespoonful each of butter and flour cooked together.

SOLE À LA NORMANDY—III

Put the fillets from three soles in a buttered saucepan with half a wineglassful of white wine, three tablespoonfuls of mushroom liquor, and salt and pepper to season. Cover and cook for six minutes, drain, and arrange on a serving-dish. Boil the gravy for five minutes, add a cupful of Allemande Sauce, a dozen oysters, and six sliced mushrooms. Take from the fire, add a tablespoonful of butter and the juice of half a lemon, pour over the fish, and serve.

SOLE À LA NORMANDY—IV

Butter a baking-dish and put the fish into it with two dozen oysters, a dozen mussels, a chopped onion, a sprig each of thyme and parsley, a tablespoonful of butter, and salt and pepper to season. Add one cupful each of red wine and stock, cover, and cook until nearly done. Drain and keep warm, lay the oysters and mussels over the sole. Add to the liquid enough stock to make the required quantity of sauce, strain, and thicken with flour cooked in butter. Take from the fire, add the beaten yolks of two eggs, pour over the fish, and serve.

FILLETS OF SOLE À LA NORMANDY

Put the fillets in a buttered saucepan with salt and pepper to season, a tablespoonful of butter, a chopped onion, and half a cupful of white wine. Cover and cook for ten minutes, then take up the fish and drain carefully. Cook together without browning, two tablespoonfuls each of butter and flour, add the liquid drained from the pan and enough oyster liquor and white stock to make three cupfuls of sauce. Cook until thick, stirring constantly, skim, take from the fire, and add the yolks of four eggs well-beaten, two tablespoonfuls of butter in small bits, the juice of half a lemon, and a few cooked oysters, mussels, and scallops cut fine. Pour the sauce over and serve.

FILLETS OF SOLE À L'ORLY

Marinate the prepared fillets for half an hour in lemon-juice with pepper and salt to season. Put the trimmings of the fish into a saucepan with a bunch of sweet herbs and white wine to cover. Season with salt and pepper, boil rapidly for fifteen minutes and strain. Dredge the fillets with flour, fry in boiling fat, and serve the sauce separately.

FILLETS OF SOLE À LA PROVENCE

Simmer the fillets in white wine to which a little olive-oil has been added, seasoning with minced parsley and garlic, grated nutmeg, salt, and pepper. Drain, sprinkle with lemon-juice, and serve with a border of fried onions.

FILLETS OF SOLE À LA ROUEN

Put the prepared fillets into a buttered baking-pan and squeeze lemon-juice over them. Cover with buttered paper and bake. Cook together one tablespoonful each of butter and flour, add one cupful of fish stock and half a cupful of cream, and cook until thick, stirring constantly. Season with salt, paprika, and lemon-juice. Pour over the fish and serve.

FILLETS OF SOLE À LA TROUVILLE

Put the prepared fillets into a buttered pan with salt, pepper, grated nutmeg, half a cupful of white wine, and half a cupful of stock. Cover and cook quickly, then drain the fish and keep warm. Put into the pan in which the fish was cooked two dozen large oysters, two cupfuls of scallops, and a dozen large mushrooms. Simmer slowly until cooked, drain, and cover the fish with them. Add stock if necessary to make the required quantity of sauce, and thicken with two tablespoonfuls each of butter and flour cooked together. Pour the sauce over, sprinkle with crumbs, dot with butter, and brown in the oven.

FILLETS OF SOLE À LA VÉNITIENNE—I

Put the prepared fillets into a buttered pan with salt, pepper, nutmeg, a chopped onion, and half a cupful of white wine. Cover and cook for ten minutes. Add two cupfuls of stock and thicken with a tablespoonful each of butter and flour cooked together. Take from the fire, add the yolks of four eggs beaten with the juice of half a lemon, and two tablespoonfuls of butter. Pour the sauce over the fish, sprinkle with chopped parsley, and serve.

FILLETS OF SOLE À LA VÉNITIENNE—II

Simmer the fillets for ten minutes in a saucepan with clarified butter, lemon-juice, white pepper, and salt. Simmer other fillets without trimming in the same manner. Drain and cool. Cut the untrimmed fillets into dice, mix with thick Allemande Sauce, grated Parmesan cheese, and salt, white pepper, and grated nutmeg to season. Spread this preparation very thinly on an earthen dish, and when it is cool cut into pieces the size and shape of the fillets; dip in crumbs, then in egg, then in crumbs, and fry in fat to cover. Warm the fillets and arrange in a circle alternately with the breaded ones. Serve with any preferred sauce.

SOLE AU GRATIN—I

Make a paste of bread-crumbs and chopped mushrooms, seasoning with pepper, salt, and minced parsley, and using cream for the liquid. Butter a serving-dish, spread with a layer of the paste, lay the fish upon it, and pour over it a wineglassful of white wine and an equal quantity of veal or chicken stock. Cover with crumbs, dot with butter, and brown in the oven. Serve in the dish in which it was cooked.

SOLE AU GRATIN—II

Butter a baking-pan, sprinkle with crumbs, chopped onion, and minced parsley. Season the fish with salt, pepper, and ginger, and stuff with whole oysters, shrimps, and mushrooms. Cover with a layer of bread-crumbs, parsley, and butter, add half a wineglassful of white wine, and bake until done.

SOLE AU GRATIN—III

Put the prepared fish into a buttered baking-dish, season with salt and pepper, sprinkle with minced parsley, add enough white wine to keep from burning, and bake. Take up carefully, cover with Italian Sauce, sprinkle thickly with crumbs, and brown in the oven.

SOLE AU GRATIN—IV

Cook together in butter a chopped onion, half a dozen mushrooms, a tablespoonful of minced parsley, and a bean of garlic, with salt and pepper to season. Spread on the bottom of a buttered baking-dish and lay the seasoned fillets upon it. Add half a wineglassful of white wine and bake for five minutes. Cover with fresh mushrooms, pour over a cupful of Spanish Sauce, sprinkle with crumbs, dot with butter, and brown in the oven. Squeeze the juice of half a lemon over it and serve.

STEWED SOLES WITH OYSTER SAUCE

Soak the fish for two hours in seasoned vinegar and simmer until done in salted and acidulated water. Serve with Oyster Sauce.

FILLETS OF SOLE WITH ANCHOVIES

Fry the fillets in olive-oil, seasoning with salt and pepper, cool, and cut into small pieces. Add four anchovies cut into small bits, pour over a French dressing and serve with toasted crackers.

FILLETS OF SOLE IN CASES

Fry in butter one cupful of chopped mushrooms, two tablespoonfuls of chopped onion, and one tablespoonful of minced parsley, seasoning with pepper and salt. Cut the soles in fillets, spread with the mixture, tie with thread, put into a buttered pan, cover, and bake. Put each fillet into a small paper case, fill with Cream Sauce, lay a mushroom on the top of each, and serve.

FILLETS OF SOLE WITH FINE HERBS

Prepare according to directions given for Fillets of Sale à la Joinville—II, adding to the sauce a chopped onion and two shallots browned in butter, with twice the quantity of chopped mushrooms, and a bean of garlic. Season with salt, pepper, and minced parsley.

SOLES WITH FINE HERBS

Trim the fish and put into a buttered baking-pan, sprinkling with chopped mushrooms, parsley, and grated onion. Season with salt, pepper, and grated nutmeg, add enough white wine to keep from burning, cover with buttered paper, and bake. Take up the fish and add the drained liquid to a cupful of Allemande Sauce and reheat. Take from the fire, add a tablespoonful of butter, the juice of half a lemon, and a teaspoonful of minced parsley. Pour over the fish and serve.

FILLETS OF SOLE WITH MUSHROOMS

Bake the fillets for ten minutes and cool. Cook together one tablespoonful each of butter and flour, add half a cupful of stock and half a cupful of cream. Cook until thick, stirring constantly. Add a pound of fresh mushrooms chopped fine and simmer until the mushrooms are cooked. Cool the mushroom mixture and spread upon the fillets. Set the baking-pan into another of hot water, reheat in the oven, and serve with Hollandaise Sauce.

FILLETS OF SOLE WITH OYSTERS

Fry the fillets in butter and cover with Allemande Sauce to which chopped cooked oysters have been added.

FILLETS OF SOLE WITH RAVIGOTE SAUCE

Fry the fillets in seasoned butter, adding a little lemon-juice when done. Pour over Ravigote Sauce and serve.

FILLETS OF SOLE IN TURBANS

Put the bones and trimmings cut from fillets of sole in cold water to cover, simmer for half an hour, strain, and add a pinch of salt to the liquid. When it boils, put in the fillets rolled up, and fastened with a toothpick. Simmer for ten minutes and prepare a Cream Sauce, using for liquid half fish stock and half milk or cream. Pour over the fish and serve.

FILLETS OF SOLE WITH WINE

Butter a baking-pan, lay the fillets in it, season with salt and pepper, and spread with butter. Add half a cupful of white wine, cover with buttered paper, and bake for five or ten minutes. Take up the fish carefully and add to the liquid a teaspoonful each of butter and flour cooked together. Take from the fire, add the yolk of two eggs, beaten smooth with half a cupful of cream; pour over the fish and serve.

ROLLED FILLETS OF SOLE

Beat together until smooth two tablespoonfuls of anchovy paste, a teaspoonful of lemon-juice, a pinch of mustard, a dash of cayenne, and two tablespoonfuls of fresh butter. Spread long narrow fillets of sole with the butter, roll and fasten with wooden tooth-picks. Sprinkle with salt, pepper, and lemon-juice, and bake, wrapping in buttered paper if desired. These fillets may be fried in butter with parsley and onions, or dipped in egg and crumbs, and fried in deep fat, or cooked with wine and lemon-juice in stock made from the bone and trimmings, and served with the strained stock thickened with butter and flour cooked together.

STUFFED FILLETS OF SOLE

Wind long, thin, narrow fillets of sole around small carrots to keep their shape, fastening with tooth-picks. Simmer the trimmings of the fish for half an hour in two cupfuls of boiling water to cover, seasoning with salt and paprika. Cover the fillets with one cupful of this stock and half a cupful of white wine. Simmer for twenty minutes. Cook together one tablespoonful each of butter and flour, add one-half cupful of fish stock and cook until thick, stirring constantly. Take from the fire, add one-half cupful of chopped shrimps and one-half cupful of chopped oysters, the yolk of one egg well beaten, and Worcestershire, salt, and Tabasco Sauce to season. Take out the carrots and replace with the cooked mixture. Cool, dip the fillets in egg and crumbs, fry in deep fat, and serve with any preferred sauce.

CHAUDFROID OF SOLES

Marinate the fillets of three soles in seasoned lemon-juice. Chop half a dozen mushrooms and cook for five minutes in butter, seasoned with pepper and salt. Add enough bread-crumbs to make a smooth paste, cool, and spread on the fillets. Fold each piece of fish so that the stuffing will be in the middle, arrange on a buttered baking-dish, cook in a moderate oven, and cool. Cook together one tablespoonful each of butter and flour, and add one cupful of fish stock made from the bones and trimmings of the soles. Take from the fire, add a little cream, and stir until cold. Pour the sauce over the fillets, garnish with lemon, parsley, and hard-boiled eggs, and serve very cold.

FRITTERS OF SOLE

Rub two tablespoonfuls of butter into half a pound of flour, add a pinch of salt, the beaten yolk of an egg, and enough cold water to make a very stiff paste. Roll the paste very thin and cut into pieces large enough to wrap fillets of sole, which have been seasoned with pepper and salt, and lemon-juice. Fry in deep fat and serve with Tartar Sauce.

TWENTY-FIVE WAYS TO COOK STURGEON

BOILED STURGEON—I

Cover a cut of sturgeon with salted and acidulated water. Add an onion, six cloves, a slice of carrot, three bay-leaves, a small bunch of parsley, and a cupful of wine. Simmer slowly until done, drain, and serve with some of the cooking liquor thickened with flour, browned in butter.

BOILED STURGEON—II

Boil the fish in court bouillon and serve with Drawn-Butter Sauce.

BROILED STURGEON STEAKS—I

Parboil sturgeon steaks for fifteen minutes, drain, wipe dry, season with salt and pepper, and broil. Serve with melted butter or Maître d'Hôtel Sauce.

BROILED STURGEON STEAKS—II

Skin and soak for an hour in cold salted water. Drain, wipe dry, and soak for an hour in a marinade of oil and vinegar. Drain and broil. Serve with melted butter and lemon-juice.

BROILED STURGEON STEAKS—III

Skin the steaks and soak in cold, salted water for an hour, drain, season, and broil, basting with melted butter as required. Season with melted butter and garnish with lemon quarters and parsley. Or, brown a tablespoonful of flour in butter, add half a cupful of cold water and cook until thick, stirring constantly. Season with salt, lemon-juice, and Worcestershire Sauce, or anchovy essence. Bring to the boil, pour over the fish, and serve.

FRIED STURGEON—I

Parboil slices of sturgeon in milk for fifteen minutes, drain, dip in beaten egg, then in seasoned flour, and fry brown in butter.

FRIED STURGEON—II

Cut the fish into cutlets, dredge with flour, dip into egg and crumbs, and sauté in a frying-pan. Drain off the fat, add a little flour and cook to a smooth paste. Add boiling water to make a sauce, and cook until thick, stirring constantly. Season with grated onion, pepper and salt and sweet herbs. Reheat the fish in the sauce, squeeze in the juice of half a lemon, and serve.

FRIED STURGEON—III

Cut sturgeon steaks into small cutlets. Dip into egg and crumbs, fry in fat to cover, and serve with any preferred sauce.

BAKED STURGEON—I

Skin a large cut of sturgeon, parboil for fifteen minutes, drain, cover with a marinade of oil and vinegar, and let stand for an hour. Gash the surface deeply and fill the incision with a force meat of bread-crumbs and minced salt pork, seasoning with lemon-juice, pepper, and minced parsley, and adding enough melted butter to make smooth. Cover, add enough boiling water to keep from burning, and bake, basting frequently.

BAKED STURGEON—II

Skin a large cut of sturgeon, parboil for fifteen minutes, drain, and cool. Rub with a marinade of oil and vinegar, cover, and bake with enough water to keep from burning. Serve with Caper Sauce.

BAKED STURGEON—III

Skin a six-pound cut of sturgeon and parboil for twenty minutes. Drain and put into a baking-pan on a layer of thinly sliced bacon. Add enough boiling water to keep from burning, and bake until done, basting often.

BAKED STURGEON—IV

Skin a six-pound cut of sturgeon, soak in salted water for an hour, drain, and parboil in fresh water. Make a stuffing of bread-crumbs, chopped salt pork, sweet herbs, and enough melted butter to make a smooth paste. Score the upper-side of the fish deeply and fill the gashes with the stuffing. Put in a buttered baking-pan with enough water to keep from burning, and bake for an hour, basting as required. Serve with Drawn-Butter Sauce, seasoned with capers and catsup.

BAKED STURGEON—V

Cover a buttered baking-pan with thin slices of salt pork. Sprinkle with chopped carrot, turnip, and onion, and lay a thick cut of sturgeon upon it. Season the fish with salt, pepper, and lemon-juice, and cover with thin slices of pork. Cook for ten minutes, then add one cupful of boiling water, and cook slowly, basting as required. Dredge with seasoned flour after each basting, and add more boiling water if necessary. After the fish has cooked for an hour, remove the pork, and drop it into the pan. Pour a wineglassful of Sherry over the fish, spread with butter, and dredge thickly with flour. Bake until the fish is a rich brown color. Take out the pork and add enough boiling water to the liquid in the pan to make the required quantity of sauce. Thicken with butter and flour cooked together, strain, and serve with the fish.

STURGEON À LA CARDINAL

Clean two pounds of sturgeon, bind into shape with tape, and put it into a buttered saucepan with acidulated water to cover. Add an onion, four cloves, a blade of mace, a sliced carrot, and a bunch of sweet herbs. Simmer gently until the fish is done and serve with Lobster Sauce.

STURGEON À LA FRANÇAISE

Skin and clean a five-pound cut of sturgeon, and tie into shape with strings. Put into a buttered saucepan with sliced carrots and onions, a bunch of parsley, three blades of mace, three cloves of garlic, and salt and pepper to season. Add red wine and white stock in equal parts to cover. Simmer until done, drain, and keep warm. Take enough of the strained liquid to make a sauce, and thicken with butter and flour cooked together. Take from the fire, add a tablespoonful of anchovy essence, a dash of paprika, two tablespoonfuls of butter, and the juice of a lemon. Pour over the fish and serve.

STURGEON À LA NORMANDY

Remove the skin from a five-pound cut of sturgeon, cover with thin slices of salt pork, and tie into shape with a string. Put into a saucepan with sliced vegetables, two tablespoonfuls of butter, one cupful of white wine, two cupfuls of white stock, a little oyster or mussel liquor, and salt and sweet herbs to season. Cover and cook slowly for an hour, basting with the liquid frequently. When done, drain the fish, and keep warm. Strain the liquid, skim off the fat, thicken with a tablespoonful each of butter and flour cooked together, take from the fire, add the yolks of four eggs beaten with the juice of a lemon, and two tablespoonfuls of butter in small bits. Take the pork off the sturgeon, pour the sauce over, and serve.

STURGEON À LA RUSSE

Soak two pounds of sturgeon in salted water to cover for ten or twelve hours. Drain and marinate in vinegar for an hour. Put it into a fish-kettle with boiling water to cover, adding two onions, a bunch of sweet herbs, and a little salt. When nearly done drain, dredge with flour, and brown in the oven, basting with melted butter. Bone and skin two anchovies and put them into a saucepan with a wineglassful of white wine, a small onion, a bit of lemon-peel, and a cupful of stock. Boil for five minutes, strain, thicken with flour and butter cooked together, take from the fire, add two tablespoonfuls of cream, and pour over the fish, or serve separately.

STEWED STURGEON—I

Marinate slices of sturgeon in vinegar for ten minutes. Drain, dry, dredge with flour, and fry brown in hot fat. Add enough veal stock to cover the fish, and a wineglassful of Madeira; cover and simmer for an hour. Add a tablespoonful of capers and serve.

STEWED STURGEON—II

Cut sturgeon steaks into small pieces and parboil for fifteen minutes. Drain, season with salt and pepper, and cook slowly in butter until done. Add one cupful of milk, bring to the boil, and add one tablespoonful of flour rubbed smooth in a little cold water. Cook until thick, stirring constantly, and serve.

STURGEON STEAK—I

Put a large sturgeon steak into a buttered baking-pan with salt, pepper, sliced onion, a bunch of parsley, and some sweet herbs. Add Claret and white stock to cover. Cover with a buttered paper and cook slowly until done. Drain and serve with any preferred sauce.

STURGEON STEAK—II

Cover a sturgeon steak with boiling water, let stand for five minutes, and drain. Marinate for five hours in melted butter, lemon-juice, and vinegar, seasoning with salt and pepper. Drain, dip in egg and crumbs, and fry in deep fat. Beat the yolks of two eggs, add a teaspoonful of made mustard and the marinade drained from the fish. Cook over hot water until thick, pour over the fish, and serve.

GRILLED STURGEON

Cut the sturgeon into slices an inch thick. Dip in flour, then into egg and crumbs, and broil, basting with oil as needed. Season with salt and pepper and serve with any preferred sauce.

PANNED STURGEON

Cut two pounds of sturgeon into squares, parboil, drain, and cool. Cook together one tablespoonful each of butter and flour, add two cupfuls of milk, and some of the liquid drained from the fish. Cook until thick, stirring constantly. Season with salt and pepper, pour over the fish and serve.

PICKLED STURGEON

Skin a six-pound cut of sturgeon and soak in cold water for half an hour. Drain, cover with boiling water, parboil for fifteen minutes, drain, and cool. Bring to the boil three pints of vinegar to which has been added a sliced onion, two bay-leaves, a dozen cloves, three blades of mace, a tablespoonful of mustard seed, a dozen pepper-corns, a small red pepper, and two tablespoonfuls of sugar. Boil for fifteen minutes, pour over the sturgeon, and let stand covered for two or three days before using.

ROASTED STURGEON

Clean and skin a six-pound cut of sturgeon, season with salt and pepper, and wrap in a large sheet of buttered paper with carrots and onions sliced, two bay-leaves, sprigs of chive and parsley, the juice of a lemon, and a tablespoonful of olive-oil. Tie up and bake for an hour in a moderate oven. Unwrap the paper, take out the vegetables, and serve with any preferred sauce.

FIFTY WAYS TO COOK TROUT

BROILED TROUT—I

Clean and split the fish and let stand for an hour in melted butter, seasoned with salt, pepper, and sweet herbs. Sprinkle with crumbs, broil, squeeze lemon-juice over, then serve.

BROILED TROUT—II

Gash a cleaned trout and marinate in oil and lemon-juice, seasoning with salt and pepper, minced chives, and parsley, and a little thyme. Drain, sprinkle with crumbs and chopped herbs, and broil carefully. Serve with any preferred sauce.

BROILED TROUT À LA MAÎTRE D'HÔTEL

Clean the fish but do not split. Score deeply on both sides, dip in seasoned oil, broil, and serve with Maître d'Hôtel Sauce.

BROILED BROOK-TROUT

Clean and split the fish, wipe dry, dip in seasoned oil and broil. Serve with any preferred sauce.

BROILED TROUT WITH BACON

Wash, clean, and split a trout, and remove the back-bone. Put a strip of bacon in place of the bone, tie the fish into its original shape and broil over a clear fire. Garnish with fried parsley.

BOILED TROUT—I

Put the fish into cold court bouillon, bring to the boiling point, and simmer for six minutes, drain, and serve with Cream Sauce.

BOILED TROUT—II

Tie a large trout in a cloth and boil it in salted and acidulated water to cover, adding an onion, a stalk of celery, and a bunch of parsley. When done, drain and keep warm. Stick blanched almonds into the fish, sharp side down, and pour over a Cream Sauce to which chopped hard-boiled eggs and parsley have been added.

BOILED BROOK-TROUT—I

Put the cleaned trout in a saucepan with enough Claret to cover. Add a slice of lemon, two cloves, four pepper-corns, a blade of mace, and a pinch of salt. Simmer slowly until done and let cool in the liquid. Take out, strain a little of the liquid over them, and serve.

BOILED BROOK-TROUT—II

Prepare and clean four large trout, pour over then two cupfuls of boiling vinegar, two cupfuls of white wine, and enough water to cover. Add an onion, three cloves, three stalks of celery, four bay-leaves, a small bunch of parsley, a teaspoonful of peppercorns, and a little salt. Cover, boil until done, drain, and serve with any preferred sauce.

FRIED TROUT—I

Roll the cleaned fish in seasoned flour and fry in deep fat.

FRIED TROUT—II

Clean the fish, split, season with salt, dredge with flour, and sauté for five minutes in hot butter.

FRIED TROUT—III

Salt the fish and dip in equal parts of flour and corn-meal, thoroughly mixed. Sauté in salt pork fat.

FRIED BROOK-TROUT

Clean and split the fish, dip in seasoned flour or corn-meal, and sauté in butter or salt pork fat.

FRIED FILLETS OF TROUT—I

Remove the fillets from slices of sea-trout, dip in beaten egg, then in seasoned crumbs, and fry in deep fat. Serve with Tartar Sauce.

FRIED FILLETS OF TROUT—II

Boil and cool a trout and divide into fillets, removing the bone. Season with lemon-juice, chopped onion, and minced parsley, and cover with a very thick Cream Sauce. Dip into crumbs, then into beaten egg, then into crumbs, fry in deep fat, and serve with any preferred sauce.

FRIED TROUT WITH MUSHROOM SAUCE

Dip slices of sea-trout in beaten egg, then in seasoned crumbs, and fry in deep fat. Serve with the sauce given in the recipe for Baked Trout with Mushroom Sauce.

TROUT WITH REMOULADE SAUCE

Sauté a small trout in butter, drain on brown paper, and serve with Remoulade Sauce.

FILLETS OF TROUT À L'AURORE

Sauté the fillets of a cleaned trout in butter, seasoning with salt and pepper. Drain and serve with Aurora Sauce.

BAKED TROUT—I

Scrape and clean the trout, stuff with seasoned crumbs, and put into a buttered baking-dish. Lay a thin slice of salt pork on each fish, sprinkle with three or four tablespoonfuls of chopped onions, add a can of mushrooms drained from the liquor, a tablespoonful of minced parsley, three tablespoonfuls of butter, and one cupful of stock. Bake, basting frequently. Thicken the liquid with butter and flour cooked together, pour over the fish, and serve.

BAKED TROUT—II

Clean a large sea or lake trout. Prepare a stuffing of bread-crumbs, seasoning with chopped onions, celery, salt, pepper, and melted butter. Cook the stuffing for ten minutes, using as little water as possible. Stuff the fish, put into a buttered baking-pan with enough hot water to keep from burning. Cover the fish with thin slices of salt pork and bake until done, adding more hot water if required. Brown two tablespoonfuls of flour in butter, add half a cupful of cream, and enough boiling water to make a smooth thick sauce. Season with salt and pepper, add a few capers, pour around the fish, and serve.

BAKED TROUT—III

Stuff a large sea or lake trout with mashed potatoes, seasoning with butter, pepper, salt, and grated onion. Butter a baking-pan and cover the bottom with thin slices of tomatoes. Lay the fish upon it, sprinkle with salt and pepper, add two tablespoonfuls of butter and enough water to keep from burning. Bake until done and serve with the tomatoes and sliced hard-boiled eggs.

BAKED BROOK-TROUT—I

Clean and score small trout, dip in seasoned melted butter, and put in a buttered baking-pan. Cover with buttered paper and bake, basting with their own liquid until done. Serve with any preferred sauce.

BAKED BROOK-TROUT—II

Chop fine three or four large mushrooms and a truffle, fry for a moment in butter, season with salt and cayenne, add enough melted butter to make a smooth paste, and stuff large brook-trout with the mixture. Put in a buttered baking-pan, sprinkle with minced parsley, and pour over half a cupful of stock to which two tablespoonfuls of butter have been added. Bake for half an hour, basting as required.

BAKED BROOK-TROUT—III

Soak a cupful of bread-crumbs in milk, squeeze dry, add two tablespoonfuls of butter, the yolk of an egg, and pepper, salt, thyme, and lemon-juice to season. Stuff the fish, sew up, put in a buttered baking-pan, dredge with flour, dot with butter, and bake.

BAKED TROUT WITH WHITE WINE—I

Put the cleaned fish in a small buttered baking-pan with white wine to moisten, and salt and pepper to season. Cover with buttered paper and bake, basting with the liquid. Take up the fish, thicken the liquid with butter and flour cooked together, add a little more butter, pour over the fish, and serve.

BAKED TROUT WITH WHITE WINE—II

Take the fillets from a three-pound trout and bake for ten minutes in a buttered baking-pan. Fry a chopped onion in butter, add a tablespoonful of flour and half a cupful of white wine. Cook until thick, stirring constantly, and add two tablespoonfuls of butter, broken into bits. Pour the sauce over the fillets and bake for fifteen minutes longer.

BAKED TROUT À LA CHAMBORD

Split and bone the cleaned fish and put in a buttered baking-pan skin side down. Sprinkle with salt, pepper, and crumbs, and put into the oven. Cover the bones and trimmings with cold water, adding two tablespoonfuls of butter, a sliced onion, and two cupfuls of stock. Boil for half an hour, strain, add a can of mushrooms, chopped, and enough crumbs to thicken. Season with salt, pepper, and anchovy paste. Take up the fish carefully, put on a serving-dish, cover with the sauce, put in the oven for a few moments, and serve.

TROUT WITH FINE HERBS

Put half a dozen cleaned trout in a buttered baking-dish with half a glassful of white wine, and a finely chopped shallot. Bake for ten minutes, strain the liquid, and add to it one cupful of Allemande Sauce. Add also a small chopped onion, two shallots, twice the quantity of mushrooms, and a bean of garlic, all minced and fried in butter. Season with salt, pepper, minced parsley, and lemon-juice; pour over the fish and serve.

BAKED TROUT WITH MUSHROOM SAUCE

Butter a baking-dish, sprinkle with bread-crumbs, lay a sea-trout upon it, cover with crumbs, dot with butter, squeeze over the juice of half a lemon, and bake, adding enough water to keep from burning. Brown a tablespoonful of flour in butter, add the liquid drained from the fish, one cupful each of mushroom and oyster liquor, and a wineglassful of Madeira. Cook until thick, stirring constantly, take from the fire, and add a few cooked oysters, shrimps, and mushrooms. Season with salt and pepper and serve separately.

BAKED TROUT WITH POLISH SAUCE
Put a cleaned trout into a buttered baking-pan, rub with butter, and season with salt and pepper. Fry a chopped onion in butter, add half a cupful of white wine and two tablespoonfuls of minced parsley, and pour over the fish. Sprinkle with crumbs, dot with butter, and bake slowly until done. Melt one and one-half cupfuls of butter and add a tablespoonful of minced parsley, and three hard-boiled eggs chopped very fine. Serve the sauce separately.

STUFFED TROUT
Clean, split, and stuff a trout, using seasoned crumbs or chopped oysters. Put in a buttered baking-dish, lay in the fish, season with salt and pepper, cover with crumbs, dot with butter, pour over a little white wine, and bake in the oven. Serve in the dish in which they were baked.

TROUT BAKED IN PAPERS
Stuff trout with seasoned crumbs, cover each one with a thin slice of salt pork, and wrap in buttered paper, fastening the papers securely; bake and serve in the papers.

BROOK-TROUT IN PAPER CASES
Stuff the fish with seasoned crumbs or chopped oysters or raw fish pounded to a pulp and mixed to a paste with the beaten white of egg and a little cream. Lay a very thin slice of salt pork on each fish and wrap in buttered paper. Bake in a hot oven. Remove the string and serve in the paper. Serve any preferred sauce separately.

TROUT IN CASES
Clean, parboil, and trim the fish, wrap in buttered paper, bake, and serve with Fine Herb Sauce.

TROUT À L'AURORE
Boil and skin the fish, put on a serving-dish, cover with Allemande Sauce, and the chopped yolks of hard-boiled eggs. Brown in the oven and serve with Aurora Sauce.

TROUT À LA CAMBACERES
Prepare six trout according to directions given in the recipe for Trout with Shrimp Sauce. Serve with one cupful of Spanish Sauce, adding two chopped truffles, half a dozen chopped mushrooms, a dozen chopped olives, and three tablespoonfuls of stewed and strained tomato. Pour over the fish and serve.

TROUT À LA CHAMBORD

Stuff cleaned trout with chopped oysters or seasoned crumbs, and put into a buttered baking-dish. Add half a wineglassful of white wine, a sprig of celery, a bay-leaf, a sprig of thyme, two cloves, and salt and pepper to season. Bake in the oven, basting frequently. Take up the fish, strain the liquid, and add it to a cupful of Spanish Sauce, with a chopped truffle, four cooked mushrooms, chopped, and a dozen cooked oysters. Pour the sauce over the fish and serve.

TROUT À LA CHEVALIÈRE

Boil, skin, trim the fish, cover with very thick Cream Sauce and let cool. Dip in crumbs, then in egg, then in crumbs, sprinkle thickly with grated Parmesan cheese, and bake in a buttered baking-dish, basting with melted butter as required. Serve with Allemande Sauce, seasoned with white wine, chopped cooked mushrooms, and anchovy essence.

TROUT À LA GENEVA

Dip the trout in a marinade of oil and lemon-juice seasoned with salt, pepper, and grated onion. Broil carefully. Heat one cupful of stock with a teaspoonful of anchovy essence and a tablespoonful each of minced parsley and Claret. Pour over the fish and serve.

TROUT À LA GASCONNE

Prepare the fish according to directions given in the recipe for trout à l'Italienne, and pour over it a Sauce à la Gasconne.

TROUT À LA HUSSAR

Stuff a cleaned trout through the mouth with butter mixed with finely chopped sweet herbs. Dip in seasoned oil and broil.

TROUT À L'ITALIENNE

Boil a large sea-trout in salted water, drain, skin, and serve with Italian Sauce, seasoned with butter, anchovy paste, nutmeg, and lemon-juice.

TROUT À LA PROVENCE

Cook the cleaned trout in salted and acidulated water with a sliced carrot, a bay-leaf, and a sprig of thyme. Drain, and cover with a sauce made by boiling for fifteen minutes one cupful of stewed tomatoes, a chopped onion, two sprigs of parsley, two truffles, and half a dozen mushrooms. Strain over the fish, garnish with olives, and serve.

TROUT À LA ROYALE

Stuff a large trout with seasoned crumbs, and cover it with Claret, adding mushrooms, parsley, chopped onion, thyme, a bay-leaf, pepper-corns, and mace to season. Drain the fish and reduce the liquid by rapid boiling to one cupful. Strain, mix with Allemande Sauce, seasoning with anchovy paste, red pepper, and lemon-juice.

TROUT À LA VÉNITIENNE

Clean a large trout and score it deeply. Fill the openings with butter highly seasoned with chopped sweet herbs, and marinate for an hour in oil. Drain, sprinkle with seasoned bread-crumbs mixed with chopped sweet herbs, and broil. Serve with any preferred sauce.

TROUT AU GRATIN—I

Parboil, drain, and skin. Put on a buttered baking-dish, season with pepper, salt, minced parsley, chopped shallots, and chopped mushrooms. Cover with Brown Sauce, pour over half a cupful of Sherry and bake. Sprinkle with crumbs, dot with butter, and brown. Squeeze lemon-juice over and serve in the same dish.

TROUT AU GRATIN—II

Clean and bone a two-pound trout. Put in a buttered baking-pan, skin side down. Dot with butter, season with cayenne, sprinkle with chopped anchovies, cover with half a pound of grated American cheese, and pour over one cupful of sour cream. Bake for half an hour, basting as required.

TROUT AU BEURRE NOIR

Clean and score the fish, dip in seasoned flour, sauté in hot butter, and take up. Brown half a cupful of butter, take from the fire, add the juice of a lemon and a teaspoonful of minced parsley, pour over the fish, and serve.

TROUT WITH SHRIMP SAUCE

Put the cleaned trout on the grate in a fish kettle, adding salted water to cover. Add also a sliced carrot, a sprig of thyme, two bay-leaves and half a wineglassful of white wine. Simmer until done, drain, and serve with Shrimp Sauce.

TENDERLOIN OF TROUT WITH WINE SAUCE

Cut a large sea-trout in pieces and simmer until done in salted and acidulated boiling water to which a large sliced onion has been added. Drain and keep warm. Cook together two tablespoonfuls each of butter and flour and add enough of the liquid drained from the fish to make a thick sauce. Cook until thick, stirring constantly, take from the fire, add one cupful of Madeira wine and three eggs well-beaten. Put the fish in a buttered baking-pan, sprinkle with seasoned crumbs, cover with mushrooms, then with oysters and shrimps. Pour the sauce over and bake until the oysters are done. Serve in the dish in which it was baked.

STEAMED TROUT

Lay the prepared fish in a steamer and place over boiling water, steam until done and serve with plenty of melted butter or Egg Sauce.

STEAMED BROOK-TROUT

Clean the fish, season lightly with salt and pepper and steam until tender. Serve with Hollandaise or Tartar Sauce.

TROUT EN PAPILLOTES

Stuff cleaned trout with chopped oysters and seasoned crumbs. Wrap a thin slice of salt pork around each one, season with salt and pepper, wrap in buttered paper, fasten firmly, and bake in a slow oven for twenty minutes. Serve in the papers.

ESCALLOPED TROUT

Boil two trout in salted water, drain and flake, removing all the bones. Fry a small chopped onion in butter, add a tablespoonful of flour and two cupfuls of milk. Cook until thick, stirring constantly. Put a layer of the boned fish in a buttered baking-pan, add a layer of the sauce, sprinkle with minced parsley, and repeat until the dish is full. Cover with crumbs, dot with butter, and brown in the oven.

FIFTEEN WAYS TO COOK TURBOT

BOILED TURBOT

Wash the fish carefully and soak it for an hour in salted water, drain, and rinse in fresh water. With a sharp knife score the black skin in a straight line from head to tail. Boil the fish in salted and acidulated water to cover, drain, garnish with parsley and lemon, and serve with any preferred sauce.

BROILED TURBOT

Clean a small turbot and marinate for an hour in seasoned oil and vinegar or lemon-juice. Drain, broil, and serve with any preferred sauce.

BROILED TURBOT À LA PROVENCE

Soak the fish for four hours in a marinade of oil and lemon-juice, seasoned with sliced carrot, onion, bay-leaf, thyme, parsley, and garlic. Drain, broil the fish on one side, and put in a buttered baking-dish with the marinade. Add two cupfuls of white wine, and bake, basting frequently. Take up the fish, and add the remainder of the bottle of wine to the liquid. Boil for five minutes, rub through a sieve, thicken with butter and flour cooked together, season with anchovy paste, minced parsley, and capers. Pour over the fish and serve.

BAKED TURBOT

Rub a small cleaned turbot with melted butter, sprinkle with minced parsley, powdered mace, and salt and pepper to season. Let stand for an hour and put into a buttered baking-dish. Brush with beaten egg, sprinkle with crumbs, dot with butter, bake, and serve with any preferred sauce.

TURBOT À LA BÉCHAMEL

Reheat cold flaked turbot in a Béchamel Sauce, adding a few cooked oysters.

TURBOT AU BEURRE NOIR

Cut cold cooked turbot into small fillets. Brown half a cupful of butter, add tarragon vinegar to taste, and pepper, salt, and minced parsley to season. Reheat the fish in the sauce and serve.

TURBOT À LA CRÈME—I

Reheat cold flaked turbot in a Cream Sauce, seasoning with grated nutmeg and lemon-juice.

TURBOT À LA CRÈME—II

Cook together three tablespoonfuls each of butter and flour, add a quart of cream and cook until thick, stirring constantly. Season with pepper, salt, minced parsley, and grated onion. Butter a baking-dish, put in a layer of cold cooked turbot flaked fine, cover with sauce, and repeat until the dish is full, having sauce on top. Sprinkle with crumbs, dot with butter, and brown in the oven. Sprinkle with chopped eggs and parsley.

TURBOT AU GRATIN—I

Remove the skin, fat, and bone from cold turbot, and flake fine with a fork. Fry in butter a slice of onion chopped, a small slice of carrot minced, a bit of bay-leaf, and a pinch of mace. Add a tablespoonful of flour, one cupful of milk, and half a cupful of stock or water. Cook until thick, stirring constantly. Season with salt and pepper and rub through a sieve. Put a layer of the flaked fish in the bottom of a buttered baking-dish, spread with the sauce, sprinkle with grated Parmesan cheese, and repeat until the dish is full. Cover with crumbs, sprinkle with cheese, dot with butter, and brown in the oven.

TURBOT AU GRATIN—II

Boil a fish, drain, and cool. Flake with a fork, and mix with Bechamel Sauce to which has been added the yolks of four eggs well-beaten, half a cupful of grated Parmesan cheese, and lemon-juice and grated nutmeg to season. Mix lightly, put into a buttered baking-dish, cover with crumbs, sprinkle with Parmesan cheese, dot with butter, and brown in the oven. Cream may be poured over the fish before sprinkling with the crumbs.

TURBOT À LA HOLLANDAISE

Clean a medium sized turbot and make a deep incision down the back from head to tail. Rub with lemon-juice and boil in salted and acidulated water until tender. Drain and serve with Hollandaise Sauce.

FILLETS OF TURBOT À L'INDIENNE

Cut a small turbot into fillets and fry in butter with a little curry powder to season. Serve with Velouté Sauce.

FILLETS OF TURBOT À LA MARÉCHALE

Clean and boil the fish and cut into convenient pieces for serving. Cool, cover with a very stiff Cream Sauce, sprinkle with crumbs, dip in beaten egg, then in seasoned crumbs, and fry. Serve with any preferred sauce.

FILLETS OF TURBOT À LA RAVIGOTE

Sauté the prepared fillets in butter, seasoning with salt, pepper, and lemon-juice. Drain, and serve with Ravigote Sauce.

FILLETS OF TURBOT

Soak a medium sized turbot in salted water for half an hour, drain, rinse in fresh water, and cut into fillets. Dip in seasoned melted butter and broil or sauté in melted butter. Serve with Maître d'Hôtel Sauce.

FILLETS OF TURBOT WITH CREAM

Separate cold cooked turbot into fillets and reheat in a Cream Sauce.

FIVE WAYS TO COOK WEAKFISH

FRIED WEAKFISH

Clean, wash, wipe dry, dip in milk, roll in flour, fry in hot fat to cover, and serve with any preferred sauce.

BAKED WEAKFISH—I

Arrange the fish on a buttered baking-dish with minced onion, parsley, and mushrooms, and salt, pepper, and grated nutmeg to season. Moisten with equal parts of white wine and white stock. Cover with small bits of butter, bring to the boil, and finish cooking in the oven. Take up the fish and thicken the sauce with crumbs, dot with butter, and brown in the oven. Squeeze lemon-juice over and serve in the baking-dish.

BAKED WEAKFISH—II

Clean and split the fish, season with salt and pepper, and put into a buttered baking-pan, skin side up. Rub with butter and bake. Pour over melted butter, sprinkle with minced parsley, and serve.

FILLETS OF WEAKFISH IN CASES

Spread the fillets with chapped oysters mixed with the unbeaten white of egg. Season with salt and pepper, sprinkle with chapped shallots, parsley, and mushrooms. Cover with crumbs, dot with butter, wrap in buttered paper, and bake slowly far half an hour. Serve with Velouté Sauce, seasoned with lemon-juice.

FILLETS OF WEAKFISH À L'ORLY

Season the fillets with salt, pepper, and lemon-juice, dip in flour, then in well-beaten eggs to which two tablespoonfuls of olive-oil have been added, and then in crumbs. Fry in deep fat and serve with Tomato Sauce.

FILLETS OF WEAKFISH À LA HAVRAISE

Season the fillets with salt and pepper and fry for a few minutes in butter. Drain and keep warm. Add to the butter two cupfuls of Velouté Sauce and a wineglassful of white wine. Boil for five minutes, take from the fire, add the yolks of three eggs beaten with the juice of half a lemon, and three tablespoonfuls of butter. Reheat, but do not boil. Add a few cooked mushrooms or oysters to the sauce, pour over the fish, and serve.

TURBANS OF WEAKFISH

Take the fillets of four small weakfish, remove the skin and most of the bones. Spread with chopped oysters mixed with seasoned crumbs, roll up, fasten with skewers, put in a buttered baking-pan, cover with buttered paper, and bake until done. Take out the skewers, cool, dip in crumbs, then in beaten egg, then in crumbs, fry in deep fat, drain, and serve with Ravigote Sauce.

FOUR WAYS TO COOK WHITEBAIT

FRIED WHITEBAIT—I

Heat together one cupful of lard and one cupful of olive-oil. Sprinkle the whitebait thickly with seasoned flour and shake free of all that does not adhere readily. Fry quickly in a frying-basket, season with salt and cayenne, and serve immediately.

FRIED WHITEBAIT—II

Wash the whitebait in ice-water, drain, wipe dry, dip in milk, then in equal parts of cracker dust and seasoned flour. Fry in deep fat, season with salt and cayenne, and serve.

FRIED WHITEBAIT—III

Cover the fish with cold water, drain, and throw them into a cloth strewn with sifted flour. Shake them in the cloth to make the flour adhere to them, then toss them in a sieve. The fish will not stick together if they are fresh. Have ready plenty of boiling beef fat, and fry the whitebait in a wire basket, a few at a time. When they are crisp without being brown they are done enough. Drain, sprinkle with salt, and serve immediately.

DEVILLED WHITEBAIT

Fry the whitebait according to directions previously given, season very highly with cayenne pepper, and serve.

TWENTY-FIVE WAYS TO COOK WHITEFISH

BOILED WHITEFISH

Boil a large whitefish in salted and acidulated water, adding a bunch of parsley and a sliced onion to the water. Drain, and serve with any preferred sauce.

BOILED WHITEFISH À LA MACKINAC

Clean and split the fish and put into a buttered dripping-pan, skin-side down. Add enough salted water barely to cover, and simmer for half an hour. Serve with Maître d'Hôtel Sauce and garnish with hard-boiled eggs.

FRIED WHITEFISH—I

Clean and trim the fish and cut into convenient pieces for serving. Dip in seasoned flour and sauté in hot lard in a frying-pan.

FRIED WHITEFISH—II

Cut the fish in slices, dip in beaten egg, then in seasoned crumbs, and fry in fat to cover. Serve with any preferred sauce.

FRIED WHITEFISH—III

Clean and dry the fish, cut into fillets, dip in seasoned crumbs, then in egg, then in crumbs, and fry quickly in fat to cover. Serve with Tartar Sauce.

BROILED WHITEFISH—I

Clean, trim, and split a large whitefish, season with salt, pepper, and oil, and broil. Garnish with lemon and parsley and serve with Tartar Sauce.

BROILED WHITEFISH—II

Put a cleaned and split whitefish on a wire broiler, season with salt and cayenne, lay a few thin slices of bacon on top, put the broiler on a baking-pan, and cook in the oven without turning. Put on a platter, add a little butter, and rub hard-boiled eggs through a sieve over the fish. Garnish with parsley and lemon.

BROILED WHITEFISH—III

Clean and split the fish, season with salt and pepper, sprinkle with lemon-juice, and broil. Pour over melted butter and serve.

BAKED WHITEFISH—I

Clean and split a large fish, remove the bone, and put in a buttered baking-pan skin-side down. Season with salt, cayenne, and lemon-juice, sprinkle with crumbs, dot with butter, and bake. Serve with any preferred sauce.

BAKED WHITEFISH—II

Make a stuffing of one and one-half cupfuls of dry bread-crumbs, seasoning with salt and pepper. Add a heaping tablespoonful of butter and one egg well-beaten. Stuff the fish and sew it up. Put in a buttered baking-pan, pour in one cupful of vinegar, and bake until done, basting with butter and hot water. Take up the fish and thicken the gravy with two tablespoonfuls of flour browned in butter and rubbed smooth with a little cold water.

BAKED WHITE FISH—III

Dip the fillets of whitefish in beaten egg, then in crumbs, then in egg, then in crumbs, and lastly in beaten egg. Bake in a buttered dripping-pan for twenty-five minutes and serve with Cream Sauce.

BAKED FILLETS OF WHITEFISH

Cut a large cleaned whitefish into fillets, removing as much as possible of the bone. Season with salt and pepper, dip into beaten egg, then in crumbs, then in beaten egg, then in crumbs, and lastly in beaten egg. Bake in a thickly buttered baking-dish, drain on brown paper, garnish with fried parsley, and serve with Parsley Sauce.

BAKED WHITEFISH À LA BORDEAUX

Stuff a large whitefish with seasoned crumbs, put into a buttered baking-pan, rub with butter, dredge with seasoned flour, add one cupful of Claret, and bake. Take up the fish, strain the liquid, add a little more Claret, thicken with flour, brown in butter, season with red pepper, and serve separately.

STUFFED WHITEFISH

Make a stuffing of bread-crumbs, seasoning with salt, pepper, sweet herbs, and melted butter. Add a beaten egg to bind, stuff the fish, and sew up. Bake slowly, basting with melted butter and water, and serve with Tartar Sauce.

STUFFED WHITEFISH WITH OYSTER SAUCE

Make a stuffing of two cupfuls of bread-crumbs, half a cupful of chopped salt pork fried crisp, a chopped hard-boiled egg, half a cupful of vinegar, and salt, pepper, butter, sage, and mustard to season. Stuff the fish, tie in mosquito netting, and steam until done. Pour over a Cream Sauce to which cooked oysters and a little lemon-juice and minced parsley have been added.

WHITEFISH À LA CRÈME—I

Cook the fish until done in boiling salted water, drain, and remove the large bones. Cook together two tablespoonfuls each of butter and flour, add two cupfuls of milk, and cook until thick, stirring constantly. Season with salt, pepper, grated onion, minced parsley, and grated nutmeg, take from the fire and add half a cupful of butter. Add also the white of an egg well-beaten. Put the fish on a serving-dish, spread the sauce over it and brown in the oven.

WHITEFISH À LA CRÈME—II

Clean a whitefish and simmer until done in salted, boiling water. Drain, remove the large bones. Put into a buttered baking-pan, sprinkle with chopped onion and minced parsley, seasoning with grated nutmeg, salt, and pepper. Cover with Cream Sauce to which three tablespoonfuls of butter have been added, and put into a hot oven for ten or fifteen minutes.

WHITEFISH AU GRATIN—I

Boil a whitefish in salted water and flake fine with a fork. Bring to the boil two cupfuls of milk and thicken it with a tablespoonful of corn-starch rubbed smooth in a little cold water. Take from the fire, add salt and pepper to season, two tablespoonfuls of butter, and two eggs well-beaten. Butter a baking-dish, put in a layer of fish, cover with sauce, season with grated nutmeg, and repeat until the dish is full. Cover with crumbs, dot with butter, and brown in the oven.

WHITEFISH AU GRATIN—II

Skin and bone the fish, cut into small squares, and season with salt and pepper. Brown two tablespoonfuls of flour in butter, and add gradually two cupfuls of stock or milk. Cook until thick, stirring constantly, seasoning with salt, pepper, lemon-juice, minced parsley, grated onion, and a tablespoonful of vinegar. Butter a baking-dish, put in a layer of the fish, cover with sauce, and repeat until the dish is full. Cover with crumbs, dot with butter, and brown in the oven.

WHITEFISH À LA MAÎTRE D'HÔTEL

Clean, split, and bone a large whitefish, dip in seasoned oil, broil, and serve with Maître d'Hôtel Sauce.

WHITEFISH À LA POINT SHIRLEY

Clean, split, and bone the fish, and put into a buttered baking-pan, skin-side down. Season with salt, red pepper, and lemon-juice, add enough boiling water to keep from burning, and bake. Serve with Maître d'Hôtel Sauce.

PLANKED WHITEFISH—I

Butter a fish-plank and tack a large cleaned and split whitefish on it, skin side down. Rub with butter, season with salt and pepper, and cook in the oven or under a gas flame. Put a border of mashed potato mixed with the beaten white of egg around the fish, using a pastry tube and forcing bag. Put into the oven for a few minutes to brown the potato, and serve with a garnish of lemon and parsley.

PLANKED WHITEFISH—II

Clean and split a large whitefish, remove the bone, and tack on a buttered fish-plank, skin-side down. Season with salt, pepper, butter, and lemon-juice, and bake in the oven.

CREAMED WHITEFISH À LA MADISON

Steam a large whitefish until tender, take out the bones, and flake fine. Cook together one tablespoonful of butter and two of flour, add two cupfuls of milk, and cook until thick, stirring constantly. Season with parsley, thyme, grated onion, salt, and pepper, take from the fire, add two eggs well-beaten, and three tablespoonfuls of butter. Put in a buttered baking-dish a layer of fish, then a layer of sauce, and repeat until the dish is full, having crumbs and butter on top. Brown in the oven.

JELLIED WHITEFISH

Boil two pounds of whitefish in salted and acidulated water, with four bay-leaves, a tablespoonful of pepper-corns, and half a dozen cloves. Take out the fish, strain the liquid, and reduce by rapid boiling to a quantity barely sufficient to cover the fish. Add the juice of a lemon and two ounces of dissolved gelatine. Flake the fish with a fork, removing all skin, fat, and bone, mix with the liquid, pour into a fish mould, wet with cold water, and put on ice until firm. Serve with Mayonnaise or Tartar Sauce.

WHITEFISH CROQUETTES

One cupful of cold boiled fish flaked fine. Add to it half a cupful of mashed potatoes, half a cupful of bread-crumbs, half a cupful of cream, the beaten yolks of two eggs, and salt and pepper to season. Shape into croquettes, dip into the beaten white of eggs, then into crumbs, and fry in deep fat. Garnish with parsley and serve with any preferred sauce.

WHITEFISH WITH FINE HERBS

Put a large whitefish in a buttered baking-pan with salt, pepper, grated nutmeg, minced parsley, chopped onions, and mushrooms to season. Moisten with white wine and white stock, and bake, basting frequently. Cover with Velouté Sauce, sprinkle with crumbs, dot with butter, bake brown, squeeze lemon-juice over, and serve.

EIGHT WAYS TO COOK WHITING

BROILED WHITINGS

Trim the fish and score on both sides, dip in oil, broil, and serve with Maître d'Hôtel Sauce.

BOILED WHITINGS

Clean and trim the fish, boil in salted water, drain, and serve with any preferred sauce.

FRIED WHITINGS

Trim and skin the fish, skewer in a circle, dip into beaten eggs, then in seasoned crumbs, and fry in fat to cover. Serve with any preferred sauce.

FILLETS OF WHITING À LA MAÎTRE D'HÔTEL

Sauté the prepared fillets in fresh butter, seasoning with pepper and salt. Drain, and serve with Maître d'Hôtel Sauce.

FILLETS OF WHITING À LA MARÉCHALE

Parboil the prepared fillets, drain, cool, spread with very thick Cream Sauce, dip in crumbs, then in beaten eggs, then in crumbs, and fry in fat to cover. Serve with any preferred sauce.

FILLETS OF WHITING À L'ORLY

Fillet the whitings and remove the skin from each. Marinate for two hours in oil and vinegar with pepper, salt, thyme, bay-leaf, parsley, and shallot to season. Drain, dip in flour, and fry in deep fat.

FILLETS OF WHITING À LA ROYALE

Prepare according to directions given in the recipe for Fillets of Whiting à l'Orly, dipping in batter before frying.

WHITING WITH FINE HERBS

Clean and skin the fish well and fasten them with their tails in their mouths. Put on a buttered baking-dish, season with salt, pepper, and powdered sweet herbs, pour over a little melted butter, cover, and bake. Allow one fish for each person and serve in the dish in which they are baked.

ONE HUNDRED MISCELLANEOUS RECIPES

BAKED FISH

Prepare a Cream Sauce, seasoning with grated onion, minced parsley, and powdered mace. Take from the fire, add the yolks of two eggs, and salt and pepper to taste. Put a layer of cold cooked flaked and seasoned fish into a buttered baking-dish, spread with the sauce, and repeat until the dish is full, having sauce on top. Sprinkle with crumbs, dot with butter, and brown in the oven. This may be baked in individual dishes if desired.

FISH BALLS

Prepare a fish stock from the skin, bones, and trimmings of fish, seasoning with bay-leaf, onion, mace, cloves, and garlic. Boil slowly for an hour in water to coyer. Chop the raw fish with a few blanched almonds and a little garlic. Season with salt, pepper, and mace, and shape into small balls. Strain the stock, bring it to the boil, drop the balls in, and simmer slowly for twenty minutes. Skim out the balls and put on ice. Beat six eggs thoroughly with a little cold water and add them gradually to the boiling stock. Cook in a double-boiler until smooth and thick. Take from the fire, add the juice of two lemons, and a tablespoonful of tarragon vinegar. Pour the sauce over the balls, sprinkle with capers and minced parsley, and serve very cold.

COLD BOILED FISH

Clean and skin a large fish and put on a piece of buttered paper in the bottom of a fish-pan. Add a sliced onion, two beans of garlic, and enough salted water to cover. Simmer until done. Take it up and squeeze over it the juice of a lemon. Boil two eggs hard, chop the whites fine and sift the yolks. Cut cold boiled beets in fancy shapes. Put a row of the chopped whites of eggs down the middle of the fish, on each side of that a row of the yolks, and next to the yolks a row of the beets. Pour over a French dressing, garnish with lettuce leaves, and serve.

FISH À LA BRUNSWICK

Cook any large fish in salted water, adding one cupful of vinegar, and sliced onions, celery root, and parsley to season. For the sauce mix the yolks of two hard-boiled eggs with the yolks of two raw eggs, add a teaspoonful of prepared mustard, and a little salt, pepper, vinegar, lemon-juice, chopped parsley, onion, capers, shallots, and chopped pickle. Mix to a smooth paste with oil, add the finely chopped whites of the eggs, spread over the drained fish, and serve.

FISH AUX BOUILLABAISSE

Heat a tablespoonful of sweet oil, cut a small piece of onion into bits, and let brown in the oil, add a cupful of strained tomatoes, a tiny bit of garlic, a bay-leaf, a little thyme, a lemon-peel, a dash of tabasco, a little tomato catsup, salt, pepper, parsley, and white wine; let this boil for half an hour, then add the fish and boil for twenty minutes. Serve on buttered toast with the sauce poured over. Garnish with parsley.

BOUILLABAISSE—I

Cut into pieces and remove the bones from three pounds of fish, add six shrimps or one lobster or two crabs, cooked, and cut into large pieces, add one-half pint of olive-oil; fry lightly, and add one lemon and two tomatoes, one onion, and one carrot, all sliced, one pinch of saffron,—as much as lies on a ten cent piece,—a bay-leaf, and some parsley. A bean of garlic is used, unless the casserole is rubbed with it before cooking. Stir for ten minutes, add one cupful of stock and one wineglassful of white wine or cider. Cook for fifteen minutes longer, pour out into a bowl, place slices of toast in the casserole, and cover with the fish and vegetables, allowing the sauce sufficient time to soak into the toast, and adding salt and pepper to taste.

BOUILLABAISSE—II

Put into a saucepan about four pounds of different varieties of fish, including one lobster. The fish should be cleaned and cut into small square pieces; the lobster should be cut in sections, leaving the shell on. Add a bunch of parsley, three sliced tomatoes, one large whole clove of garlic, chopped fine, three bay-leaves, half a dozen cloves, one teaspoonful of saffron, three sliced onions, one cupful of olive-oil, salt and pepper to season, and enough water to cover. Bring to the boil, and simmer for thirty minutes. Line a soup tureen with thin slices of toasted bread, pour the contents of the sauce over it, and serve in soup plates, with both forks and spoons. This is a genuine French recipe.

CANAPES OF FISH

Toast small squares of bread and make a border of stiffly beaten white of egg around each one, using a pastry bag and tube. Bake in a quick oven until light brown. Fill the centre with creamed fish and serve very hot.

FISH CAKES—I

Season hot mashed potatoes with salt, pepper, and butter, and add one beaten egg to each two cupfuls of potatoes. Add an equal amount of cold cooked flaked fish and enough Cream or Drawn-Butter Sauce to make a smooth mixture. Shape into small flat cakes, dredge with seasoned flour, and sauté in bacon fat. Serve with a garnish of fried bacon.

FISH CAKES—II

Chop the cooked fish and season with grated onion, sweet herbs, powdered mace, and salt and pepper. Add half as much bread-crumbs as fish, mix with the unbeaten white of egg and a little melted butter, shape into small flat cakes, dredge with flour, and fry in butter.

FISH CHOPS

Mix cold cooked flaked fish with a little very thick Cream Sauce, and season with lemon-juice and minced parsley. Shape into chops, dip in egg and crumbs, and fry in deep fat. Stick a small piece of macaroni in the small end of each chop to represent the bone. Serve with Tartar Sauce.

CHARTREUSE OF FISH—I

Butter a small mould and put in alternate layers of seasoned mashed potatoes, cold cooked flaked fish, seasoned, and sliced hard-boiled eggs. Pour over enough cream to moisten, cover with potatoes and steam for twenty minutes. Turn out on a hot platter, garnish with parsley, and serve with any preferred sauce.

CHARTREUSE OF FISH—II

Mix one cupful of stale bread-crumbs with two cupfuls of cold cooked flaked fish and two eggs well-beaten. Season to taste, adding a little Worcestershire Sauce. Put into a buttered mould, steam for thirty minutes, and serve with any preferred sauce.

FISH CHOWDER

Skin three or four pounds of fresh fish and cut into convenient pieces for serving. Cut a quarter of a pound of fat salt pork into dice, and fry crisp. Skim out the dice and fry two sliced onions brown in the fat. Strain the fat into a deep kettle, cover with sliced raw potatoes, add the fish, salt and pepper to season, and enough boiling water or fish stock to cover. Simmer slowly until the fish is almost done, add two tablespoonfuls of butter, half a dozen split Boston crackers, four cupfuls of boiling milk, and the onion and pork dice. Reheat and serve.

COQUILLES OF FISH

Flake cold boiled fish and mix it with Cream Sauce. Season with anchovy essence, salt and pepper, then fill buttered shells with the mixture, cover with fried crumbs, heat thoroughly in the oven, and serve.

COURT BOUILLON FISH

Slice the fish in pieces (red fish is best), season with salt and pepper, and boil until done. Put two tablespoonfuls of butter into a frying-pan, when hot slice in one large onion and brown it, add one-half can of tomatoes, season with one teaspoonful of pepper, one-half teaspoonful of allspice, some finely chopped parsley, and one-half cupful of tomato catsup. Just before it begins to boil add one wineglassful of good Claret. Cut some bread into small cubes, fry in butter to garnish the dish. Place the fish in the centre of the platter, pour the gravy over and garnish with the bread cubes.

FISH À LA CRÈME—I

Reheat cold cooked fish, flaked, in a Cream Sauce.

FISH À LA CRÈME—II

Butter a stoneware platter and put upon it cold cooked flaked fish mixed with Cream Sauce. Sprinkle with crumbs, dot with butter, and surround with a border of mashed potato mixed with beaten egg, using a pastry bag and tube. Sprinkle with cheese and bake in the oven.

FISH À LA CRÈME—III

Scald one quart of milk in a double-boiler with a blade of mace, a bay-leaf, and a sprig of parsley. Thicken with one tablespoonful each of corn-starch and butter rubbed together. Take from the fire, add salt and pepper to season, and the beaten yolks of two eggs. Put a layer of fish in a buttered baking-dish, then a layer of sauce, and repeat until the dish is full, having sauce on top. Cover with crumbs, dot with butter, and brown in the oven.

CREAMED FISH

Mix cold cooked flaked fish with Cream Sauce and season to taste. Peel large cucumbers, cut in two lengthwise, boil until tender in salted water, scoop out the pulp, and fill with the hot fish. Cover with crumbs, dot with butter, and brown in the oven.

CREAMED FISH WITH OYSTERS

Reheat cold cooked flaked fish with an equal quantity of oysters in Cream Sauce. Simmer until the edges of the oysters curl.

CREAMED FISH ON TOAST

Mix cold cooked flaked fish with Cream Sauce, season with lemon-juice, pour over hot buttered toast, and serve.

FISH À LA CRÈOLE

Chop an onion and a clove of garlic and fry in lard. Add three tablespoonfuls of flour, cook until brown, and add one can of strained tomatoes. Have the fish cut into convenient pieces for serving, dredge with seasoned flour, and sauté in butter until brown. Pour the sauce over, simmer until done, and serve.

FISH CROQUETTES—I

Mix cold cooked flaked fish with one-third the quantity of mashed potatoes and add enough Drawn-Butter Sauce to make a smooth paste, season with salt, pepper, and Worcestershire, cool, shape into croquettes, dip in egg and crumbs, and fry in deep fat.

FISH CROQUETTES—II

Prepare a very thick Cream Sauce and mix it with twice as much cold cooked fish flaked fine. Season to taste and cool. Add bread-crumbs or an egg, or both, if the mixture is not stiff enough. Shape into croquettes, dip in egg and crumbs, fry in deep fat, and serve with any preferred sauce.

CURRIED FISH—I

Fry two chopped onions in butter and add a tablespoonful of flour mixed with a teaspoonful of curry powder. Add two cupfuls of water or stock and cook until thick, stirring constantly. Reheat in this sauce cold cooked flaked fish; take from the fire, season with salt, pepper, and lemon-juice, and serve in a border of boiled rice.

CURRIED FISH—II

Season cold cooked flaked fish with grated onion and lemon-juice and reheat in Curry Sauce.

CURRIED FISH—III

Fry two chopped onions in butter and add enough flour to make a smooth paste. Add enough stock to make the required quantity of sauce, and cook until thick, stirring constantly. Season highly with salt, pepper, lemon-juice, cayenne, curry powder, and a little sugar. Reheat cold boiled fish in this sauce and serve with boiled rice.

CURRIED FISH—IV

Fry a chopped onion in butter, and add enough curry powder to season highly. Add a cupful of stock or milk, and cold cooked fish cut into small slices. Simmer for ten minutes, sprinkle with chopped parsley, and serve.

CURRIED FISH IN RAMEKINS

Reheat cold cooked flaked fish in Curry Sauce, fill buttered individual dishes, cover with crumbs, dot with butter, sprinkle with grated cheese, and brown in the oven.

FISH CUTLETS

Mix cold cooked flaked fish with very thick Cream Sauce and season to taste. Shape into cutlets, dip in egg and crumbs, and fry in deep fat.

DEVILLED FISH—I

Make a paste with a teaspoonful of dry mustard, two tablespoonfuls of butter, and lemon-juice, seasoning with salt and cayenne. Fill small buttered shells with cold cooked flaked fish, spread with the paste, cover with crumbs, dot with butter, and brown in the oven.

DEVILLED FISH—II

Mix cold cooked flaked fish with Cream Sauce and chopped hard-boiled eggs, seasoning with salt, pepper, minced parsley, and made mustard. Fill small shells—clam shells are usually used—and cool. Brush the tops with beaten egg, sprinkle with crumbs, and fry in deep fat. Serve with Tartar Sauce.

DEVILLED FISH—III

Mix together one tablespoonful each of mustard, lemon-juice, and hot water, add a teaspoonful of Worcestershire, and salt and paprika to season. Broil the fish until it begins to brown, spread with the mixture, dip in crumbs, and finish broiling. Serve with Tartar Sauce.

ESCALLOPED FISH—I

Reheat equal quantities of cold cooked flaked fish and cold cooked maraconi cut small in equal parts of tomato sauce and oyster liquor. Season with salt and pepper, grated onion, paprika, and minced parsley. If desired, this mixture may be put into a buttered baking-dish, covered with crumbs, dotted with butter, and browned in the oven.

ESCALLOPED FISH—II

Fill a buttered baking-dish half full of cold cooked flaked fish seasoned to taste. Cover with Cream Sauce, seasoned with grated onion, chopped celery, minced parsley, and clove. Cover with mashed potato, beaten light with the stiffly beaten white of egg, dot with butter, and brown in the oven. Cream may be used instead of the Cream Sauce.

ESCALLOPED FISH—III

Mix cold baked flaked fish with the remnants of the stuffing. Arrange in a buttered baking-dish with alternate layers of seasoned cracker crumbs, having crumbs on top. Pour over enough cream to moisten, and bake brown.

ESCALLOPED FISH—IV

Into a well-buttered baking-dish put a layer of cold baked fish flaked. Add a layer of the stuffing, if any, sprinkle with crumbs, dot with butter, and repeat until the dish is full, having crumbs and butter on top. Pour over enough cream or Cream Sauce to moisten, and bake until well browned.

ESCALLOPED FISH AU GRATIN

Add one egg well-beaten to three cupfuls of seasoned mashed potato. Make a border of the potato around a stoneware platter. Put a layer of Béchamel Sauce on the bottom of the platter, then a layer of cold cooked flaked fish, cover with sauce, sprinkle with crumbs and grated cheese, dot with butter, and brown in the oven. Serve in the same dish.

ESCALLOPED FISH IN SHELLS

Allow one cupful of Cream Sauce to each cupful of cold cooked flaked fish, seasoning with salt, pepper, grated onion, and lemon-juice. Add chopped hard-boiled eggs if desired, or the yolk of one egg beaten smooth with a little hot cream. Fill buttered shells with the mixture, cover with crumbs, dot with butter, and brown in the oven. Sprinkle also with minced parsley or grated Parmesan cheese, or sweet green pepper.

FILLED FISH

Clean a fish thoroughly and take the flesh carefully from the skin. Do not injure the skin. Take out the bones, chop the meat fine, and mix with an equal quantity of bread-crumbs. Season with grated onion, salt, pepper, grated nutmeg, and minced parsley. Add half a cupful of butter, half a cupful of blanched and pounded almonds, three whole eggs, and the yolks of two more. Fill the skin, preserving the natural shape of the fish, and sew up. Simmer in court bouillon until done, drain, and stick the body of the fish full of blanched almonds shredded. Strain the liquid in which the fish was cooked, thicken with butter and flour cooked together, season with lemon-juice, pour around the fish, and serve.

FISH FRITTERS

Mix any cold cooked flaked fish with an equal quantity of mashed potatoes, seasoning with grated onion. Make into a paste with beaten egg, shape into balls, dredge with flour, and fry in deep fat. Dip in egg and crumbs before frying if desired.

FISH IN GREEN PEPPERS

Prepare Creamed Fish according to directions previously given. Cut a slice from the pointed ends of green peppers, and remove the seeds carefully. Stuff with the fish mixture, sprinkle with crumbs, and lay a bit of butter on top of each one. Put into a baking-pan with a little hot water and bake carefully, basting as required.

FISH HASH

Cut salt pork into dice, fry crisp, and skim out the pork. Mix together equal parts of cold cooked flaked fish and cooked potatoes, cut small. Season to taste and cook slowly in the pork fat until brown. Arrange the dice around the platter as a garnish.

JELLIED FISH SALAD

Mix cold flaked fish, which has been cooked in court bouillon, with Mayonnaise. Add sufficient soaked and dissolved gelatine to make the mixture very hard. One package of gelatine will solidify one quart of the mixture. Pour into a mould wet in cold water and put on the ice to harden. Turn out and serve with a garnish of hard-boiled eggs and lettuce.

KEDJEREE—I

Prepare a Cream Sauce, take from the fire, season to taste, and add two eggs well-beaten. Add cold cooked flaked fish and boiled rice in equal parts, seasoning the rice with salt, pepper, cayenne, mace, and melted butter. Reheat and serve.

KEDJEREE—II

Moisten cold flaked fish with one egg beaten with two tablespoonfuls of milk and a tablespoonful of melted butter. Heat thoroughly in a double-boiler, season to taste, and serve with rice which has been cooked for ten minutes in stock.

CRÉOLE KEDJEREE—I

Cook together for five minutes one cupful of cold cooked flaked fish, one cupful of cold boiled rice, one hard-boiled egg chopped fine, a tablespoonful of butter, and salt, red pepper, and curry powder to season. Serve on buttered toast.

CRÉOLE KEDJEREE—II

Prepare according to directions given above, adding chopped onion and garlic, and a little lemon-juice to the seasoning.

FISH LOAF

Line a buttered baking-dish with mashed potato that has been well seasoned with pepper and salt, and made light with well-beaten eggs. Fill the centre with Creamed Fish, seasoned to taste, cover with more mashed potato, rub with butter, and bake until the top is nicely browned. Serve in the same dish.

FISH WITH LEMON SAUCE

Put to boil in a wide porcelain-lined kettle sufficient water to cook the fish. Add one-half cupful of vinegar, and one-half cupful of wine. Add a heaping tablespoonful of butter, and when melted, put in the slices of fish, which have already been seasoned. Boil until the fish is tender. In the meantime, beat the yolks of four eggs until light with half a cupful of sugar, and the juice of two lemons. Remove one cupful of fish stock from the kettle with the fish. Let boil until thoroughly mixed, shaking the pan to prevent curdling. Put on a serving-dish, and garnish with slices of lemon and parsley.

BAKED FISH WITH LEMON SAUCE

Bake the fish in a pan with water and butter, taking care to add water when all in the pan has been absorbed. When the fish is done, drain off all the gravy which is in the pan, and put on the stove to boil with one cupful of white wine. Beat the yolks of four eggs with one-half cupful of sugar, stir a little wine in, add the juice of two lemons, put back on the stove to thicken, and just before serving, pour the sauce over the fish. Half the quantity of sauce can be used for a small family.

CREAM LEMON FISH

Boil the sliced fish until tender, in enough water to cover, to which a lump of butter, half a cupful of vinegar, and salt and pepper have been added. Beat the yolks of two eggs and two teaspoonfuls of sugar, and add the juice of one lemon. Take the fish out of the water, and put on the platter in which it is to be served. Thicken the gravy with flour that has first been dissolved in a little water. When thick, pour two cupfuls of the gravy over the eggs and lemon, stirring all the time. When cold, add one-half cupful of cream whipped stiff, and pour over the fish.

MASKED FISH

Cover the bottom of an earthen baking-dish with sliced onion, add a thick layer of sliced raw potatoes, seasoning with salt and red pepper. Cover with a layer of fish, add a layer of sliced tomatoes, cover with raw potato, and fill the bowl with stock or water in which one-half cupful of butter has been melted. Bake for two hours in a slow oven.

STEWED FISH À LA MARSEILLES

Cook three pounds of fish with a crab in equal parts of hot water and cider, seasoning with minced garlic, parsley, and thyme, a bay-leaf, and a clove. Cook for half an hour and thicken with a tablespoonful each of butter and flour cooked together. Add the yolks of two eggs beaten with a little cold water, and salt, pepper, and lemon-juice to season. Add a green pepper chopped fine, and two pods of okra. Simmer for fifteen minutes and serve in the dish in which it is cooked.

FISH EN MATELOTE—I

Cut any firm-fleshed fish into strips and season with salt and pepper. Parboil two sliced onions, drain, season, add a cupful of hot water and half a cupful of

Sherry. Add the fish and simmer until done. Thicken with butter cooked in flour, and serve.

FISH EN MATELOTE—II

Cut three or four kinds of fish into convenient pieces for serving, and sprinkle with salt and pepper. Cover with water and Claret in equal parts, and add parsley, thyme, and bay-leaves to season. Simmer until done. Take the fish up carefully and strain the cooking liquor. Fry a dozen or more small white onions brown in butter. Add two tablespoonfuls of flour and the liquid drained from the fish. Cook until thick, stirring constantly, and add boiling water or stock, if too thick. When the onions are done, take from the fire, season with lemon-juice, add a few cooked mushrooms, pour over the fish, and serve.

MATELOTE OF FISH À LA NORMANDY

Fry brown in butter with sliced onions two pounds of fresh sliced fish, using several kinds. Add two tablespoonfuls of flour, half a dozen sliced mushrooms, salt, pepper, and lemon-juice to season, a pinch of sweet herbs, and Claret and stock in equal parts to cover. Simmer for half an hour and serve in a casserole.

FISH MOUSSELINES

Mince enough uncooked white fish to make two cups, add one cupful of soft bread-crumbs and one-half cupful of cream. Press through a colander, season with salt, pepper, lemon-juice, a suspicion of mace, and Worcestershire Sauce. Fold in carefully the beaten whites of four eggs. Turn into buttered moulds (round bottomed ones) and steam one-half hour. Turn out on separate plates, surround with the sauce, and drop tiny balls of boiled potato in the sauce. For sauce, make a stock of the fish bones and add to it two tablespoonfuls of butter and two of flour cooked together. There should be one and one-half cupfuls of stock. Add one-half cupful of cream; and, when boiling, salt, pepper, and one tablespoonful of grated horse-radish soaked in lemon-juice.

MOULD OF FISH

Line a buttered mould with seasoned mashed potato and fill the centre with alternate layers of Creamed Fish and sliced hard-boiled eggs. Cover with the potato and steam or bake. Turn out and serve with any preferred sauce.

FISH PATTIES—I

Mix cold cooked flaked fish with Cream Sauce and put into buttered patty-shells with alternate layers of crumbs. Sprinkle with crumbs, dot with butter, and brown in the oven.

FISH PATTIES—II

Reheat cold cooked flaked fish in Béchamel Sauce, adding a few cooked mushrooms. Fill patty-shells and brown in the oven.

FISH AND OYSTER PIE

Butter a baking-dish and put in a layer of cold cooked fish, seasoning with pepper and salt. Sprinkle with bread-crumbs, add a layer of oysters, and season with nutmeg and minced parsley. Repeat until the dish is full. Cover with crumbs and dot with butter, or with a rich biscuit dough, and bake. If the biscuit crust is used, rub with butter, and bake until brown.

FISH PIE

Soak one cupful of stale bread-crumbs in milk, add two tablespoonfuls of melted butter, salt, pepper, minced parsley, and thyme to season, and beat until smooth. Skin and bone two medium-sized fish, using bass, cod, flounder, or mackerel. Scrape and pound half of the flesh and add it to the bread paste. Cut the rest of the fish into slices, season it, and arrange in layers in a deep baking-dish, spreading each layer with the paste and seasoning. Cover with thin slices of bacon and pour over one cupful of stock. Cover the pie with pastry, leaving a hole in the middle for the steam to escape. Cover with buttered paper and bake for three hours in a slow oven. Take off the paper, brown the crust, and pour into the hole half a cupful of stock to which a tablespoonful of Sherry or white wine has been added. Serve cold.

NORMANDY FISH PIE

Fill a baking-dish with any kind of fish, freed from skin, fat, and bone, and cut into small pieces. Season with minced parsley, grated nutmeg, salt, cayenne, black pepper, and mushroom catsup. Moisten with white wine and brandy in equal parts, cover, bake, and serve very hot.

FISH PIQUANT

Boil the fish whole in water seasoned well with onion, celery, salt, red pepper, and a tiny bit of garlic. When tender, drain, and put on a platter. Mix a lump of butter the size of an egg with three tablespoonfuls of flour, then add the juice of one or two lemons (according to size). Stir into this three cupfuls of the water in which the fish was boiled, put back on the stove, and stir until thickened. Remove from the fire, pour over the well-beaten yolks of two eggs, add some cut up pickles and olives, pour over the fish, and garnish with parsley or celery tops.

PICKLED FISH—I

Cut any kind of fish into pieces, dredge with flour, and fry. Cover with hot vinegar, adding a sprig of mint, and a pod of pepper. Let cool in the liquid, drain, and serve very cold.

PICKLED FISH—II

Cut any firm-fleshed fish into small pieces, dredge with seasoned flour, and fry brown in butter. Cover with boiling water to which half a cupful of vinegar has been added. Add a chopped onion, two tablespoonfuls of olive-oil, and a teaspoonful each of ground mace, cloves, and allspice. Simmer for an hour and serve very hot.

POTTED FISH—I

Pound cold cooked flaked fish to a paste, seasoning highly with salt, mustard, red and black pepper. Add melted butter to moisten, pack closely in small stone jars or cups and steam for half an hour. Cover with melted butter and keep in a cool place until ready to use.

POTTED FISH—II

Cut the fish into convenient pieces for serving. For every six pounds of fish allow one-fourth cupful each of salt, black pepper, and stick cinnamon, one-eighth cupful of allspice and one teaspoonful of clove. Put a layer of the fish in the bottom of an earthen pot, dredge with flour, sprinkle with spices, dot with butter, and continue until the dish is full. Fill the jar with equal parts of vinegar and water, cover tightly, and bake for five hours in a slow oven. Serve cold.

POTTED FISH—III

Clean, skin, split, bone, and cut in small pieces three shad or half a dozen small mackerel. Pack in layers in a small stone jar, sprinkling each layer with salt, cayenne, and whole spices. Cover with vinegar, close the jar tightly, and bake for five or six hours in a slow oven. Let stand for two or three days before using. All the small bones will be dissolved.

RÉCHAUFFÉ OF FISH—I

Take two cupfuls of cold cooked flaked fish and put into the chafing dish with two tablespoonfuls of butter, one cupful of crumbs, salt and pepper to season, and one egg beaten smooth with half a cupful of cream. Simmer for five or six minutes.

RÉCHAUFFÉ OF FISH—II

Reheat one cupful of cooked flaked fish and one cupful of cooked macaroni in butter. Season with salt, pepper, and tabasco sauce, and add one cupful of stewed and strained tomatoes. Heat thoroughly and serve.

RÉCHAUFFÉ OF FISH—III

Prepare a Cream Sauce, using for liquid equal parts of cream and fish stock. Add cold cooked flaked fish which has been seasoned with salt, pepper, oil, and lemon-juice. Reheat, season with anchovy paste and minced parsley, and serve.

RÉCHAUFFÉ OF FISH—IV

Allow one cupful of Egg Sauce and four cupfuls of mashed potato to each two cupfuls of cold cooked flaked fish. Put a layer of potato in a baking-dish, lay the fish upon it, add the sauce, cover with potato, spread with melted butter, and brown in the oven.

RÉCHAUFFÉ OF FISH—V

Brown a tablespoonful of flour in butter, add two cupfuls of milk, and cook until thick, stirring constantly. Season with salt, pepper, cayenne, ginger, and mace. Reheat cold cooked flaked fish in the sauce.

RÉCHAUFFÉ OF FISH—VI

Reheat one and one-half cupfuls of stewed and strained tomatoes, seasoning with salt and pepper. Warm cold cooked flaked fish in the sauce, take from the fire, add the yolk of an egg beaten with a little cold water, and serve. The fish may be put on a serving-dish and the sauce poured over it if desired.

FISH À LA REINE—I

Mix one pound of cold cooked flaked fish with Cream Sauce, seasoning with salt, pepper, and minced parsley. Add three chopped mushrooms and the yolk of one egg well-beaten and reheat, but do not boil. Serve in paper cases or shells.

FISH À LA REINE—II

Reheat cold cooked flaked fish in a Cream Sauce, seasoning with pepper, salt, and minced parsley. Add a cupful of chopped cooked mushrooms, and when very hot, take from the fire and stir in the beaten yolks of two eggs. Serve in patty-shells or individual dishes.

FISH RISSOLES—I

Flake cold cooked fish, add one-third the quantity of grated bread-crumbs, season with salt, pepper, grated onion, and melted butter, and add enough well-beaten yolk of egg to make a smooth paste. Cut pie-paste into three-inch squares. Place a teaspoonful of the minced fish in each square and cover with the paste. Wet the edges to make sure they adhere. Dip the rissoles in egg and crumbs, and fry in deep fat.

FISH RISSOLES—II

Season a cupful of cold cooked flaked fish with salt, pepper, and melted butter. Soak a French roll soft in half a cupful of milk, add the fish, and beat until smooth. Season with a little grated onion and mix with two eggs well-beaten. Bake in small buttered cups, turn out, and serve with any preferred sauce.

FISH SALAD

Cut a large fish into slices and boil the trimmings in water to cover with a chopped onion, a little butter, and pepper and salt to season. Boil for fifteen minutes, strain, and simmer the sliced fish in it until done. Take up the fish carefully and squeeze the juice of three lemons into the liquid. Season with cayenne, take from the fire and add the yolks of six eggs and the whites of three beaten with a little cold water. Reheat but do not boil; pour over the fish and let cool. Serve very cold.

FISH SALAD À LA TYROLIENNE

Add one cupful of cooked shrimps, cut into dice, to two cupfuls of cold cooked flaked fish. Mix with four tablespoonfuls of vinegar, two tablespoonfuls of capers, a pinch of celery seed, and a little pepper. Add one green pepper freed from seeds and shredded. Mix with Mayonnaise and serve on lettuce leaves with a garnish of hard-boiled eggs.

STEWED FISH—I

Cover the trimmings of a large fish with cold water, boil for half an hour, and strain. Add two fried onions and cover the fish with the liquid. Add the juice of half a lemon and one tablespoonful of butter and two tablespoonfuls of flour cooked to a smooth paste. Simmer until the fish is done, season with salt, pepper, minced parsley, and mushroom catsup, add one quart of parboiled oysters, and serve.

STEWED FISH—II

Boil three sliced onions in water to cover until tender, and drain. Season the onions with salt, pepper, cloves, mace, and allspice. Cover with thick slices of fish. Add white wine or Claret and water in equal parts to cover, and bring to the boil. Simmer until the fish is done, and thicken the liquid with butter and flour cooked together.

STEWED OR SHARP FISH

Put in a fish-kettle on the stove one tablespoonful of fresh butter, when melted add half an onion cut fine, a tiny piece of garlic, cut fine; let brown, then add a tablespoonful of flour, lightly browned, and enough water to cook the fish. To this liquor add some cut up celery or celery seed, some finely chopped parsley, two cloves, one bay-leaf, a tiny pinch of mace, a small pinch of cayenne pepper, some black pepper, a little ginger, and one tablespoonful of fresh butter. When this mixture begins to boil, add the fish, which has been cut up, and salted. Cook until done. Remove the fish to a platter, and add to the liquor one cupful of sweet milk, stirring constantly; boil for one minute, then pour over the beaten yolks of two eggs, stirring all the time. Slice a lemon over the fish, then pour the liquor over. Serve hot or cold.

SWEET SOUR FISH

First cut up and salt the fish. Shad or trout is best. Put in a fish-kettle with one and one-half cupfuls of water and one cupful of vinegar, add one onion cut in slices, one dozen raisins, one lemon cut in slices, two bay-leaves, and six cloves. When this mixture begins to boil, put in the fish and cook thoroughly. When done, remove the fish to a platter. Put the liquor back on the stove, add three tablespoonfuls of granulated sugar (which has been melted and browned in a frying pan), then add two tablespoonfuls of flour which has been rubbed smooth with a little water. Let boil well and pour over the fish. If not sweet enough, add more sugar. Serve cold.

SWEET SOUR FISH WITH WINE

Put to boil in a fish-kettle one cupful of water, one-half cupful of vinegar, two tablespoonfuls of brown sugar, six cloves, one-half teaspoonful of ground cinnamon, and one onion cut in slices. Boil thoroughly, then strain and add to it one lemon cut in slices, one wineglassful of red wine, one dozen raisins, and one tablespoonful of pounded almonds. Return to the fire, and when it comes to a boil, add the fish, cut up and salted. Cook until done, remove the fish to a platter, and to the liquor add a small piece of Leb-kuchen or ginger cake, and stir in the well-beaten yolks of four eggs; stir carefully or it will curdle. If not sweet enough, add more sugar. Pour over the fish. Shad or trout is the best fish to use.

SPICED FISH—I

Cook together for ten minutes one cupful of vinegar, one tablespoonful of sugar, and six each of whole allspice, cloves, and peppercorns. Strain over two cupfuls of cold cooked flaked fish, and serve very cold.

SPICED FISH—II

Cool five pounds of sliced fish in salted water, drain, cool, and skin. Boil together a quart of vinegar, two blades of mace, a small onion sliced, a small red pepper, two tablespoonfuls of grated horse-radish, six cloves, a bay-leaf, a tablespoonful of mustard seed, and half a cupful of water. Put the fish into an earthen jar, pour over the hot spiced vinegar and let stand in a cold place for two days before using.

FISH TIMBALES

Pound in a mortar one pound of fresh raw fish and press through a purée sieve. To every cupful of fish pulp add a tablespoonful of bread-crumbs soaked until soft in cream. Add also the beaten yolk of one egg, and salt, pepper, grated onion, and nutmeg to season. Beat thoroughly, and for every cupful of pulp, fold in the whites of two eggs beaten stiff. Fill a well-buttered mould three-quarters full, set it into a pan of warm water, cover with buttered paper, and bake for twenty minutes. Do not let the water boil. Turn out on a platter and serve with any preferred sauce.

FISH TIMBALE—I

Run through a meat-chopper twice half a pound of white fleshed fish. Add one cupful of soft bread-crumbs which have been boiled to a smooth paste in a little milk. Cool, add to the fish, press through a sieve, add six tablespoonfuls of cream, and salt and pepper to season. Fold in carefully the stiffly beaten whites of five eggs. Butter a small timbale mould, fill with the mixture, and put in a baking-pan half full of boiling water. Cover with buttered paper, bake for twenty minutes, and serve with Cream Sauce.

FISH TIMBALE—II

Chop cold cooked fish fine and mix to a smooth paste with bread-crumbs soaked in milk. Season with melted butter and grated onion and moisten with the beaten yolks of eggs. Bake in buttered individual moulds, turn out, and serve with a sauce made of one cupful of stewed and strained tomatoes mixed with a wineglassful of Sherry and half a cupful of cream, and thickened with the beaten yolks of two eggs. Add a few shrimps and cooked oysters to the sauce, pour around the timbales, and serve.

FISH TIMBALES—III

Chop fine one cupful of raw fish and rub it through a sieve. Season with salt, pepper, and grated onion, and add a dozen blanched almonds, chopped fine. Fold in one cupful of whipped cream and the whites of four eggs beaten very stiff. Fill small buttered moulds, set into a pan of hot water, and bake carefully.

FISH TIMBALE—IV

Add one cupful of cold cooked flaked fish to one cupful of very thick Cream Sauce and season with salt, cayenne, lemon-juice, and minced parsley. Take from the fire, add the yolks of three eggs, well-beaten, and cool. Fold in the whites of three eggs beaten stiff, fill buttered individual moulds two-thirds full, set into a pan of hot water, and bake for fifteen or twenty minutes. Serve with any preferred sauce.

TURBAN OF FISH—I

Prepare a Cream Sauce, seasoning with grated onion, powdered mace, minced parsley, and lemon-juice. Add the yolks of two eggs. Put a layer of cold cooked flaked fish in a buttered baking-dish, season with salt, pepper, and lemon-juice, spread with the sauce, and repeat until the dish is full. Cover with crumbs, dot with butter, sprinkle with grated Parmesan cheese, and brown in the oven.

TURBAN OF FISH—II

Cut thin slices of fish into narrow strips, remove the skin, dip in seasoned oil, and roll up, fastening with wooden toothpicks. Dip in seasoned flour or in beaten egg and crumbs, fry in deep fat, and serve with any preferred sauce. If preferred do not roll the fish, but fry the strips straight.

FISH TURBOT

Reheat any kind of cold cooked fish in a Cream Sauce, adding the beaten yolk of an egg to the sauce. Put into a buttered baking-dish, cover with crumbs, dot with butter, sprinkle with grated Parmesan cheese if desired, and bake brown, or put the fish and the sauce in the baking-pan in separate layers.

FISH TOAST

Mix cold cooked flaked fish with Cream Sauce, seasoning with salt, pepper, lemon-juice, and minced parsley. Add the yolks of two eggs, beaten with a little milk, and heat thoroughly, but do not boil. Spread on very hot buttered toast.

FISH À LA VINAIGRETTE

Flake cold cooked fish and arrange on a platter with a border of lettuce leaves. Pour over it a French dressing to which chopped olives, capers, and pickles have been added.

Echo Library

www.echo-library.com

Echo Library uses advanced digital print-on-demand technology to build and preserve an exciting world class collection of rare and out-of-print books, making them readily available for everyone to enjoy.

Situated just yards from Teddington Lock on the River Thames, Echo Library was founded in 2005 by Tom Cherrington, a specialist dealer in rare and antiquarian books with a passion for literature.

Please visit our website for a complete catalogue of our books, which includes foreign language titles.

The Right to Read

Echo Library actively supports the Royal National Institute of the Blind's Right to Read initiative by publishing a comprehensive range of large print and clear print titles.

Large Print titles are in 16 point Tiresias font as recommended by the RNIB.

Clear Print titles are in 13 point Tiresias font and designed for those who find standard print difficult to read.

Customer Service

If there is a serious error in the text or layout please send details to feedback@echo-library.com and we will supply a corrected copy. If there is a printing fault or the book is damaged please refer to your supplier.

Printed in the United Kingdom
by Lightning Source UK Ltd.
119334UK00002B/118

9 781406 837728